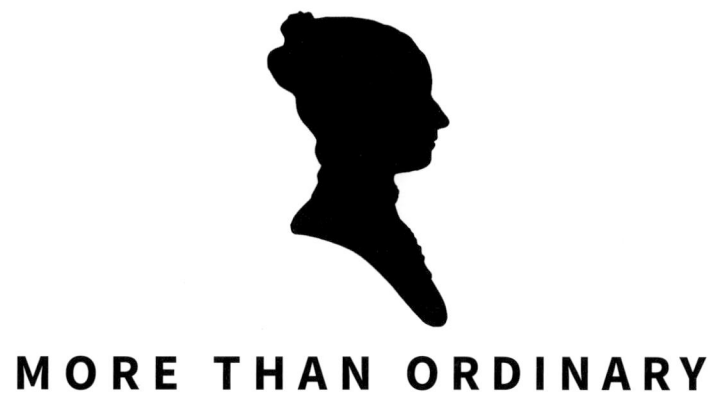

MORE THAN ORDINARY

EARLY ST. LOUIS ARTIST ANNA MARIA VON PHUL

BY HATTIE FELTON

MISSOURI HISTORICAL SOCIETY PRESS
ST. LOUIS
DISTRIBUTED BY UNIVERSITY OF CHICAGO PRESS

To Mumsy, for your steadfast support and friendship.
You are a more than ordinary woman.

© 2021 by Missouri Historical Society Press

All rights reserved 25 24 23 22 21 • 1 2 3 4 5

Library of Congress Cataloging-in-Publication Data

Names: Missouri History Museum, author. | Felton, Hattie, 1991- author. | Levine, Frances, writer of foreword.

Title: More than ordinary : early St. Louis artist Anna Maria von Phul / Hattie Felton.

Description: St. Louis : Missouri Historical Society Press, 2021. | Includes bibliographical references. | Summary: "The first complete catalog of Anna Maria von Phul's existing work, all of which is in the collections of the Missouri Historical Society. An essay examines her work, and a full catalog showcases her watercolors, silhouettes, and copywork of the early 19th century Midwest"-- Provided by publisher.

Identifiers: LCCN 2021017861 | ISBN 9781883982997 (paperback)

Subjects: LCSH: Von Phul, Anna Maria, 1786-1823--Catalogues raisonnés. | Missouri Territory--In art--Catalogs. | Saint Louis (Mo.)--In art--Catalogs. | Art--Missouri--Saint Louis--Catalogs. | Missouri History Museum--Catalogs.

Classification: LCC N6537.V625 A4 2021 | DDC 709.778/66--dc23

LC record available at https://lccn.loc.gov/2021017861

Designed by Steve Hartman

Printed and bound in the United States by Modern Litho, St. Louis

Image on cover: *Miss M. Von Phul* silhouette, unknown artist and date (possible self-portrait)

Image on inside cover: Landscape with stream and castle ruins, by Anna Maria von Phul, unknown date

Unless otherwise specified, all images are from the Missouri Historical Society Collections

CONTENTS

4. Introduction by Dr. Frances Levine
6. More than Ordinary
29. Catalog

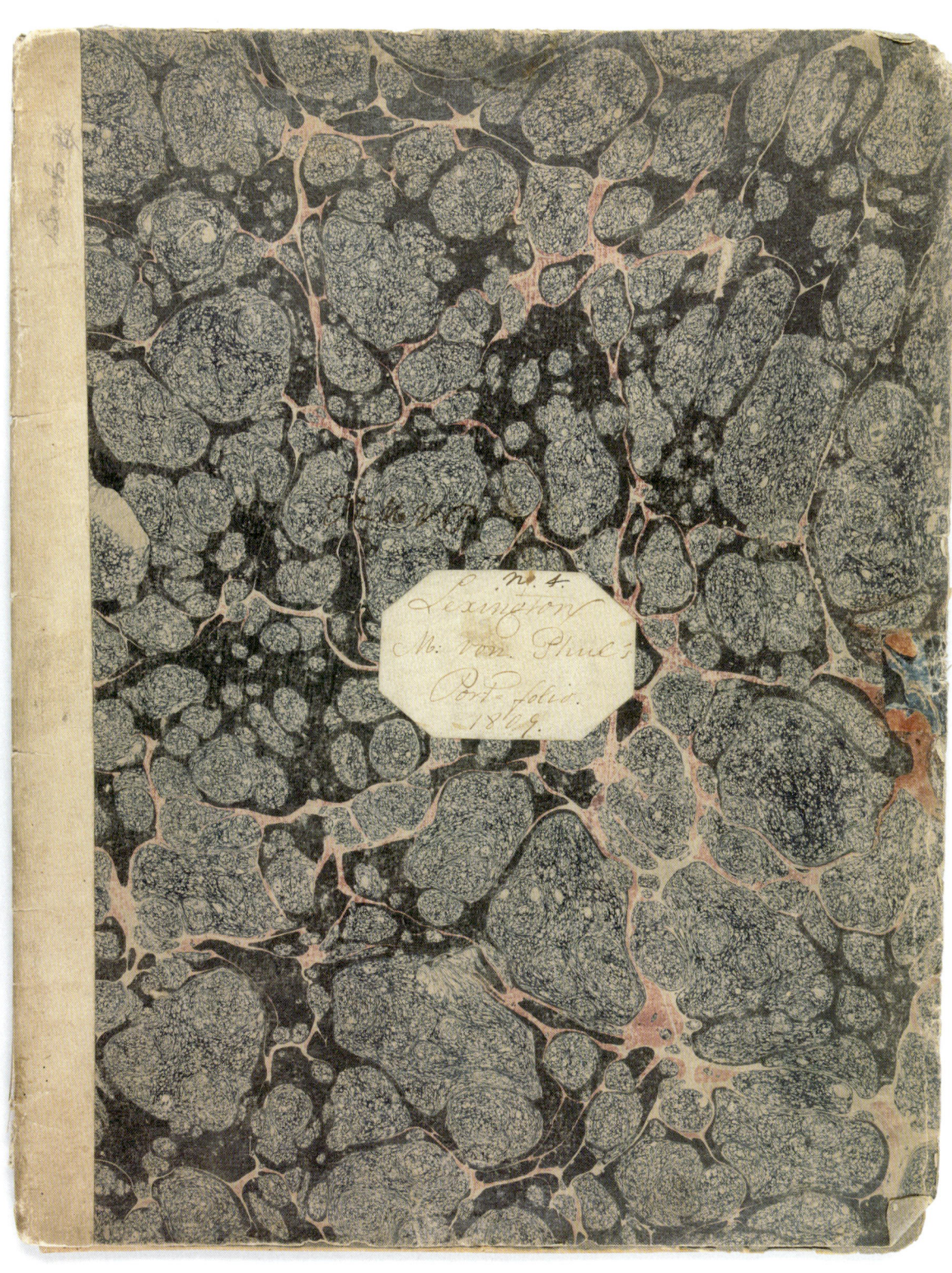

INTRODUCTION

WHY AND HOW DO MUSEUMS COLLECT?

Dr. Frances Levine
President and CEO
Missouri Historical Society

The Anna Maria von Phul watercolors and sketches featured in this volume provide a unique perspective of early St. Louis history. They are the only contemporaneous images painted of French Creole St. Louis during the early 19th century, and they were created by a woman who lived here for only a short time. These images are the closest things we have to eyewitness views before the invention of photography. Anna Maria von Phul portrayed the landscape and domestic settings of Creole life just as Missouri was on the cusp of statehood. Did von Phul record all aspects of life in St. Louis? Certainly not. But her skill as a painter and the thoughtful consideration she brought to her surroundings captured a time before steamboat traffic hauled in goods from far and wide, before the region was transformed by the trade networks that emerged with western expansion. The Missouri Historical Society is privileged to have these delicate watercolors and sketches in our collections. They represent just a portion of the depth and breadth of our holdings that document St. Louis's past.

MHS COLLECTIONS TELL STORIES OF THEIR TIME

Curating collections of artifacts that convey the story of St. Louis and westward migration is at the very core of the Missouri Historical Society's mission. When MHS was founded in 1866, its mission articulated a grand vision "to save from oblivion the early history of the city and state." St. Louis knew something about the threat of oblivion. In 1849 the riverfront community was devasted by a fire that spread from a steamboat onto the land, decimating St. Louis's commercial district. At precisely the same time, a cholera epidemic that had emerged a year earlier was raging through families with terrifying speed, surely claiming more victims than the official count of 4,547 dead men, women, and children. As the city and state were rapidly rebuilding in the wake of the Civil War, the Missouri Historical Society's founders were indeed proposing a monumental task. They endeavored to save the long history of the region before it was lost to war, natural disaster, overzealous housekeeping, or worse, the willful destruction of historical records. The founders' efforts were impressive and resulted in amassing a number of significant collections. We continue their work today, but it is far from finished.

The Missouri Historical Society Collections hold some 175,000 objects, 100,000 library volumes, more than 7,900 linear feet of archival documents, and more than 1 million photographs and prints that chronicle centuries of the archaeological and written history of Missouri and the country's growth. This region's history reaches back to antiquity, and our collections contain some of the Mississippian culture's finest artifacts. These artifacts show the skill of artisans and the ingenuity of the people who farmed, fished, and hunted along the river between 800 and 1200 CE. The collections hold countless examples of the influence of French and Spanish colonial settlers, conveyed through the maps, wills, memoirs, letters, clothing, guns, and household items that citizens used to wrest a living from the land. Our photographic collections document the wanton destruction of 26 Mississippian mounds as settlers in the 1800s mined them for building materials and forever altered the landscape built by Indigenous peoples. It also shows St. Louis's expansion, how its neighborhoods have changed, and how social movements have shaped and reshaped our region. Television news footage and documentary films have further deepened our collections. Digital media have expanded our holdings in ways our founders never could have imagined—and in ways we are still coming to fully appreciate. It has been said that the work of curators and museum collections management staff is never done. Rather, it grows and changes with each passing year.

Some of the first artifacts collected by the Missouri Historical Society were Thomas Easterly's daguerreotypes. These early photographs captured images of landmark buildings and Native American mounds that dotted the landscape. The Missouri Historical Society broadened its mission in 1881 by opening public galleries and seeking donations to populate its first exhibits. Since that time the community has continued to shape the Missouri Historical Society Collections through generous donations that augment curators' purchases. After buying a new building in downtown St. Louis in 1886, MHS commissioned portraits of the region's most noteworthy men. Among these was a portrait of Dred Scott that had been painted from a photograph donated to MHS. The Missouri Historical Society eventually acquired many portraits of women, helping to fill that significant gap.

In its earliest years MHS focused on collecting artifacts related to the lives of St. Louis's founding families. Artifacts associated with women were usually relegated to items such as clothing and decorative arts. Over time the Missouri Historical Society Collections grew to include an extraordinary range of regional furnishings made by local artisans. The Library & Research Center holds manuscripts, maps, diaries, and letters that document early fur-trade expeditions and the experiences of those who pushed westward, as well as the city's growing and changing industrial landscape. More recently, MHS curators have broadened the scope of our collections to include the history of communities whose pasts have been overlooked or erased—a conscious effort to construct a more complete history of this region.

WHAT DO CURATORS DO?

The words "curated collection" have been applied to all manner of aesthetically beautiful things. But what does "curated" mean in a museum setting? Although curators must have an eye for fine craftsmanship and beauty, they are more than avid collectors of objects that are valuable or visually pleasing. History museum curators also strive to obtain the stories and context that make an object, letter, map, or photograph worthy of long-term care and preservation. When curators accept an object into a museum's collection, they do so with a commitment to preserving it in perpetuity—forever. So curators seek durable goods that will tell the story of a person or a community's experience in a particular time and place. At MHS, we also consider our mission: Is the artifact related to St. Louis history or the city's place in US history? Is it a better example than something we already have in our collections because of its craftsmanship, or do we know more about who owned it, how it was used, or how it conveys a community's experience? If we're deciding whether to accept a chair into our collections, for example, MHS considers if that chair is associated with the history of a singular event, or if it was produced using a woodworking tradition unique to the region. Perhaps the chair fills a gap in our region's history because it's associated with an underrepresented group or neighborhood.

Visitors often ask how certain items came into our collections. One way is through the relationships our curators and archivists cultivate with families who are interested in donating an item. Curators also keep current with auctions. Some pieces in our collections are purchased with funds bequeathed to the Missouri Historical Society, which can extend donors' legacies for a century or more. Professor Sylvester Waterhouse (1830–1902), a professor of classics at Washington University in St. Louis, bequeathed $5,000 to MHS in 1901. He directed the funds to be invested for 50 years, then the accrued amount used to create a permanent endowment. The fund supported the acquisition of items of local interest as well as *Gateway*, our biannual members' magazine, which keeps members connected to St. Louis history through long-form stories, photo essays, and articles that expound upon the artifacts in our collections. William Keeney Bixby (1857–1931) established three funds at the Missouri Historical Society, each around $1,000, to support operational needs and the acquisition of books. Throughout his life Bixby collected archives and manuscript materials, which he donated to MHS. His generosity endures as a lasting legacy of his passion for history. Other donors have established funds to support internships for minority students or local history research. MHS is grateful for the funds and gifts we have received throughout the decades that continue to support the acquisition and conservation of historical objects.

COLLECTING IN THE PRESENT FOR THE FUTURE

Modern curators have shifted their focus away from collecting curiosities or items belonging to the region's elite toward collecting artifacts, photographs, films, objects, and digital media to ensure the times we are living in are documented for future generations. Today the Missouri Historical Society is engaged in multiple initiatives that seek to expand our artifacts, oral histories, and documents that illustrate the history of specific communities. Our African American history collections have grown to encompass the history of Black neighborhoods; medical and legal professionals; sports figures and musicians; writers; teachers; and activists and civil rights workers whose leadership has moved the national agenda on voting rights, education, housing, social justice, and equity. The Gateway to Pride Initiative traces the trials and triumphs of the LGBTQIA+ community's decades-long pursuit of equality. MHS also recognizes the extraordinary role that immigrants have played throughout St. Louis history, and we are seeking to broaden our holdings to include more stories and artifacts related to refugees, migrants, and resettlement programs. These recent collecting initiatives all connect past stories to the present and connect the present to the stories that will be told about St. Louis in the future. Our curators have an awesome responsibility to shape the collections today to ensure that tomorrow's exhibitions and publications will be possible.

This volume, *More than Ordinary: Early St. Louis Artist Anna Maria von Phul*, inaugurates a series of books that will focus on the Missouri Historical Society Collections. The series will allow us to share more of the 175,000 items in our collections with the public, as well as the stories that led us to collecting these items over the past 155 years. The Missouri Historical Society staff is committed to making our collections accessible online and on-site so that we can tell more local stories than ever. Our collections serve as the basis for books, blogs, programs, and exhibitions that are in progress right now—and ones we haven't yet dreamed of. By pulling back the curtain on our collections to reveal their extraordinary depth and breadth, we hope to inspire the public to partner with us and help shape the collections of our time by identifying artifacts that will convey today's stories centuries from now.

MORE THAN ORDINARY

IN 1823 THE ILLINOIS NEWSPAPER THE *EDWARDSVILLE SPECTATOR* PUBLISHED THE LONGEST OBITUARY OF ITS SEVEN-YEAR HISTORY.

Filled with words of praise for the deceased's generous nature, astute intellect, and unwavering faith, it would be easy to assume that the remembrance paid homage to an educator or a merchant, or perhaps a religious or political figure. Rather, it marked the passing of Anna Maria von Phul, a 37-year-old woman.[1] She was unmarried, was childless, and lived in the homes of family members and friends. By most standards, Anna Maria led what looked to be a comfortable yet inauspicious life—but that was hardly the case. Although the obituary employed the florid language and religious overtones typical of the era, it also brimmed with genuine affection and admiration. Who was this woman, whose "mind was stored with information of a solid and most important kind"?

---

1 Anna Maria von Phul's obituary mistakenly gives her age as 35.

On Monday morning last, at the residence of Mr. James Mason, of this town, Miss Maria Von Phul, aged 35.

It is soothing to the feelings of a bereaved friend, to reflect on the worth of that object whose loss is deplored. The heart loves to recal[2] the scenes, in which the delights of friendship was shared with one, now covered by the clod of the valley. The very circumstances which would seem likely to aggravate grief, convey a balm to the wounded bosom.

Such is the source from which the friends of Maria Von Phul (and who that knew her was not her friend?) will derive their consolation, under the afflicting stroke, which deprives them of her society. They will remember those intellectual accomplishments, which made her the delight of all who had the happiness of her acquaintance. They will call to mind her apt improvement, of every subject presented to her contemplation, and treasure in their memory, the observations they have heard fall from her lips, on the occurrences of life, and while their sorrows are tranquilized by the remembrance, will, it is hoped, be stimulated to exertion in acquiring knowledge, and practicing virtue.

To give a correct biography of Miss Von Phul, a more intimate knowledge of the events of her life were necessary, than the writer of this small tribute of respect can claim. It is hoped that some one, whose privileges have been greater, will feel the propriety of holding up an example to succeeding, as well as to cotemporary females, which, no doubt, would be worthy of imitation.

But of her character, and in some small degree, of her acquirements, the writer feels authorized to speak.

Her mind was stored with information of a solid and most important kind. Few subjects, in which the intellect can be profitably employed, or the imagination engaged, could pass under her view, without calling forth powers of superior order. Her conversation was a feast, of which the learned, the pious and the gay, delighted to partake. She possessed the singular faculty, of conveying the most grave and important instruction, so as to gratify while it improved her auditors.

But if an occasional intercourse, was, by the powers of her mind, made thus pleasing, a close, an intimate, a continued friendship, was rendered by the warmth and sincerity of her affections, still more desirable. While her lively imagination threw a charm around the subjects of her discourse, and fascinated those who enjoyed the pleasure of her conversation, the virtues of her heart, the purity of her life, and the kindliness of her affections, drew more closely to her, all who were privileged with a closer intimacy. To such she was indeed dear.

But many as were the virtues of Miss Von Phul, it is believed she had too just a sense of that accountability we owe to our Creator, and the purity of that law by which we are to be judged, to be satisfied with her own performances, or trust in them for the rewards of eternity. She strove to keep that holy law—but she sought strength from on high to enable her to do so. She exerted herself to abstain from iniquity, but she implored Divine grace to deliver her from corruption. She aimed at the felicities of heaven, but she trusted in Christ Jesus the Son of God, as her only hope of attainting to them.

Such was Maria Von Phul. With a mind endued with more than ordinary capacity, she examined the testimony of God in behalf of His revelation, and was convinced, that none but Jehovah could have devised—none but Jehovah could have executed, a scheme so glorious—so replete with blessings to man. Let those who would display equal wisdom, examine the word of God with equal care; and let those who revere her memory, pay it such honor as she would have desired, by following her example in "searching the scriptures to see whether those things be so," of which the pious of all ages and denominations love to reflect and converse.

While the disconsolate friend of the amiable and lovely Maria, are heaving sighs of anguished and unavailing regrets for their loss, may they be accompanied by humble prayer to the God of consolation, and then shall their tears be mingled with streams from the fountain of mercy that make glad the hearts of those, who mourn without repining—who feel the rod, but bow to the hand that chastises.

—*Edwardsville Spectator,* **August 2, 1823**

---

2 To maintain the historical accuracy of the letters and newspaper excerpts reprinted in this book, we have preserved the original language and spellings.

Born in 1786, Anna Maria von Phul was the first known woman artist working in the Missouri Territory. Although only a portion of her overall body of work is extant today, what remains gives modern viewers an insight into the people and places that comprised early St. Louis years before other artists made their living depicting the city. Von Phul's life story provides an all too rare look at how one woman overcame educational inequities and family hardships to leave an artistic legacy.

The art and letters von Phul left behind reveal someone passionate and curious about people and the world around her—a woman who sought opportunities to travel and learn. Copywork and cutwork silhouettes demonstrated her artistic aptitude early on. Paintings from her years in Kentucky include the serene estate of Chaumiere du Prairie, where she lived for a time. Later pages from her sketchbooks are filled with landscapes of the Missouri Territory—portraying Native American earthworks, documenting St. Louis's built environment, capturing the mighty Mississippi River—as well as many portraits. For von Phul, art was a way to explore her surroundings and connect with friends and strangers alike. Today, her art is a conduit for modern viewers to explore and connect with people and places long disappeared. Von Phul loved to share her art with others; she was in the habit of tucking paintings and sketches into the folds of letters to friends and family. Yet for 130 years after her death, her work lay forgotten in a family attic. Descendants rediscovered and donated these pieces to the Missouri Historical Society in 1953, at last giving von Phul the chance to share her art with the world.

A 2016 survey by the National Museum of Women in the Arts revealed that most Americans could not name five women artists.[3] It is a sobering reality that women have worked in obscurity for much of history, relegated to amateur—being a "professional" artist was simply not an option for them. Perhaps even more sobering is how little has been done to bring these artists into the spotlight. Anna Maria von Phul's more than ordinary life is just one of thousands of untold stories that deserve to be known. This volume is one step in changing that narrative.

Anna Maria von Phul was born in Philadelphia, Pennsylvania, on May 17, 1786, to Johann Wilhelm "William" and Catharina "Catharine" von Phul. She was the sixth of eight known von Phul children: George, Catharine, William, Sara (later spelled Sarah), Henry, Philip, and Graff. Church records indicate there may have been a ninth child, Elizabeth, born in 1792, who died as an infant.[4] Although only three of the children survived much past age 30, the von Phuls were a tight-knit family. Catharine was the daughter of German immigrants who settled in Lancaster County, Pennsylvania. William, born into a prosperous family in Westhofen, Germany, immigrated to Lancaster County in 1764, where he met and married Catharine. Having the benefit of family money, William put himself to work in Pennsylvania, purchasing land and launching or investing in several successful businesses, including a distillery and a ferry. He also served as a private during the Revolutionary War.

After the war ended the von Phuls moved to Philadelphia, where they had a comfortable, well-appointed home in the city's North Mulberry Ward. However, the family's life was upended when William died in 1798. He had a long list of debts and a mismanaged estate, leaving Catharine and her children without the inheritance they had hoped would sustain them. In all, it took at least four years to settle his affairs. Those were days "filled with many severe misfortunes,"[5] son Graff later recalled.

Spurred by the hardships that befell her in Philadelphia, Catharine packed up Henry, Sarah, Graff, and Anna Maria and moved to the recently established frontier state of Kentucky in 1800. By this time two of the von Phul children, Catharine and William, had died, possibly in the 1793 Philadelphia yellow fever epidemic. George and Philip chose to remain in Philadelphia. The von Phuls were close with several families who had ties to both Philadelphia and Lexington, which may explain why Catharine chose to move her struggling family there. Or perhaps the allure was simpler than that: to get a fresh start in a new town hundreds of miles away from painful memories.

---

3 Katherine J. Wu, "#5WomenArtists Campaign Tackles Gender Inequity for the Fifth Year in a Row," *Smithsonian Magazine*, March 9, 2020, smithsonianmag.com/smart-news/fifth-year-row-5womenartists-campaign-tackles-gender-inequity-180974362.

4 Von Phul family tree, Ancestry.com.

5 Graff von Phul to John Breckinridge, January 27, 1819. Von Phul Family Papers, Missouri Historical Society, St. Louis. Unless otherwise noted, all letters cited are part of the Missouri Historical Society Collections.

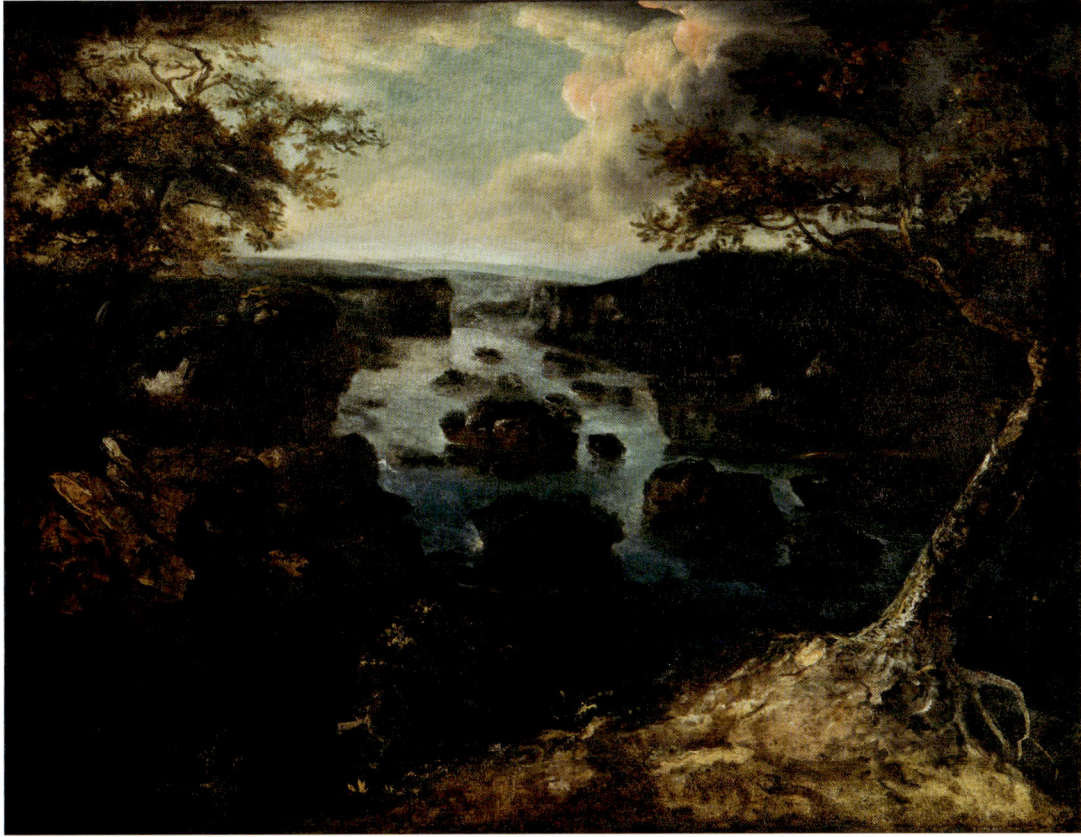

The Passage of the Pato'k thro' the blew mountain, at the confluence of that River with the Shan'h
George Beck
Oil on canvas
1797

Courtesy of Mount Vernon Ladies' Association

The transition from bustling Philadelphia (population 41,000) to Lexington (population 1,700) might have been difficult for a 14-year-old girl on the cusp of adulthood. However, Anna Maria—or Mary, as her family often called her[6]—flourished in Lexington. Though small, it was hardly a backwater or rough frontier town. By 1800 it had already developed a reputation as the "Athens of the West." A university town, Lexington attracted politicians, publishers, artists, and entrepreneurs. Poet Josiah Espy (who gave the city its Athens moniker) once remarked that "the main street of Lexington has all the appearance of Market Street in Philadelphia on a busy day."[7]

George and Mary Beck were European-born artists and educators who settled into this vibrant scene in 1804. Like the von Phuls, they had relocated from Philadelphia, where Mary ran a boarding and day school for girls and George painted and offered art instruction. George Beck's early career is replete with aggrandized accounts of his artistic achievements,[8] but not all of them are unfounded. Upon the Becks' arrival in the young United States, George quickly found some success when he painted two scenes of the Potomac River, *The Potomac River Breaking through the Blue Ridge* and *Great Falls of the Potomac*, which were purchased by George Washington. But the artist was lured westward in search of dramatic landscapes to inspire him, and Mary likely wanted to live closer to family in Cincinnati. After a meandering trip, the couple settled in Kentucky.

---

6 Based on letters addressed to her, family and friends most often called her Maria or Mary. However, Anna Maria herself generally signed her letters and work with her full given name, Anna Maria, or her initials, AM. Thus, for the purposes of this essay and catalog, her preferred usage will be honored.

7 National Park Service. "Athens of the West." Accessed January 14, 2021. nps.gov/nr/travel/lexington.

8 "A Biographical Memoir of the Late George Beck, Esq.," *The Portfolio* 2, no. 2 (August 1813): 117–122.

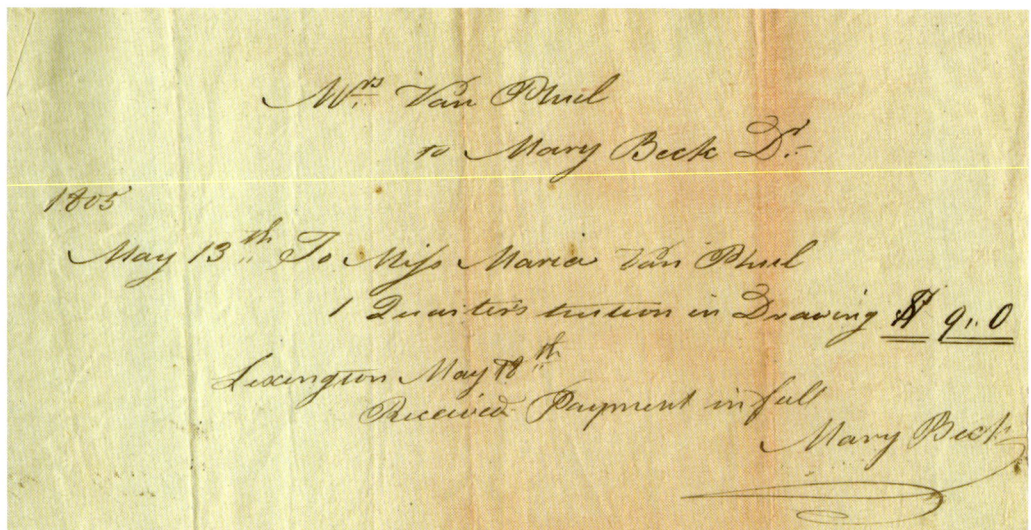

Receipt of payment for "1 Quarter's tuition in Drawing" to Mary Beck
May 13, 1805

As in Philadelphia, Mary started a school in Lexington called Mary Beck's Young Ladies' Academy, which opened in 1804 or 1805.[9] The school was one of Kentucky's first institutions providing serious education for girls. In addition to the traditional ornamental pursuits considered essential for young ladies, such as drawing and needlework, Mary also offered arithmetic, spelling, geography, logic, astronomy, and natural philosophy—subjects that pushed the boundaries of what was considered suitable for young women. George intended to operate a school for young men in Lexington but found that Transylvania University had already filled the town's niche for advanced instruction. With Mary's successful school meeting their financial needs, George turned his attention to painting, translating Greek volumes, writing poetry, and calculating astronomical occurrences.[10]

Although their time in Philadelphia overlapped by at least one year and they lived within a few blocks of each other, it is not known if Anna Maria studied with Mary in Pennsylvania. A tuition invoice indicates that Anna Maria received instruction in drawing at Mary Beck's Young Ladies' Academy as early as the first quarter of 1805, soon after the Becks moved to town. Anna Maria's earliest dated work from 1804 (Figure 26) shows that she had likely been drawing for years by the time she started taking lessons from Mary at age 20. Nevertheless, Anna Maria's artwork from the first two decades of the 1800s reveals the Becks' influence on her artistic development.

---

9 The first documented mention of Mary Beck's Young Ladies' Academy in Lexington is in the *Kentucky Gazette* on February 12, 1805. Mary states in an advertisement that her terms are not well understood by the people of Lexington, implying that the school had only recently opened.
10 "George Beck, an Eighteenth-Century Painter," *The Register of the Kentucky Historical Society* 67 (January 1969): 20–36.

(Figure 26)

Copy of a European scene
Anna Maria von Phul
Watercolor on paper
1804

Anna Maria's earliest dated painting reveals a young artist drawing inspiration from European landscapes mixed with her own fanciful interpretations of faraway places.

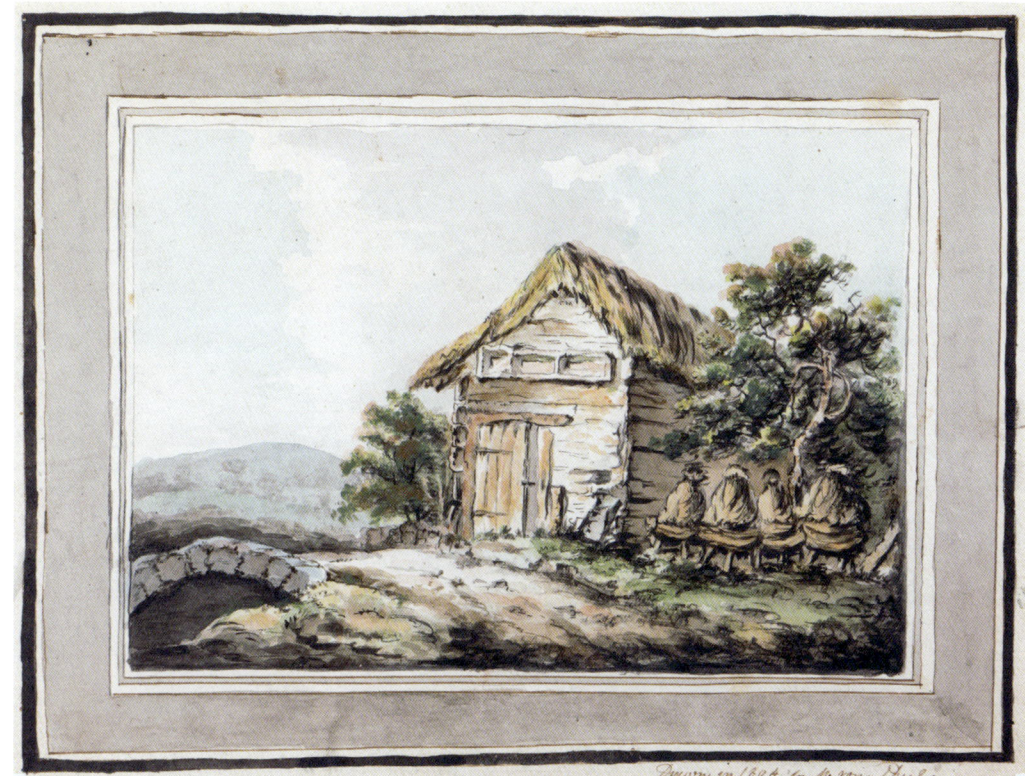

(Figure 4)

Copy of a work by George Beck
Anna Maria von Phul
Ink wash on paper
Unknown date

Although Anna Maria received instruction in drawing from Mary Beck, many examples of her work clearly reflect George's influence. By copying from his collection of prints and his original work, Anna Maria improved her composition and use of tone. Copying so many prints did not improve her use of perspective, however; her work often lacks a dynamic depth of field.

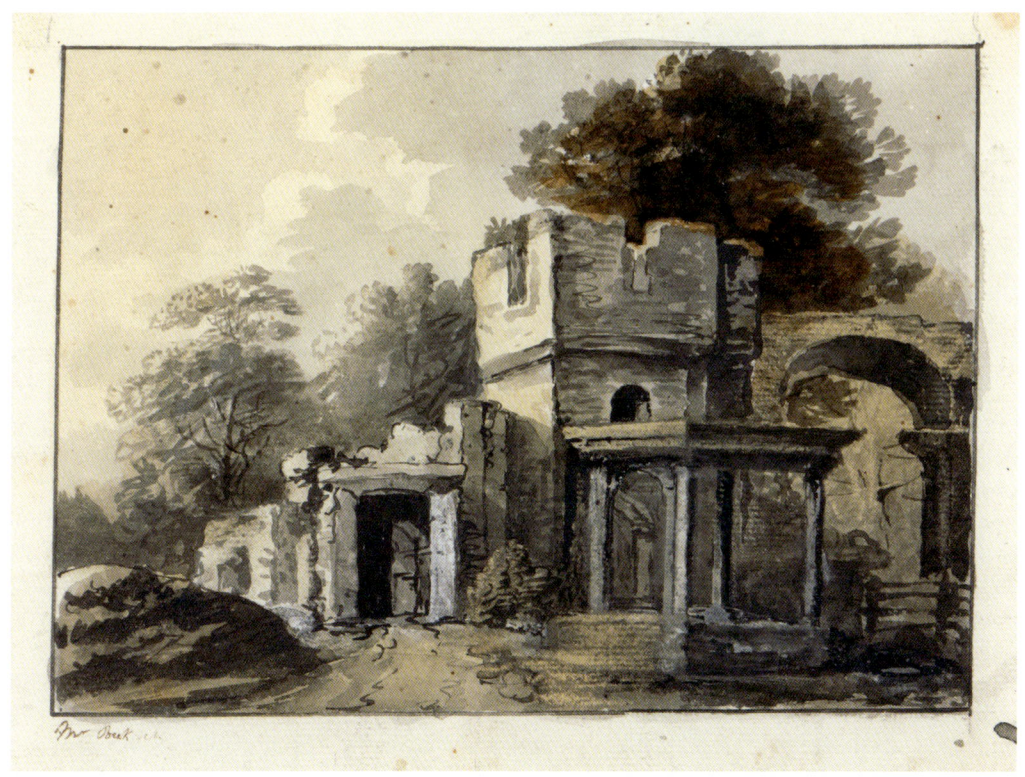

MORE THAN ORDINARY | 11

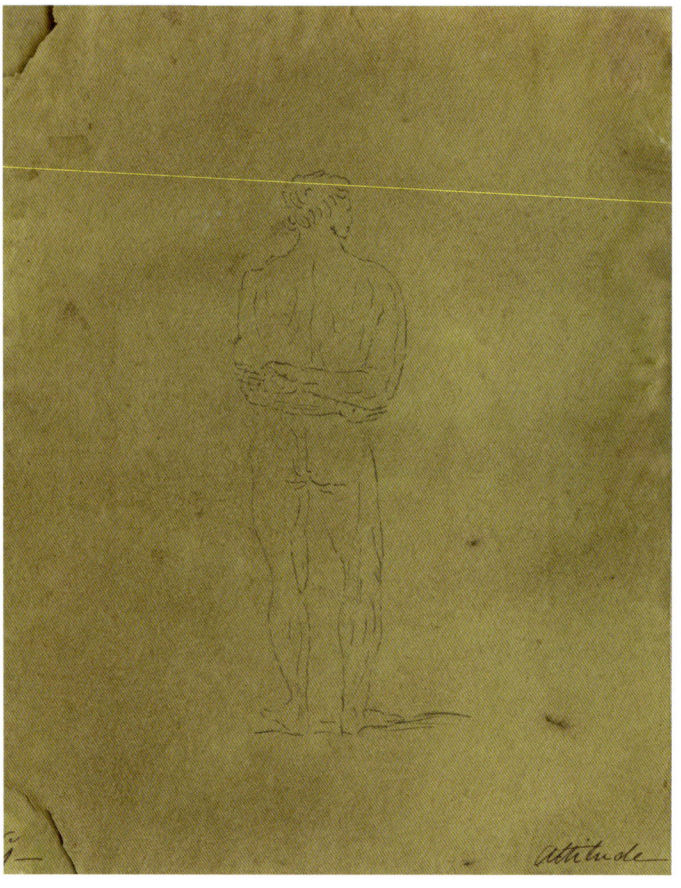 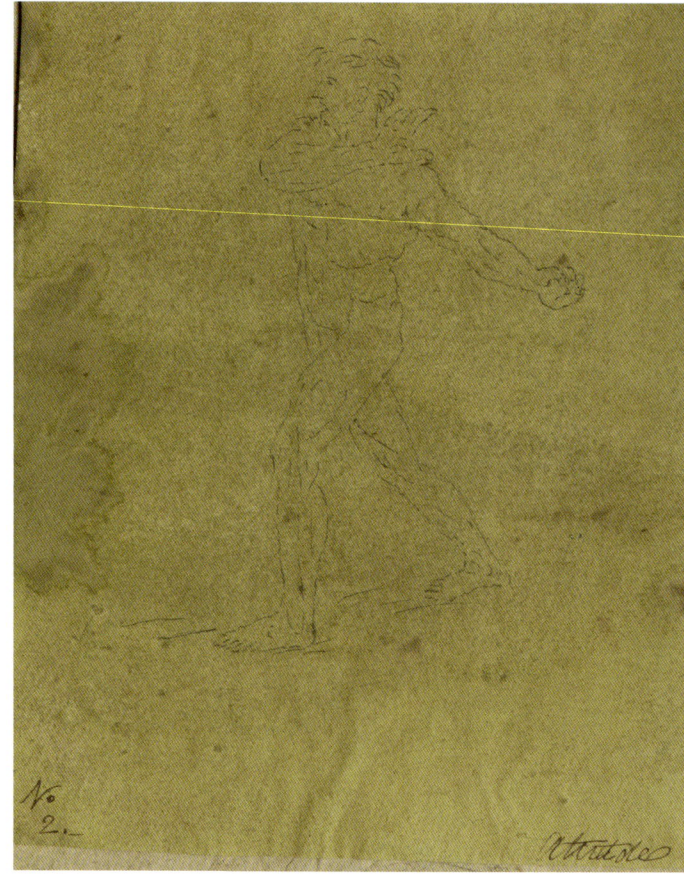

(Figures 135 and 136)

Attitude No. 1 and Attitude No. 2 (academy figure studies)
Anna Maria von Phul
Ink on paper
Unknown date

During his travels through Europe and his residence in Philadelphia, George Beck had assembled an impressive library of prints, and Anna Maria enjoyed access to his expansive collection. In a letter he wrote to her in 1812, Graff urged Anna Maria to use George's portfolios to find academy figures to serve as subjects of her work. Academy figures are studies of the human body that were made by artists who studied at European art academies during the 17th and 18th centuries. These figures were often based on a live model and were used to train aspiring artists in the nuances of depicting the human body. Because of the inequity in art education, women rarely had access to live models or training in anatomy, so Anna Maria had to copy others' figure studies to further her artistic abilities.

Graff states in a letter to Anna Maria that George "has a great number of engravings from the best masters." Always ready with artistic advice, Graff goes on to remind her to "not make finished copies, but accurate sketches of the finest parts of the best pictures." He recalls a "beautiful engraving . . . among Mr. Beck's prints of Bathing Venuses" and requests that if she can find it, to sketch it for him in India ink or bistre.

In addition to working as an art teacher, Mary Beck was a motivated artist who arranged exhibitions of her work in Kentucky and even sent some pieces to St. Louis to sell. In the late 1810s and 1820s, she arranged several shows of her paintings. Her enterprising nature is occasionally mentioned rather derisively in letters. One friend wrote to Anna Maria in 1823 that Mary was "sinking money into [the exhibition]" despite her friends opposing the idea.[11] Undaunted, she was always eager to put her art "before the citizens." After her relationship with Anna Maria evolved from one of student-teacher to one of equals, the two seemed to have encouraged creativity in each other. In her last known letter to Anna Maria, Mary discusses her plans to visit, saying: "the winter you know, my dear Maria, is not the time to walk and study from nature, which would certainly be one of our greatest pleasures, while together. It is true that congenial minds at all times feel a delight in each others company."[12] In their friendship, the women found artistic motivation and edification.

Anna Maria's early years in Lexington provided her with another close friendship—that of Ann Gist. In her letters to Ann, now part of the Kentucky Historical Society's Gist Family Papers, Anna Maria discusses silhouettes and paintings, news of Kentucky society and events, her mother's failing health, and the theatre. The letters also discuss her love of literature and poetry, and several of them contain original and transcribed verses. Dated letters span from 1806 to 1813, and the collection includes a small booklet of Anna Maria's handwritten poems. Many of the pages are filled with an affection not even seen in letters to her siblings. "You know I am not fond of finery," Anna Maria wrote in 1808, "yet I clasped your chain round my neck imediately and kist the locket which is so dear to both of us. This is what you call affection Ann but trust me those are feelings which I blush not to avow. . . ."[13]

In an undated note, she sends Ann one of her recent works, a copy of the painting *The Nightmare* by Henry Fuseli. As exemplified in other letters about her art, Anna Maria is particular about how her work is to be framed and presented. She instructs Ann to leave as much of the margins visible in the frame as possible, as her *relievo* technique would be lost if it were covered up.[14] In an amusing commentary on the artistic taste (or lack thereof) of Lexington's young women, Anna Maria laments that the painting would shock their nerves and therefore she cannot display it in a parlor.

> *You will find enclosed the Night-mare. If you should honour it with a frame let as much of the margin appear as you can. Pardon me Ann that I should dictate to your better taste, but the margin to use a technical phrase added a relievo to the picture I thought—It has been said of this picture of the Night mare by those who were extreemly fastidious you will allow, Ann; that A Lady "all in her night robe loose," was an indelicate sight. Sure it would be one among the last that I should hang in a parlor, but I can see nothing to shock the irritable nerves of the fine ladies of Lexington!—How flattered shall I be if it should obtain a place in your Chamber: Your ideas of the true delicacy are too refined and correct to exclude it on that scare.*

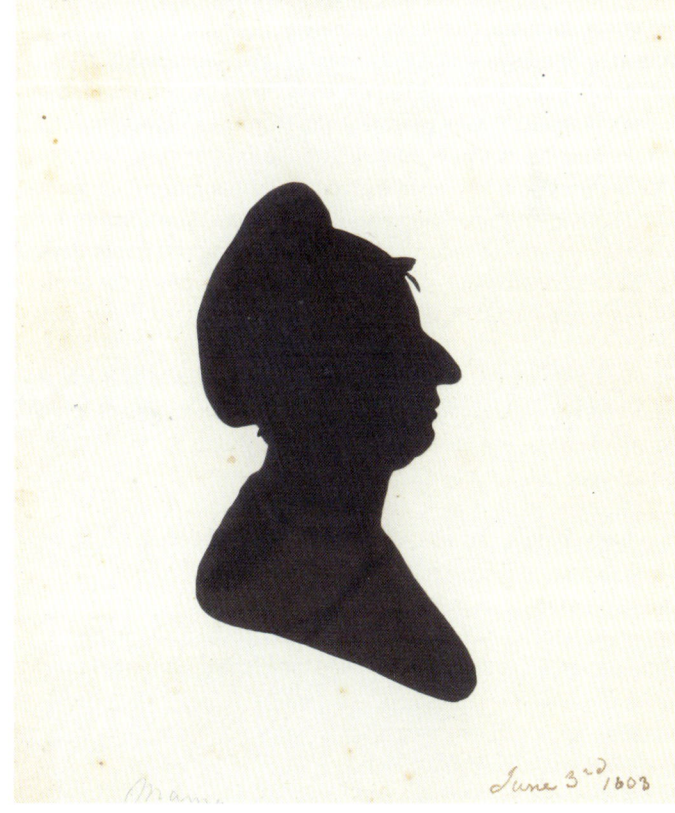

(Figure 120)

Mama (silhouette of Catharine von Phul)
Attributed to Anna Maria von Phul
Hollow cut on white paper
1803

---

11 Sarah Ward to Anna Maria von Phul, July 21, 1823.

12 Mary Beck to Anna Maria von Phul, June 15, 1823.

13 Anna Maria von Phul to Ann Gist, April 4, 1808. Gist Family Papers, 1806–1830, MSS 144, Kentucky Historical Society.

14 This technique gives art on paper a three-dimensional effect. Much like methods used by sculptors, *relievo* accentuates the subject by elevating it from the background.

Anna Maria's mother, Catharine, passed away in 1808. Her death was a harbinger of turbulent years to come. Henry, the de facto patriarch of the remaining von Phul family, left Kentucky for the Missouri Territory town of St. Louis in the early 1810s. Anna Maria's oldest brother, George, still living in Philadelphia with his wife and three young children, died in 1812. Though it is never explicitly stated in her letters, the absence of Graff, who briefly joined the military and then relocated to Baltimore, made this period especially difficult for Anna Maria. The letters they exchanged in the following years document the close bond they maintained despite their distance. In 1809 her sister Sarah married Lexington postmaster John Jordan Jr. Living independently as a single woman was not feasible, so Anna Maria moved in with the couple. John died just four years later. Newspaper records indicate that the home and the furniture it contained were sold at auction, leaving the two sisters homeless.[15] She wrote to her dear friend Ann of the family's upheaval in 1813: "Henry is now bending his way to the Missouri Teritory where danger awaits him, Graff devoted as he has ever been to us, now contrary to our wishes, and guided by military enthusiasm, the patriot wish to serve his country . . . is on duty at fort McHenry; my third brother is on the ocean: such is life's chequered path."[16]

During this period Anna Maria's letters reveal a life in limbo. In the 10 years preceding her death, Anna Maria lived with relatives and friends, only rarely remaining in the same home for more than a year or two. One long letter to her brother Henry in 1814 reported that she and Sarah were ending their current stay at a friend's home in Bourbon County, Kentucky, and they had made plans to live at the residences of two different family friends in the following month. Anna Maria entreated Sarah to take lodging at a new boardinghouse in Lexington, but the idea was deemed impossible given their financial circumstances.[17] "I do not admire living about in this way," she admitted to Henry.[18] Perhaps recording her surroundings on paper gave her a sense of stability—and her portraits of family a sense of permanence—in an otherwise uncertain life.

Having Henry settled in St. Louis opened a new world for Anna Maria. He relocated there to pursue a career as a merchant, which he felt would guarantee profitability in the young but thriving town of just over 1,600 residents. St. Louis was home to an increasingly colorful array of people—trappers, traders, Native Americans, boatmen, miners, artisans, Western explorers, freed and enslaved Black people, and French Creole families, many of whom were originally from New Orleans and French Canada. Perhaps most important for Henry's eventual success as a businessman and shop owner, St. Louisans had a taste for all things imported from the East Coast and abroad. During Henry's first decade in St. Louis, the town's population more than tripled.

Correspondence among the von Phul siblings in St. Louis and Kentucky provides insight into the excitement, culture, danger, and occasional monotony of life in the Missouri Territory—and how those farther east perceived it. It did not help Sarah's initial concerns for Henry's safety that he had chosen to relocate as war was looming. Although the War of 1812's best-known accounts focus on the eastern states and the Battle of New Orleans, skirmishes in the Missouri Territory also played a part. After one visit to Kentucky in early 1814, Sarah wrote to Henry about his return trip to St. Louis: "I have heard of your plan of arming your boat, but you cannot reasonably hope the danger will cease on the arrival. It is the opinion of the best judges that the town itself will be unsafe this summer. . . ."[19] In the letter's pages, some too damaged to surmise their full context, it is evident that the potential for attacks by Native Americans troubled Sarah. British troops had given firearms to Indigenous groups along the frontier, including the Shawnee, Sac, and Fox. Although there were no direct attacks on St. Louis during the War of 1812, violence instigated by both sides was reported in St. Charles and elsewhere across the territory.

> *I am sure I should be afraid to live in the town, much more to trust myself out of it, as it appears you young people do. Your strawberry parties would be truly delightful, but for the apprehensions of the danger attending. I dare say now you will laugh at me. . . . I was quite charm'd with your description of the prairie, and your parties—and but for the Indians, would have wish'd myself among you. It must be truly a very desirable state of society, when people can enjoy themselves with so much simplicity and innocence, without ceremony, and show and parade. . . .*[20]

Henry's social profile rose considerably after he married Rosalie Saugrain in 1816. She was part of the prestigious Saugrain family who had settled in St. Louis in 1799, and Anna Maria was thrilled to welcome a new sister into her family. In typical fashion, she commemorated the occasion with a drawing, telling Rosalie in a letter, "I enclose . . . a small butterfly, which I sketched from nature, a trifle in it self, and only presented as an offering of friendship and the only thing I could possibly convey to you in a letter." The arrival of nieces and nephews was also cause for excitement, and in 1819 she sent a "striking likeness" of her niece Rosalie to St. Louis. Henry and his wife went on to have 10 surviving children, the oldest of whom was named after Anna Maria.

---

15 *Kentucky Gazette*, November 15, 1813, 3.

16 Anna Maria von Phul to Ann Gist, May 12, 1813. Gist Family Papers, 1806–1830, MSS 144, Kentucky Historical Society.

17 The family's financial straits are also discussed in a January 5, 1817, letter from Sarah von Phul Jordan to Henry von Phul: "Maria and I find our incomes so limited that we are desirous of increasing it by every reasonable means, and have thought of selling our plate [silver]. It would add something to our little pittance."

18 Anna Maria von Phul to Henry von Phul, July 30, 1814.

19 Sarah von Phul Jordan to Henry von Phul, March 11, 1814 (presumed year).

20 Sarah von Phul Jordan to Henry von Phul, June 21, 1814.

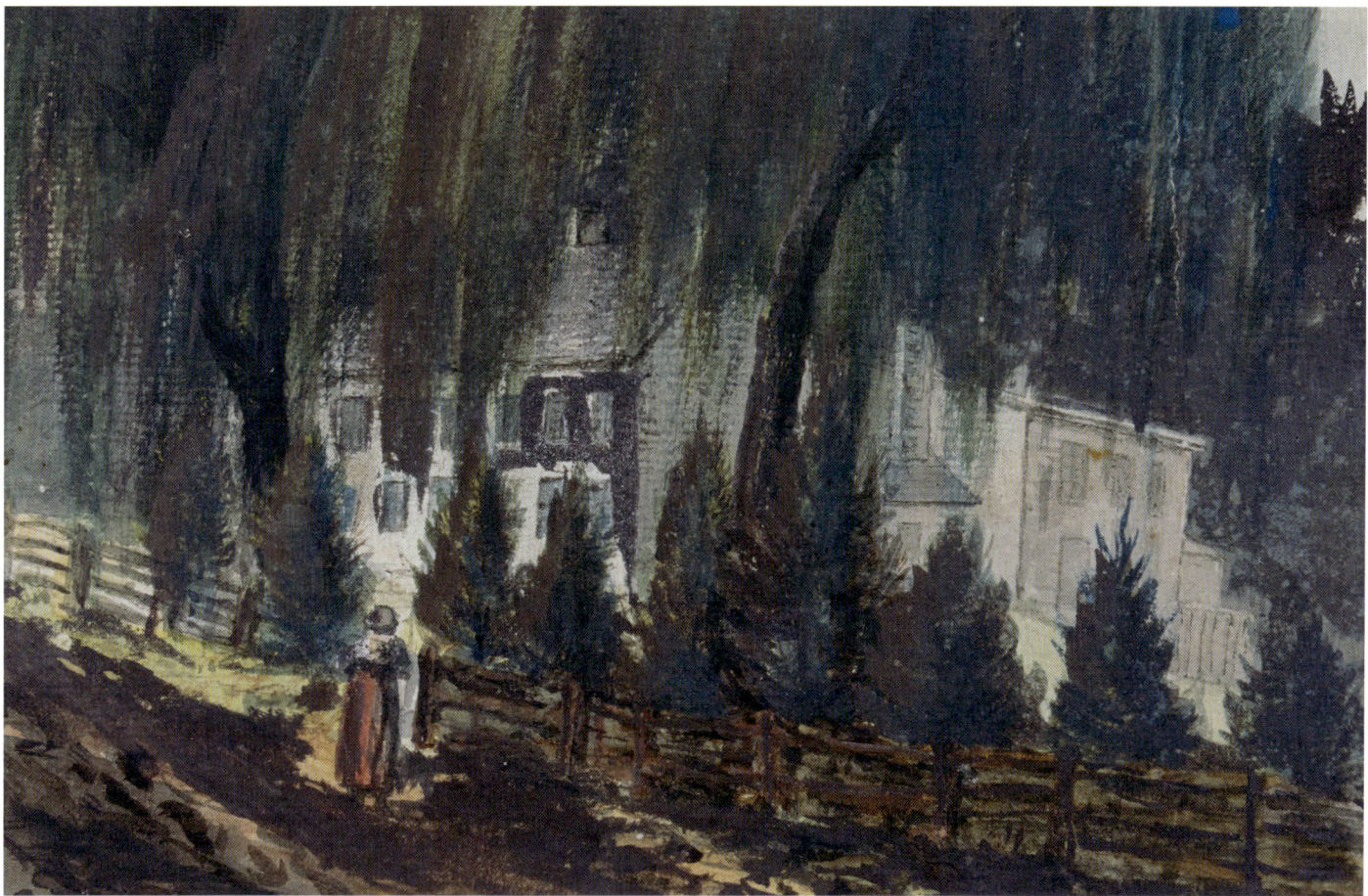

(Figure 123)

Chaumiere du Prairie
Anna Maria von Phul
Gouache on paper
Unknown date

"If ever there was a place that merited the term paradise it is this lovely spot I now enhabit. from my window where I now sit, I have a view of a lawn the most beautiful that can be conceived, flowers whose fragrance is wafted on every gale, the tulip of various dies, the splendid peony, and the immaculate gulder rose. . . ." Letter from Anna Maria von Phul to Rosalie Saugrain von Phul, May 12, 1819.

Anna Maria sketched Rosalie's butterfly from her new residence at Chaumiere du Prairie, the beautiful Kentucky estate of Colonel David Meade, located a few miles away from Lexington in Jessamine County. David and his wife, Sarah, invited Anna Maria and Sarah to stay with them in early 1815. Chaumiere would be the sisters' on-again, off-again residence over the next five years.

The Meades finished their Greek Revival home around 1800. At his "cottage in the meadow," David Meade brought to life his elaborate vision of an idyllic landscape: a lake with a small island connected to the lawn by an arched bridge (Figure 124); a seasonal waterfall; meandering walking paths; a Greek-style portico (Figure 12); a Chinese-style pavilion; and an expansive array of cherry trees, tulip trees, lilacs, honeysuckle, tulips, roses, and countless other flora. Chaumiere du Prairie became a destination for those visiting Kentucky—and for Kentuckians themselves—as well as politicians, including Aaron Burr, Henry Clay, James Monroe, Andrew Jackson, and Zachary Taylor.[21]

> *Mr. Meade never permits a gun to be fired on his grounds. The consequence is that the place is like a large Aviary, and about sun set they appear to fly on the poplar trees from every part of the country. . . . Whilst during the day, the little songsters fly from thicket to bush in the most fearless manner, the hares and squirrels like wise bound along the lawn unmolested.*[22]

---

21 Howard Downing, "Chaumiere du Prairie," National Register of Historic Places Nomination Form (Washington, DC: US Department of the Interior, National Park Service, 1975), item 8, page 3.

22 Anna Maria von Phul to Henry von Phul, May 12, 1821.

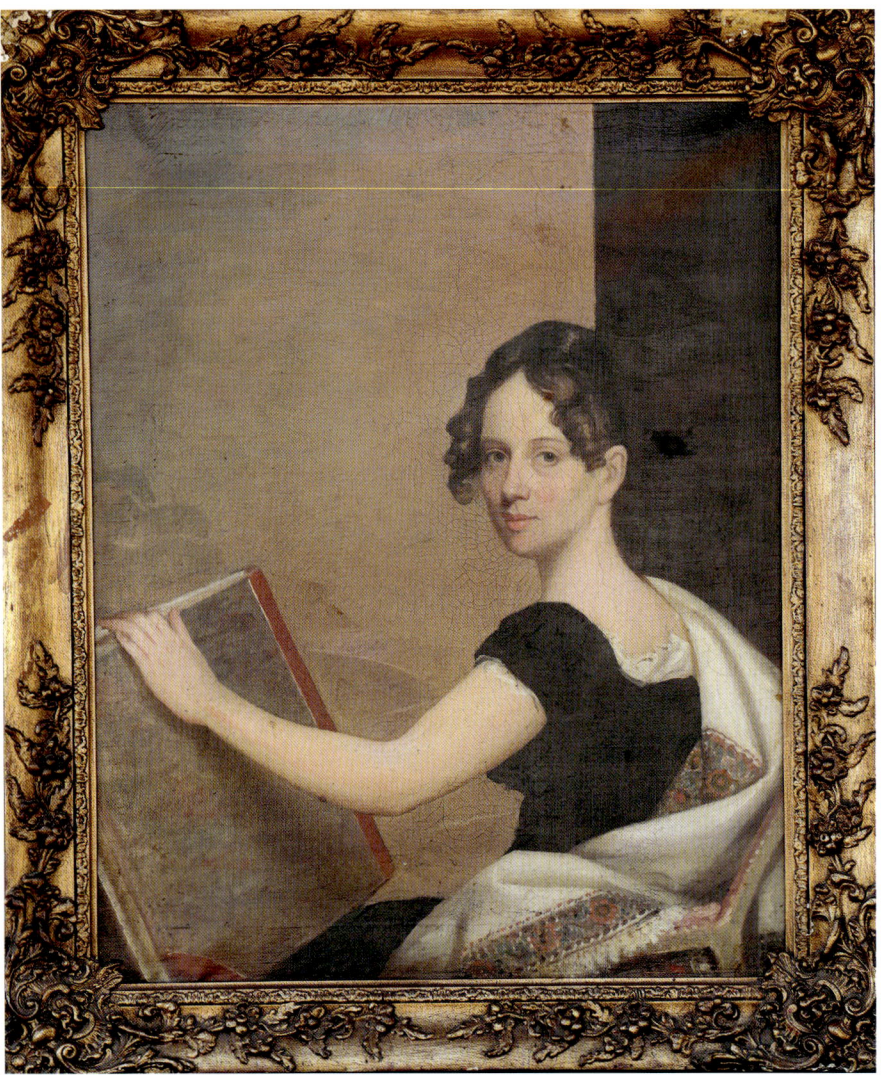

Portrait of Anna Maria von Phul
Matthew Harris Jouett
Oil on canvas
ca. 1818

Collection of Felicity Huffman

Anna Maria described Chaumiere's grounds as a paradise. However, David Meade's plan for the estate could only be fulfilled using the labor of dozens of enslaved persons: 50 in 1810 and 39 in 1820.[23] Although these men and women kept the trees pruned, gardens weeded, and grass trimmed and ensured countless other tasks were tended to, they received none of the credit for the estate's beauty.

Even as she was surrounded by spectacular scenery, Anna Maria struggled with artistic motivation and opportunity. During her early years in Lexington she befriended two young aspiring local artists, William Edward West and Matthew Harris Jouett, and during the 1810s she watched as they became successful portrait painters. West had also studied art under George and Mary Beck,[24] and by 1809 he showed such promise that he relocated to Philadelphia to learn from renowned painter Thomas Sully. During one of Henry's trips to Philadelphia in 1811, he visited West's studio to sit for a portrait miniature. Although the location of this miniature is not known today, at the time Sarah deemed it a "very correct likeness . . . executed in his best stile and with the happiest effect."[25] In the following years, West remained close with the von Phul family.

It was Matthew Harris Jouett, however, who seems to have been especially dear to Anna Maria. His name appears in several of her letters, including one written from Chaumiere in 1816, in which she tells her brother Henry that Jouett has gone to Boston to study with portrait artist Gilbert Stuart: "He wrote me a long letter which roused all my dormant ambition again and I am now drawing a picture which I intend for you." She admits that for some time she had neglected her art, but thanks to Jouett's encouragement she had "commenced drawing again."

---

23 1820 United States Federal Census, Jessamine County, Kentucky.
24 Patti Carr Black, *Art in Mississippi, 1720–1980* (Jackson: University Press of Mississippi, 1988), 45.
25 Sarah von Phul Jordan to Henry von Phul, August 8, 1811.

Letter from Anna Maria von Phul to Henry von Phul
February 11, 1818

Anna Maria stayed with her sister Sarah and brother-in-law in Edwardsville for several months before and after the birth of Sarah's first child. Anna Maria gave Henry the news in an exuberant letter, saying, "I have the agreable intelligence to communicate of Sarah's being the happy mother of a bouncing girl. . . . They will call it—no you must guess, but the first letter is M."

As much as Jouett inspired Anna Maria, she may have had a similar effect on him. Upon the artist's return to Kentucky, several of the von Phuls commissioned portraits. He depicted Anna Maria proudly holding a large portfolio of her drawings and offering a gentle gaze and slight smile—perhaps directed at the painter, rather than the viewer, in a nod to their close friendship. Although only this portrait of Anna Maria remains today, Jouett may have intended to paint a second, for in an 1819 letter Graff observed, "I see Mr. Jouett has finished your first portrait. Did you ever set for the other?"

In 1817, Sarah wed James Mason. He established himself in Edwardsville, in what was soon to become the new US state of Illinois. Sarah and Anna Maria made the journey to meet him later that year. Graff had joined Henry in St. Louis a year or two prior, so the trip would be a reunion for the four siblings. Travel was difficult. Anna Maria later remarked to her sister-in-law that if she were a bird she would visit more often, but the roads and distance frightened her. Still, she went on to make the trip between Kentucky and St. Louis many more times.

The St. Louis that unfolded before Anna Maria must have captivated her. Perhaps it was the change of scenery. Perhaps it was being reunited with her dear brothers and new sister-in-law. Whatever the reason, her creativity was reinvigorated, and she filled two known sketchbooks during her stay over the spring and summer. St. Louis in the 1810s was a city in transformation. Once a rural frontier town that French settlers built on trade, by 1818 it was evolving into a thriving American city. The cultural and economic center of the Missouri Territory, St. Louis boasted some 3,500 people in the city proper and 6,000 more in the surrounding countryside. As both a destination itself and a jumping-off point for travelers heading north, south, east, or west, St. Louis was a confluence of diverse people.

Settlers had largely expulsed the Native American presence in Kentucky by the time the von Phul family moved there, so Anna Maria's contact with Indigenous peoples had likely been limited. In St. Louis, however, Native Americans were part of everyday life. Among Anna Maria's portraits is a Native American woman, and although her appearance is striking and expressive, her identity is not known. This woman's place in Anna Maria's portfolio is a reminder of the ubiquity of Native peoples in the region. But their presence in St. Louis was not simply represented by the people who walked its streets: Their long history loomed large in the form of some two dozen earthwork mounds.

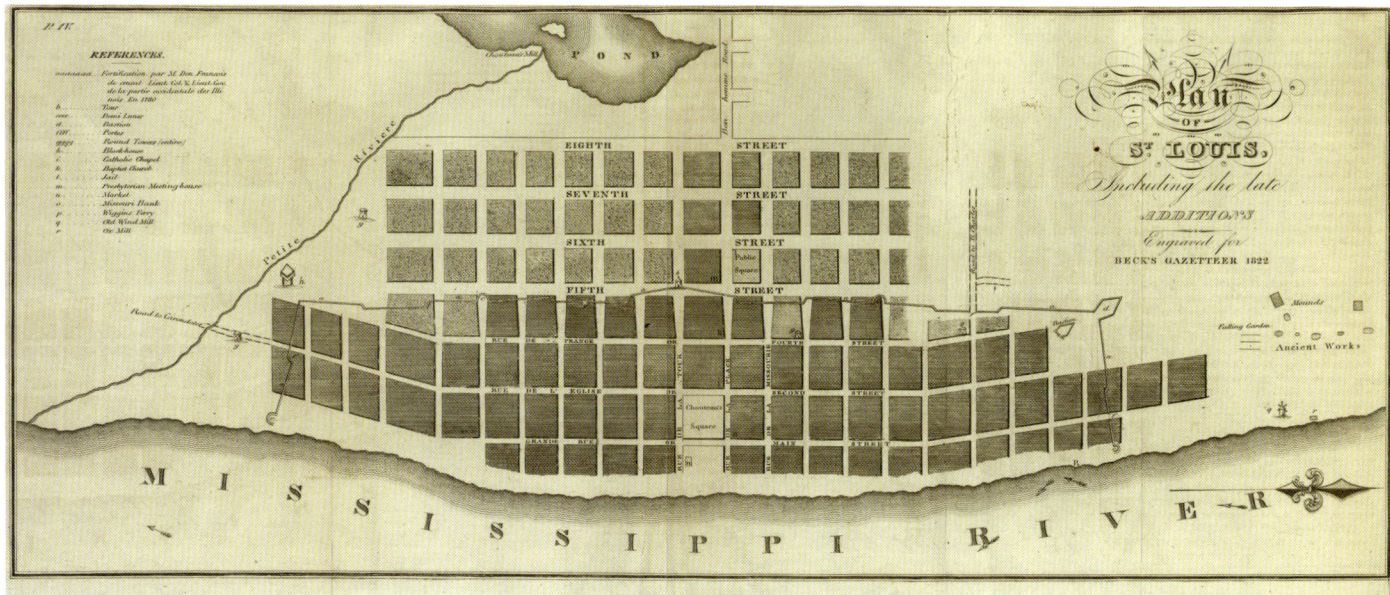

Plan of St. Louis, Including the late additions
Engraved by Lewis Caleb Beck for *Beck's Gazetteer*
1822

Nine Native American earthworks are included in Beck's map. He titled them "Ancient Works," and they are visible on the far right side of the map (see detail).

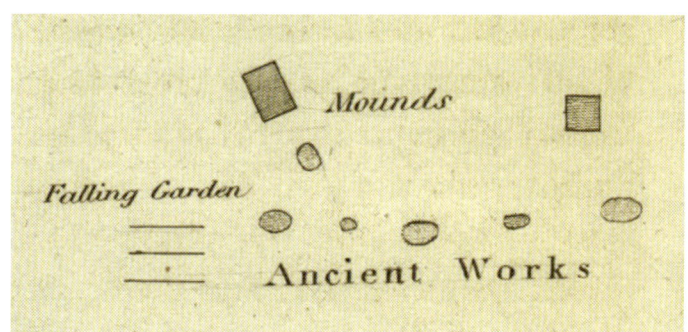

Plan of St. Louis
Detail of Native American earthworks

(Figure 33)

View of a mound near St. Louis
Anna Maria von Phul
Pencil and wash on paper
1818

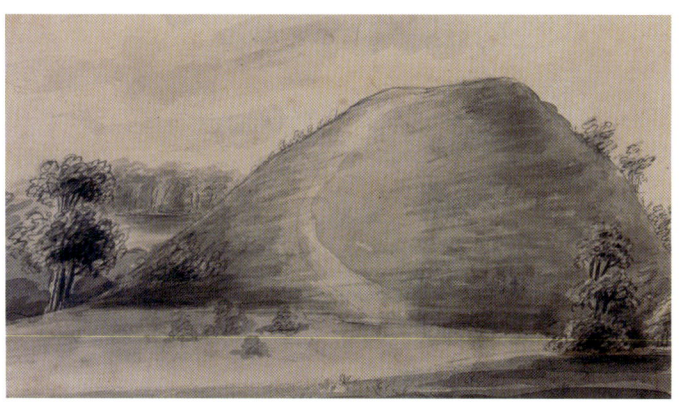

(Figure 76)

Native American woman in a point blanket
Anna Maria von Phul
Watercolor on paper
1818

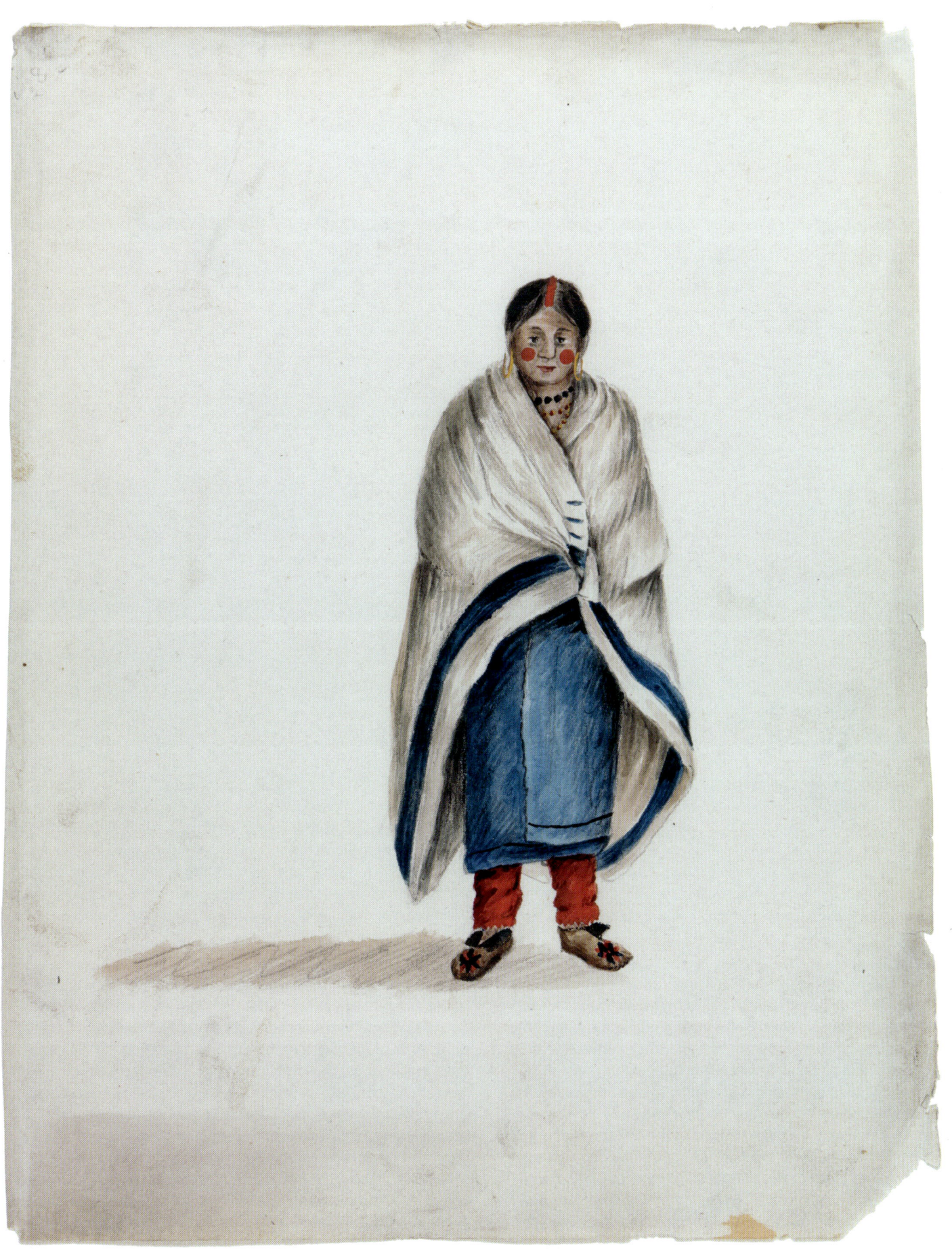

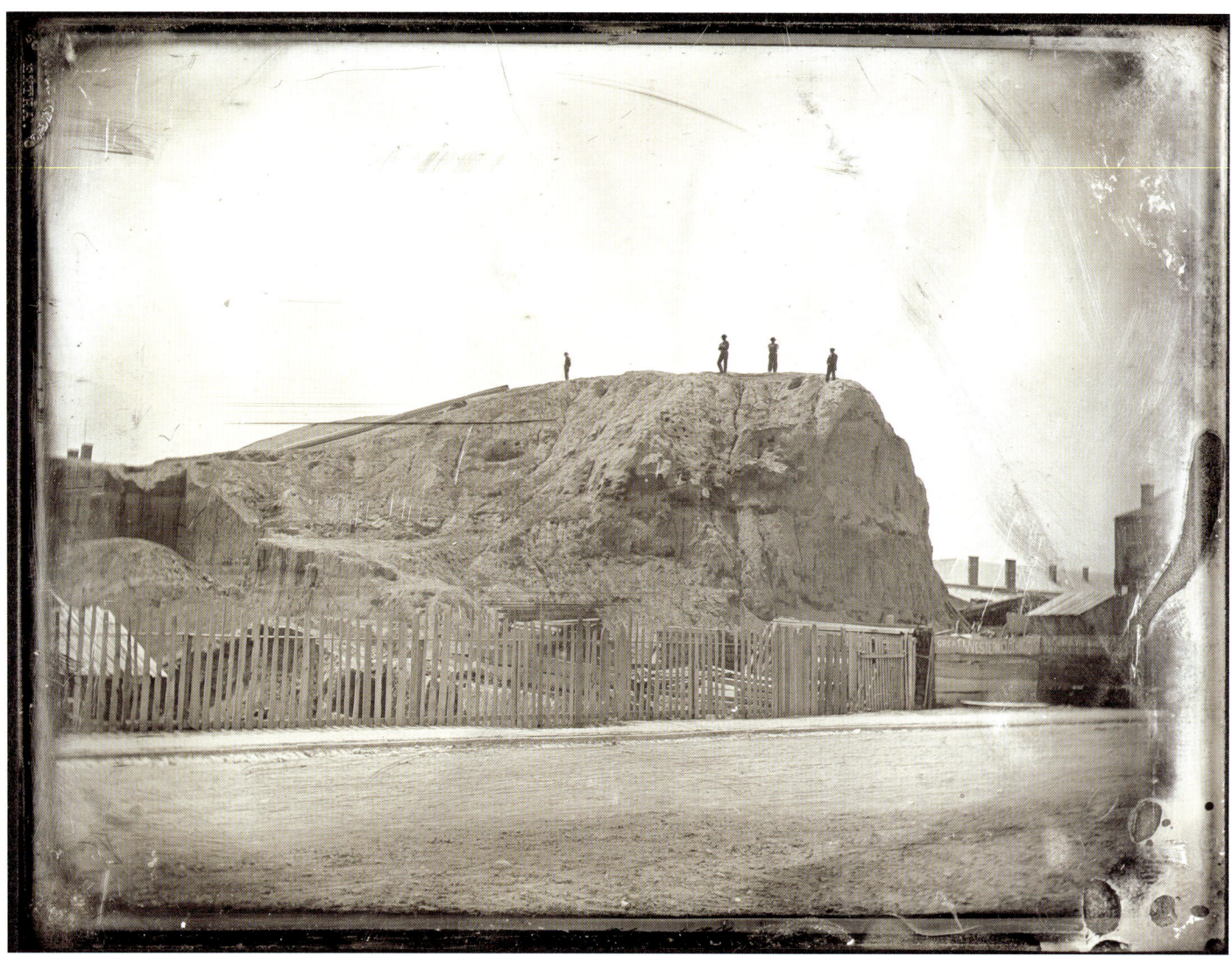

Big Mound on 5th and Mound streets
Thomas M. Easterly
Daguerreotype
ca. 1854

Daguerreotypist Thomas Easterly documented St. Louis during the 1850s and 1860s. His collection includes several daguerreotypes of the city's largest earthwork mound, commonly called Big Mound, before and during its destruction. The ceremonial chamber mound measured 319 feet long by 34 feet high. Although portions were already removed when he took this image, the people and surrounding buildings convey its imposing scale.

It's uncertain how much Anna Maria knew about the history of Indigenous peoples or the significance of their mounds, but she was undoubtedly transfixed by them. Although there were some prehistoric earthworks around Lexington, none came close to what she saw in St. Louis. These remarkable sights made their way into her 1818 sketchbooks six times. The mounds anchored the town: St. Louisans used them as markers and guideposts, and they perched upon them to observe the city and river from above (as Anna Maria did in Figure 36). One of her depictions of the mounds features a man—possibly Henry or Graff—posed in the foreground (Figure 69). Her intention with this piece is unclear, but the composition makes it seem as though the subject is posing in front of the mounds. Her "sightseeing" views of the mounds hint at their treatment as tourist attractions. By 1821 one of them was the site of Mound Garden, which was billed as "a place of entertainment and recreation." St. Louisans used the mounds for such purposes for decades until they were razed to make way for the city's expansion. Mapmakers provided early depictions of the mounds on paper, and while these were sometimes elegantly rendered, Anna Maria may have been among the first American or European artists to paint the mounds in St. Louis. However, she was hardly the last. Many later artists also documented these remaining markers of a populous and vibrant Native American society.

Another theme Anna Maria wove into her depictions of the people and places that made up St. Louis is the mix of cultures that infused the city. Originally settled by Native Americans and then French Creoles—and ruled in turn by France and Spain (then briefly France once again)—the territory was now firmly under United States control, and Missouri had its sights set on statehood. The descriptor "Creole," which is often used to label the early non-Native people and culture of Missouri, stems from the use of the word in colonial Louisiana. It encompasses people of French, West African, Caribbean, Spanish, and Native American (and sometimes even German) heritage who melded in Louisiana and formed a distinct culture and identity all their own. St. Louis's Creole milieu permeates the details of Anna Maria's art.

Domestic architecture also reflects the territory's time of transition in the 1810s and 1820s. During that era Missouri homes most closely resembled the French Creole style that was found in abundance along the more southern reaches of the Mississippi River. These homes bear features that make them immediately recognizable, including *poteaux en terre* (post in ground) construction, prominent wraparound galleries (porches) supported by columns, and wide rooflines with several dormers.

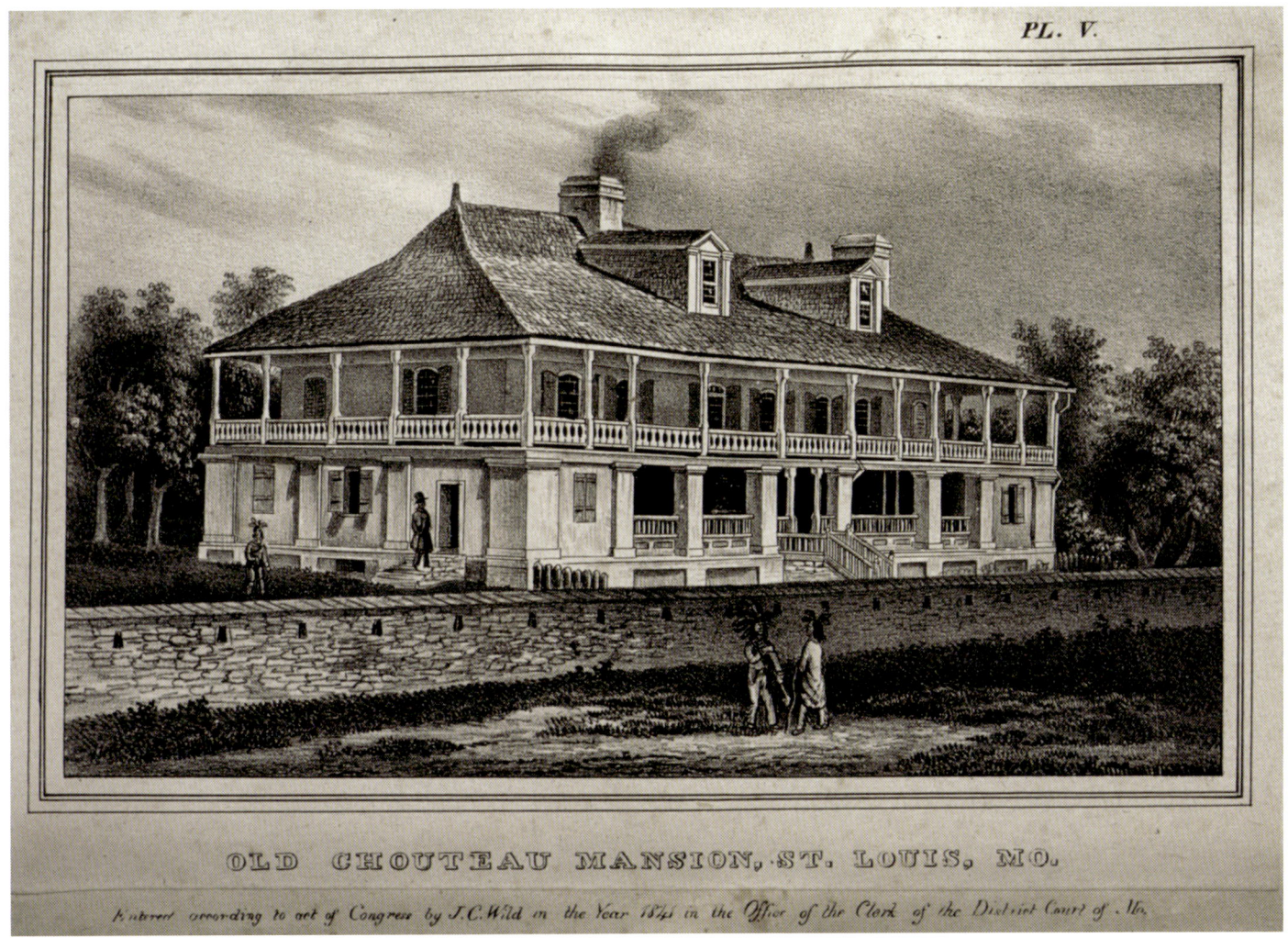

Old Chouteau Mansion, St. Louis, MO.
John Caspar Wild
Painting and lithograph
1841–1842

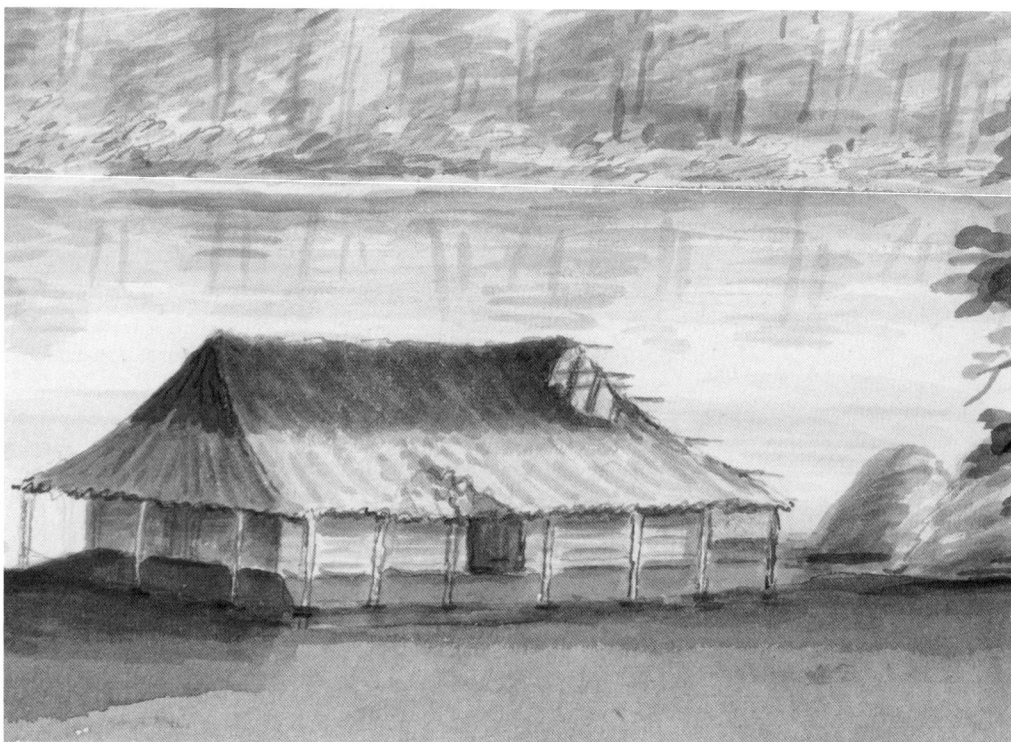

(Figure 66)

Abandoned Creole home
Anna Maria von Phul
Wash on paper
1818

As enmeshed in St. Louis culture as these Creole homes were, their dominance on the cityscape waned as the old French families found themselves surrounded by the city's new influx of Americans. By 1821 the author of St. Louis's first city directory didn't hesitate to call the French homes old-fashioned (but he was sure to note that the large porches were a nice respite from the summer heat). Eleven years prior, one newspaper reporter wasn't as charitable when describing the town's buildings, writing, "when I look at its wretched plan . . . the irregular manner, and singular taste in which its houses are built . . . I cannot but wish . . . a conflagration would seize it and burn it to the ground; and that a different and more elegant taste, giving it a new form may cause it to rival in beauty any town in the western country."[26] He offered a halfhearted apology to outraged citizens in the next issue of the paper, but it, too, was followed by a second (albeit softer) assertion that their homes did need upgrading and perhaps a fire would do the trick—if only new buildings could rise from the ashes.[27]

By the time of Missouri's statehood, brick homes—many of them in the Federal style, familiar to residents who had relocated from points east—began to change the look of St. Louis's streets. As old-fashioned as wooden buildings may have seemed to newcomers, they remained a significant part of the city's landscape, despite increasing competition from brick ones. In the southern part of the city, where many French Creole families eventually settled (descriptively called Frenchtown, located in present-day Soulard), wooden homes outnumbered brick and stone homes 223 to 78 in 1821. The Chouteau Mansion, a bastion of Creole architecture, was a fixture in the heart of downtown St. Louis until 1845.

Two of Anna Maria's pieces hint at this shift in housing (Figures 66 and 38). In the former, a lone Creole home, perched along what appears to be the Mississippi River, seems at first glance a peaceful abode. But a second look confirms that the house is abandoned, and its roof is in severe decay. The rundown house signals the end of an era—even if that wasn't the artist's intent. In the latter, two very different homes—one brick, one Creole—anchor a charming street scene filled in every corner with life and activity. Historian Bob Moore of Gateway Arch National Park extensively researched the city's layout and proposed that the two-story brick Federal-style home is the Carr Residence (built 1815) and once stood on South Main, where the Arch grounds are today.[28] It sat across from a small Creole home, built by Louis Marcheteau Desnoyers in 1766. In these two homes, St. Louis's past met its future.

---

26 *Missouri Gazette and Public Advertiser (Louisiana Gazette),* October 11, 1810, 3.
27 *Missouri Gazette and Public Advertiser (Louisiana Gazette),* October 17, 1810, 3.
28 Unpublished correspondence, Missouri Historical Society files.

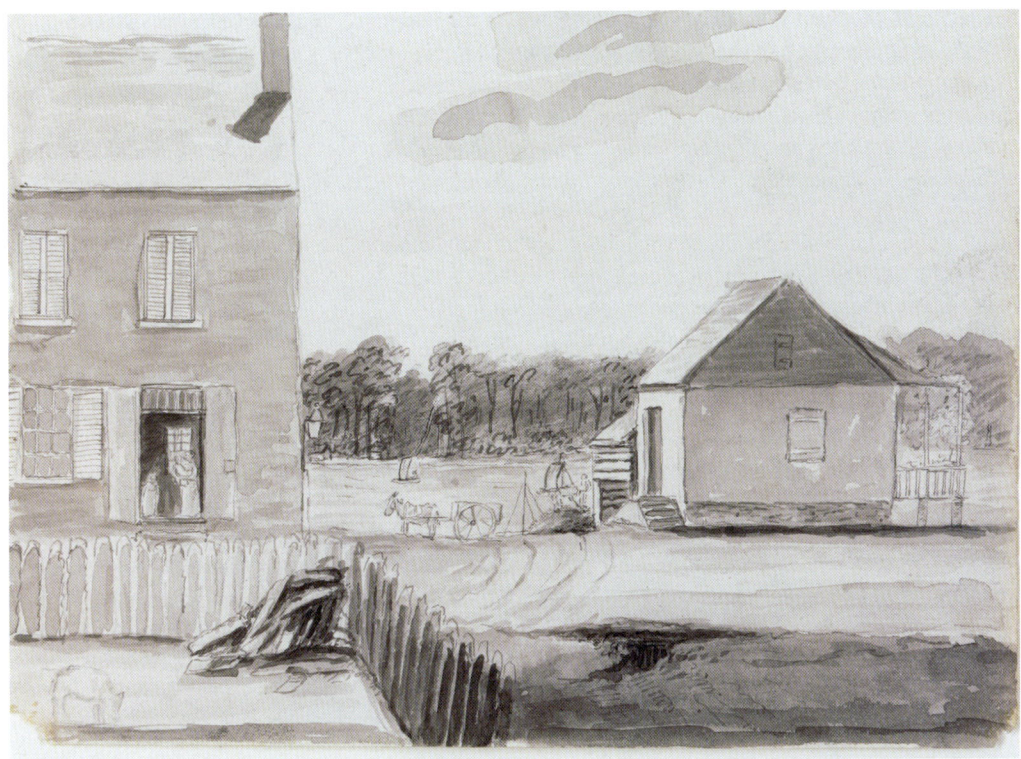

(Figure 38)

View of two St. Louis homes
Anna Maria von Phul
Wash on paper
1818

As with St. Louis's homes, Anna Maria's depictions of people and their dress was another manifestation of the city's blend of cultures. Along with the standard leather boots and shoes of the day, one also might have seen women wearing embroidered satin slippers imported from France or moccasins that combined Indigenous and American styling. Von Phul's Native American woman in Figure 76 wears moccasins decorated with a blue and red design on the upper, perhaps made of quillwork. Likewise, the working woman in Figure 74 and the cart driver in Figure 72 wear versions of moccasins.

Another striking accessory featured in Anna Maria's portraits are the headwraps worn by many of the women. During the region's colonial history the Spanish governor of Louisiana enacted sumptuary laws, commonly known as "tignon laws." Intended to limit the rights of freed women of color, this oppressive edict required Creole women of African descent to cover their hair in public to distinguish them from their white Creole counterparts. However, the tignon, which resembled the headwraps worn in West Africa, became a fashion accessory rather than a symbol of oppression. Women folded colorful fabric into elaborate shapes, infusing their tignons with creativity and style. The colonial laws and the transfer of culture along the Mississippi River from New Orleans to St. Louis were evident throughout the customs and style of early Missouri and naturally made their way into Anna Maria's art.

Nowhere does Anna Maria record the identity of her subjects with headwraps. The women she depicts wearing them have ambiguous ethnicities. At first glance they appear to be light-complected Creole women, but the cultural mix of people who lived in St. Louis makes accurately identifying their ethnicity impossible. It raises an interesting question about the origin of this style in St. Louis: Did tignons cross demographics? Another explanation could be a relatively short-lived trend of wearing turbans during the late 18th and early 19th centuries. Fashion plates and portraits from the time suggest that turbans enjoyed some popularity in Europe and along the East Coast as part of elegant ensembles and eveningwear. The two women in Figures 74 and 92 are not dressed for any special social occasion; rather, they're in everyday workwear. While the genesis of the headwraps shown in Anna Maria's art is difficult to pinpoint, the style endured in St. Louis, and some Creole women continued wearing them into the 1850s and 1860s.

Anna Maria's depictions of St. Louis are also notable for what's missing from them: steamboats. Unlike renderings of St. Louis that would soon follow, steamboats had yet to dominate the riverfront in the early 1810s. Instead, simple human-powered keelboats and small rowboats with sails make their way across her page. In August 1817 the *Zebulon Pike* was the first steamboat to arrive at St. Louis. Within a few years this efficient mode of river transportation was a mainstay, and it heralded a new age for the Mississippi and Missouri rivers—and all the towns along them. Once again, Anna Maria captured the Missouri Territory on the cusp of dramatic change.

In the 1950s, Missouri Historical Society director Charles van Ravenswaay remarked to the *St. Louis Post-Dispatch* how fortunate it was that Anna Maria von Phul chose subjects of "greatest interest to us today."[29] With housing, clothing, and transportation front and center throughout von Phul's art, van Ravenswaay's assessment remains accurate. However, as much as her work tells us about early St. Louis, there are still large swaths of everyday life on which she never focused her brush. Notably absent from her portraits are enslaved people, who made up approximately 15 percent of the population in the Missouri Territory. So while her work details certain aspects of the city, it is hardly representative of everyone's experience.

Late in the summer of 1818, Anna Maria returned to Kentucky. Not long after, Henry and Rosalie's daughter Rosalie died. A friend of Anna Maria's who had recently returned from St. Louis relayed the news before Anna Maria received the letter regarding her niece's passing. With no reliable mail service running between Kentucky and the Missouri Territory, the von Phul siblings often counted on the kindness of travelers to convey their correspondences. Henry likely felt this frustration in his business and his personal life, for in 1818 he petitioned the United States Congress to establish a mail route from Louisville.

Although a flurry of lengthy letters between Lexington and St. Louis the following year shed light on Anna Maria's life, no dated artwork exists from this time. Anna Maria had made new acquaintances when she lived in Missouri, and she endeavored to keep in contact despite the distance. However, in the case of her correspondences with Rosalie's mother, Madame Saugrain, distance was not the only barrier to communication—there was also the issue of language. To better converse with French-speaking St. Louisans, Anna Maria began taking French lessons, and she peppered her letters with short French phrases. Much to Graff's disapproval, however, she thought one semester of study would suffice. In a letter he warns her that "vanity alone can flatter herself with such hopes in speaking a language in six months—especially where it is not used by any around you." Their letters do not reveal if Anna Maria decided to continue studying the language, but with a large French-speaking population still prominent in St. Louis, it would have been helpful.

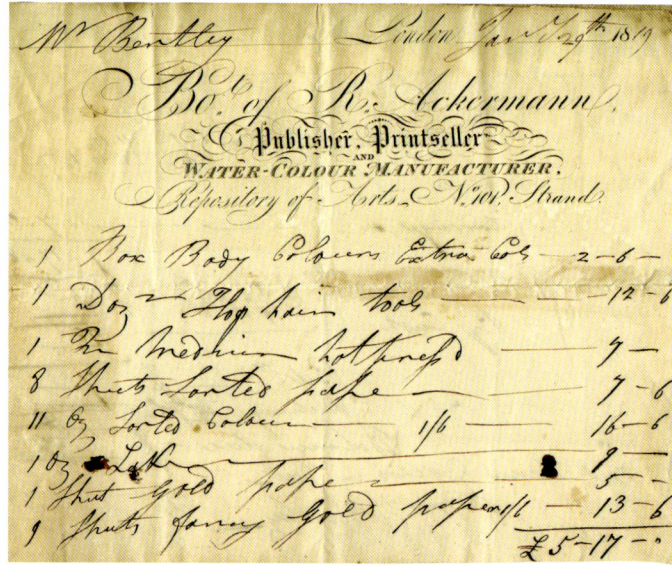

Receipt for the purchase of art supplies from R. Ackermann of London
1819

By the turn of the 18th century, watercolor was well loved by artists for painting atmospheric landscapes and portrait miniatures. Previously relegated to quick color studies and preparatory sketches, watercolor's expressive yet technical abilities quickly cemented it as a serious medium. Among other supplies, the Ackermann receipt lists one box of "Body Colours," or gouache—an opaque paint similar to watercolor—which Anna Maria frequently used in her work. In the early 1800s watercolors and gouache came dried in cakes, which artists rehydrated before use. Neatly organized carrying cases allowed artists on the move to conveniently transport their paint and supplies for outdoor painting, which is likely why Anna Maria used them during her travels.

---

29 *St. Louis Post-Dispatch*, February 4, 1954, 24.

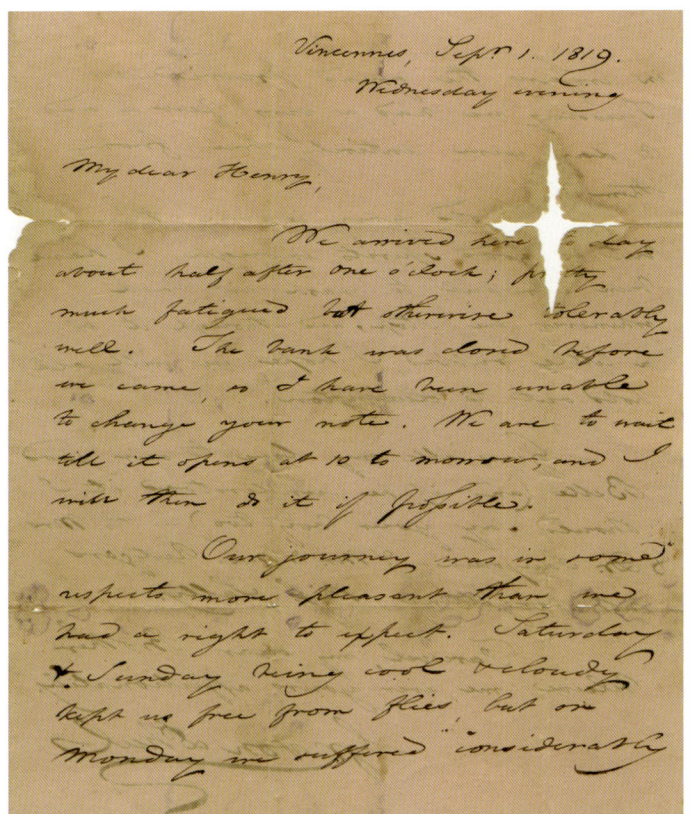

Letter from Graff von Phul to Henry von Phul
September 1, 1819

Halfway through his trip from St. Louis to Lexington, Graff paused to write Henry an update on his travels. It was the last time the siblings heard from their brother.

In addition to urging Anna Maria to keep taking French lessons, Graff also wrote to remind her not to neglect her drawing. "I have written so much to you on this subject I am weary," he gently chastised. An amateur artist himself and a steadfast supporter of her artistic endeavors, Graff eagerly compared notes about the merit of certain paintings. He also sent her details about the artworks he observed in St. Louis that were owned by people such as Auguste Chouteau and Bishop William DuBourg. DuBourg infused St. Louis with religious focus and access to fine art. He brought original works by Paolo Veronese, Peter Paul Rubens, Guido Reni, and other European masters to furnish his new brick cathedral.[30]

> First then, with regard to the pictures of Mr. Du Burg: I must repeat or confirm what I said—The Centurion of Paul Veronese—has many beauties I allow—but it has as many glaring defects—and its general effect is far from pleasing—As to the Madona I have not changed my opinion—but I must say it is entirely in consonance with that of the good Bishop—he told me he thought my judgement correct of all his pictures. . . .[31]

Graff's letters also reported the latest happenings and challenges facing the city. Graff had a propensity for relating gloomy news, and his letters from 1819 mention the passing of Henry's father-in-law, Dr. Antoine Saugrain; a plague of mosquitoes that threatened to eat him alive; and rains so heavy they collapsed Mill Creek dam, sweeping away several buildings and leaving much of the town strewn with mud and dead fish. Tiring of St. Louis, he informed Anna Maria of his intentions to return to Kentucky, but it's not clear if the visit was meant to be a permanent relocation or simply a trip to see his sister and old friends. Graff left St. Louis for Kentucky in late August, but near Vincennes, Indiana, he disappeared. Exactly what fate befell Graff is still unknown. Back in Lexington, an eager Anna Maria awaited the arrival of her brother, but in late September, she received news that his body had been found, along with a few of his personal effects: a pair of gold cufflinks, a piece of material taken from his pants, and some of his hair. She was distraught. "There are indeed but few of us left," she wrote Henry in December, "and I as ardently wish we may be again a united family—never to separate."[32]

---

30 1821 St. Louis *City Directory*.
31 Graff von Phul to Anna Maria von Phul, March 15, 1819.
32 Anna Maria von Phul to Henry von Phul, December 14, 1819.

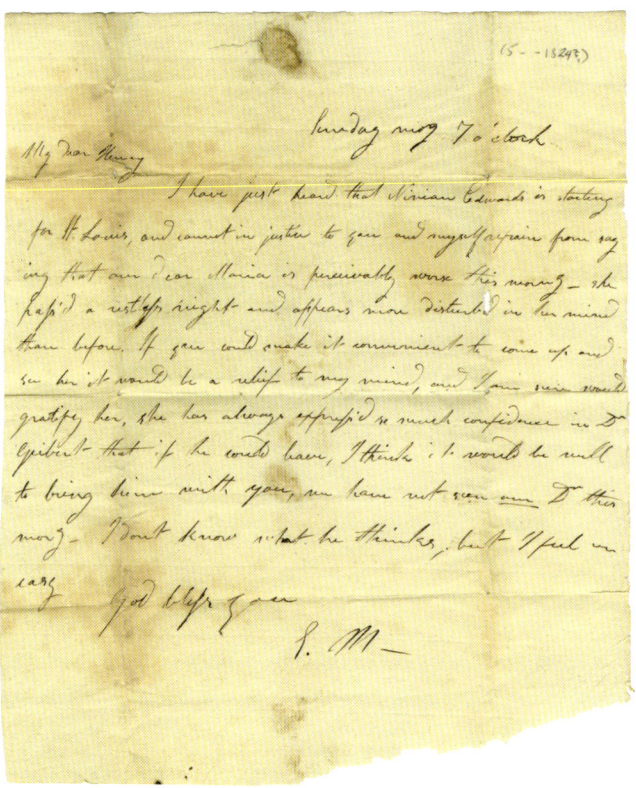

Letter from Sarah von Phul Mason to Henry von Phul
Unknown date

"Maria is perceptibly worse this morn . . . and appears more disturbed in her mind than before," Sarah wrote in a hasty note. "I feel uneasy," she ended, forebodingly.

In the spring of 1820, as soon as the weather allowed travel, Anna Maria joined her siblings once again. In Edwardsville, Sarah was not well and feared she might not survive the birth of her next child, so Anna Maria spent several months by her side. Although the trip between Missouri and Kentucky had once terrified her, the path was by now familiar. Torn between two places—each one filled with people whose company she enjoyed—Anna Maria returned to Chaumiere du Prairie the following spring. "I shall be as happy in Kentucky as this state of probation will admit," she told Rosalie, yet she seems to have gone back to Kentucky to settle some of her affairs. Whatever the reason for her return, she didn't stay for long, and by the summer of 1821 she was back in St. Louis—this time for good.

Because family letters from 1821 to 1823 are few and no dated art from this period is known to exist, piecing together the details of these years in Anna Maria's life is difficult. We do know that she remained active in both the Lexington and St. Louis art worlds. Through Henry's store she attempted to sell frames and framed prints or paintings shipped from James McIntosh, a contact she had in Lexington. McIntosh, a skilled carver and gilder, owned a frame shop in Lexington and likely helped Anna Maria frame many of her own works when she lived there. After she moved to St. Louis, he shipped her frames and pictures, hoping to establish a new market. However, the demand for such goods in Missouri was not as strong as McIntosh had hoped, and he asked Henry to sell the pieces for whatever they could bring to save the cost of shipping them back to Kentucky.

It seems incongruous with St. Louis's booming population that frames would be so difficult to sell, especially as the country was experiencing exponential growth in the appreciation and commodification of art for the middle class. An economic depression at the time, caused in part by a lack of hard currency, was likely an underlying cause. By then St. Louis boasted two known portrait painters, François Marie Guyol de Guiran and Chester Harding. Perhaps reflecting St. Louis's fickle art market and challenging economy, Guyol de Guiran supplemented his portrait commissions by tutoring students in arithmetic, geometry, trigonometry, algebra, and other subjects. By 1821 he was teaching drawing and writing at Saint Louis College—now known as Saint Louis University—but he soon left the city for New Orleans.

Still confident that St. Louis had a latent desire for art, James McIntosh wrote to Anna Maria that she should urge Matthew Harris Jouett to visit. McIntosh said that Jouett's skills had greatly improved and that "his merit would Command attention & Business" in St. Louis, writing, "I think were you to write himself a few lines on the subject it would have a tendence to fix his determination." It is not known if Anna Maria wrote Jouett to encourage him to bring his artistic abilities to Missouri. She did, however, correspond with her old friend Mary Beck. Those letters reveal that in 1821 Mary sent crates of her paintings to Anna Maria to sell or exhibit in St. Louis, but the rough terrain and long trip seem to have damaged the artwork. Mary Beck also intended to visit St. Louis in 1823 and had even planned a large exhibition of her work, but the trip was delayed, so she arranged a show in Louisville instead.

Anna Maria left St. Louis in the summer of 1823 to visit Sarah in Edwardsville. It doesn't seem as though she intended her stay to be a long one, but she fell ill. Although Anna Maria generally enjoyed good health, a letter from two years prior hinted at her susceptibility to ailments, stating, "a little illness goes a good way with me."[33] Not many details of the illness that struck her over the summer of 1823 are known, but the onset must have been sudden, for Sarah wrote to Henry in a letter dated only "Thursday night" that "she has been worse every other day since she was first attack'd." She had "bilious symptoms" and a seemingly relentless fever—symptoms too broad to hypothesize a diagnosis. The duration of her illness is also poorly documented, but it seems it was long enough for Sarah and Henry to have exchanged several concerned notes on the topic.

On Monday, July 28, 1823, Anna Maria succumbed to fever. The obituary from the *Edwardsville Spectator* provides one of the only mentions of her passing, and no record of her burial has ever been found. The loss of a dear sister, aunt, friend, and artist left her friends and family bereaved. Henry helped settle the small estate she left behind[34] and preserved her letters and sketchbooks to pass along to his children. Family memories of this charming woman lived on through the five nieces and great-nieces who bore her name.

When Charles van Ravenswaay welcomed descendants of Henry von Phul to the Missouri History Museum in 1953, his excitement must have been difficult to contain. After studying early Missouri for decades, he knew a history-making collection when he saw one. As he unpacked the boxes that John Richardson Thomas and Henry von Phul Thomas had brought to the institution, he discovered sketchbooks and letters. Turning the pages, van Ravenswaay found 1818 St. Louis crystallized in drawings and watercolor paintings.[35] He quickly pushed the story to the *St. Louis Post-Dispatch*, placed the drawings on exhibit, and got to work writing an article. He effused of the collection, "They are not the prim and mannered efforts of an untrained school girl, but the deft work of a talented artist. Many of them are no more than water color sketches in grissaile, but their artistry gives them distinction in pattern and line. Others flow with color. . . ."[36]

Although composed of just 136 pieces, the collection's ability to intrigue, inspire, and inform endures. Year after year, historians, curators, researchers, and the public turn to their favorite works by Anna Maria von Phul to illustrate life in early St. Louis. But only rarely was this collection used to tell her story. Now, nearly 200 years after her death and 70 years after her work again came to light, Anna Maria's collection is published in full. Rather than her "complete works," however, these are considered her "known works." With nearly two decades of documented productivity, more of Anna Maria's art must exist, and there may yet be additional letters to uncover. To talk about Anna Maria von Phul opens a world of possibilities, not certainties. This tension mirrors the uncertainties Anna Maria must have felt in her own life. Undiscovered as an artist in her time, her sketchbooks have now cemented her relevance in perpetuity as the earliest known woman artist working in Missouri.

---

33   Anna Maria von Phul to Rosalie Saugrain von Phul, July 23, 1821.

34   Probate record for Maria von Phul, St. Louis, Missouri, May 17, 1825.

35   Charles van Ravenswaay, "Anna Maria von Phul," *Bulletin of the Missouri Historical Society* 10, no. 3 (1953): 367–384.

36   Unpublished press release, Missouri Historical Society files.

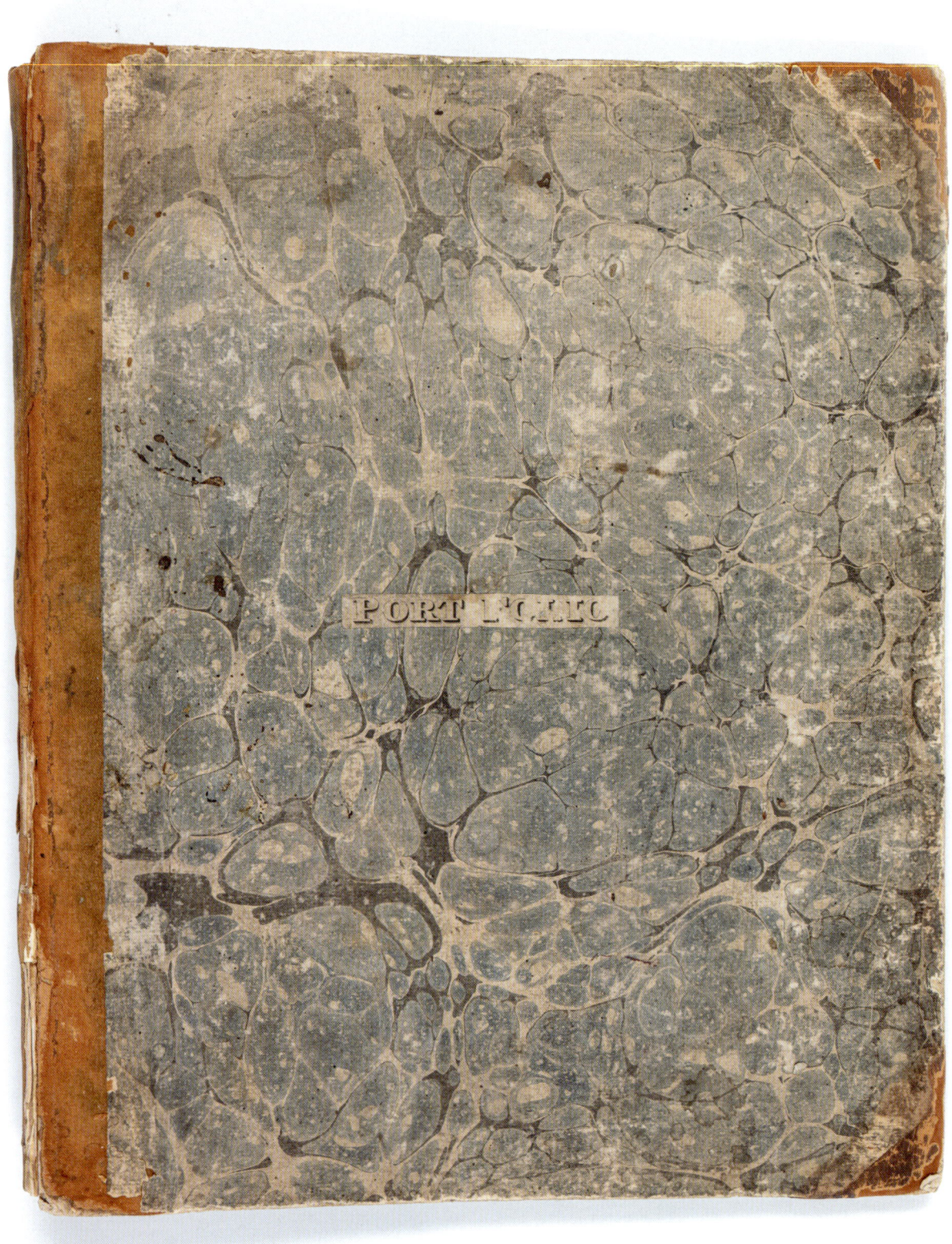

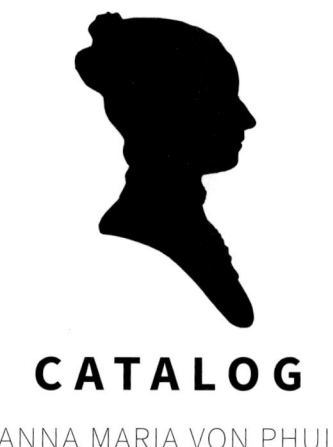

CATALOG
ANNA MARIA VON PHUL

A NOTE TO THE READER

The catalog that follows includes each piece from the Missouri Historical Society Collections that is signed by or attributed to Anna Maria von Phul. These pieces were removed from their original sketchbooks in the 1950s so that they could be exhibited and loaned individually; therefore, we cannot be sure of their original order. However, by using dated pieces, book number notations, and other details to inform their order and grouping, the author has attempted to structure the catalog in a manner both logical and accurate that reflects the original associations between art and book. Titles in italics were given by Anna Maria von Phul; others have been named descriptively.

SECTION 1: BOOK 2 AND BOOK 4

These two portfolios contain assembled works from Anna Maria von Phul's earlier years as an artist, including several scenes copied from paintings by George Beck, portraits and figures copied from prints, and multiple Kentucky landscapes. Dated works included in these two volumes span from 1804 to 1817.

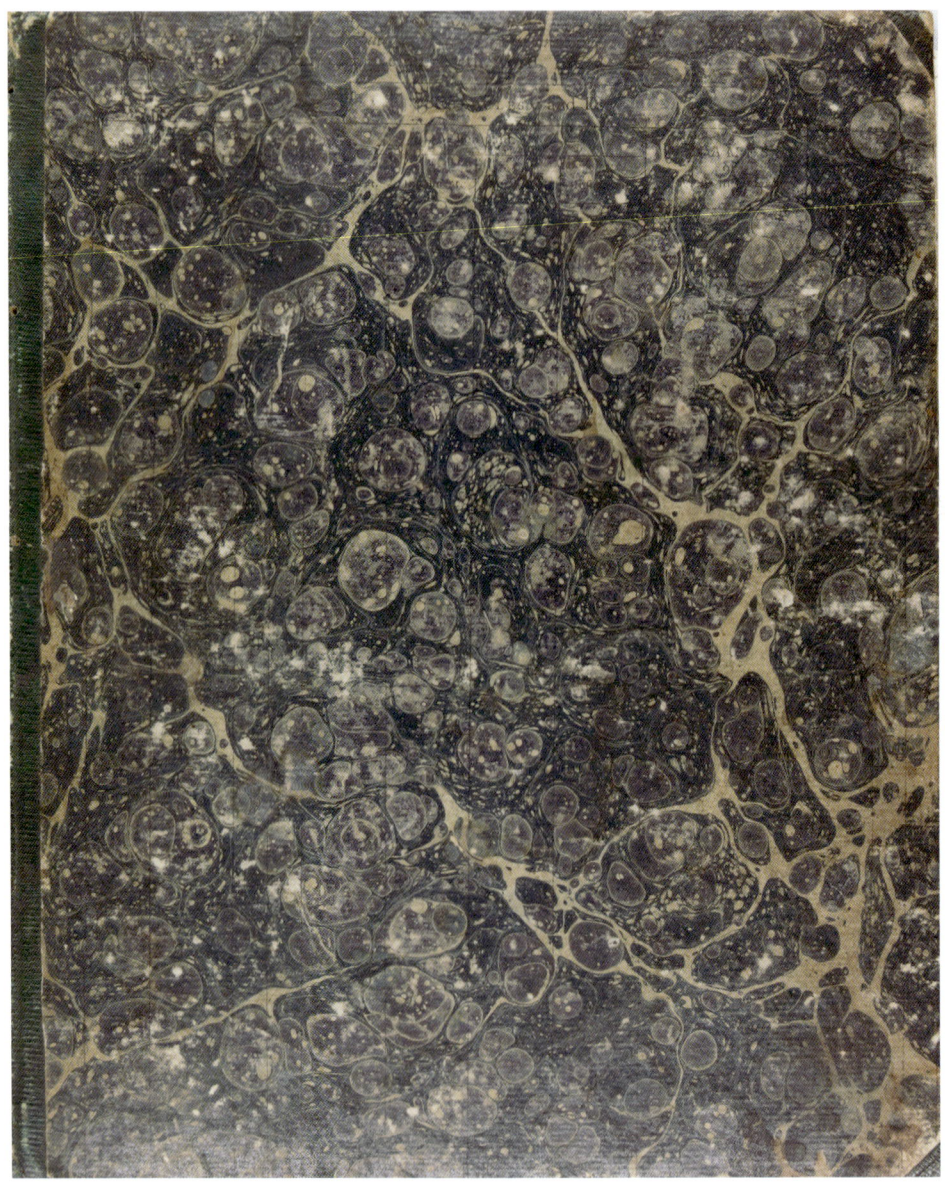

Cover of Book 2

Portfolio
8" × 10"
Unknown date

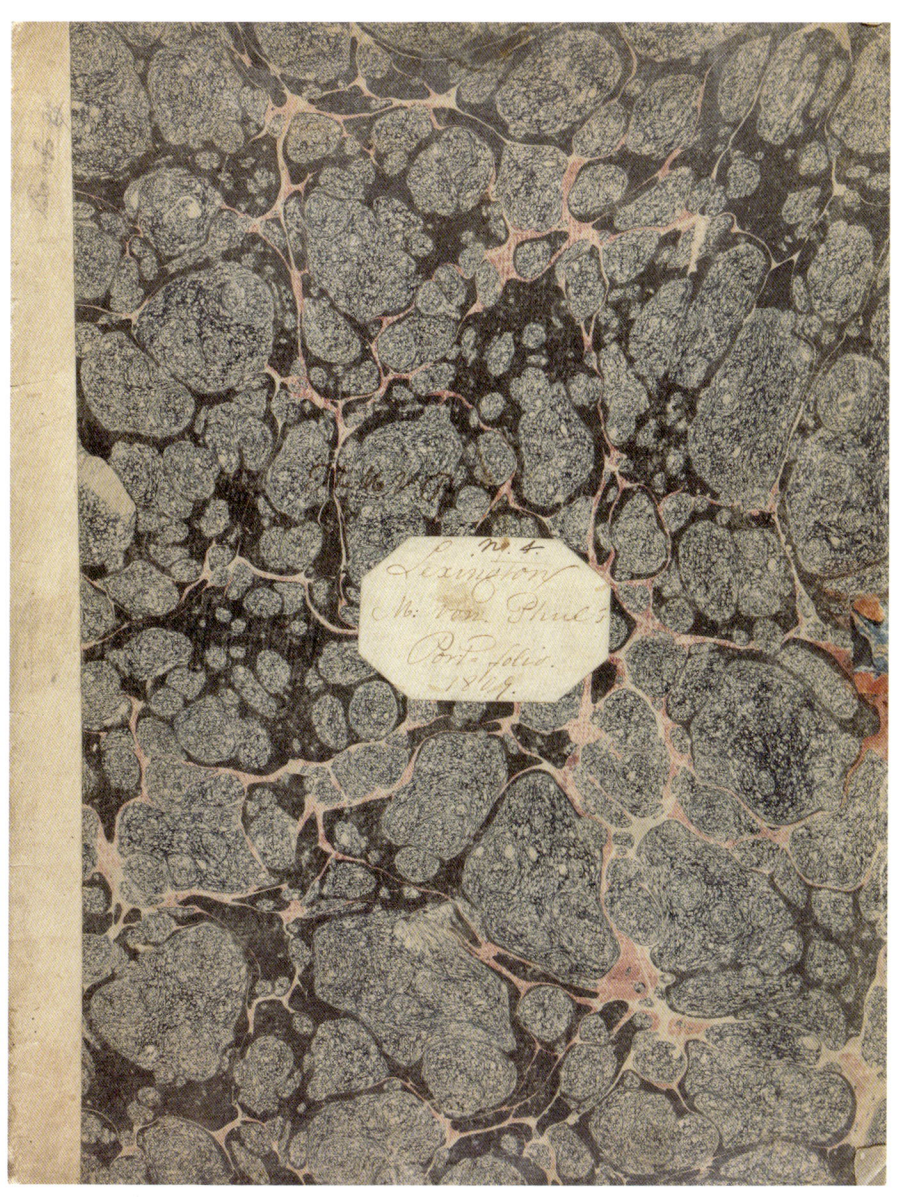

Cover of Book 4

No. 4 Lexington, M. von Phul's Port-folio
10¼" × 13½"
1809

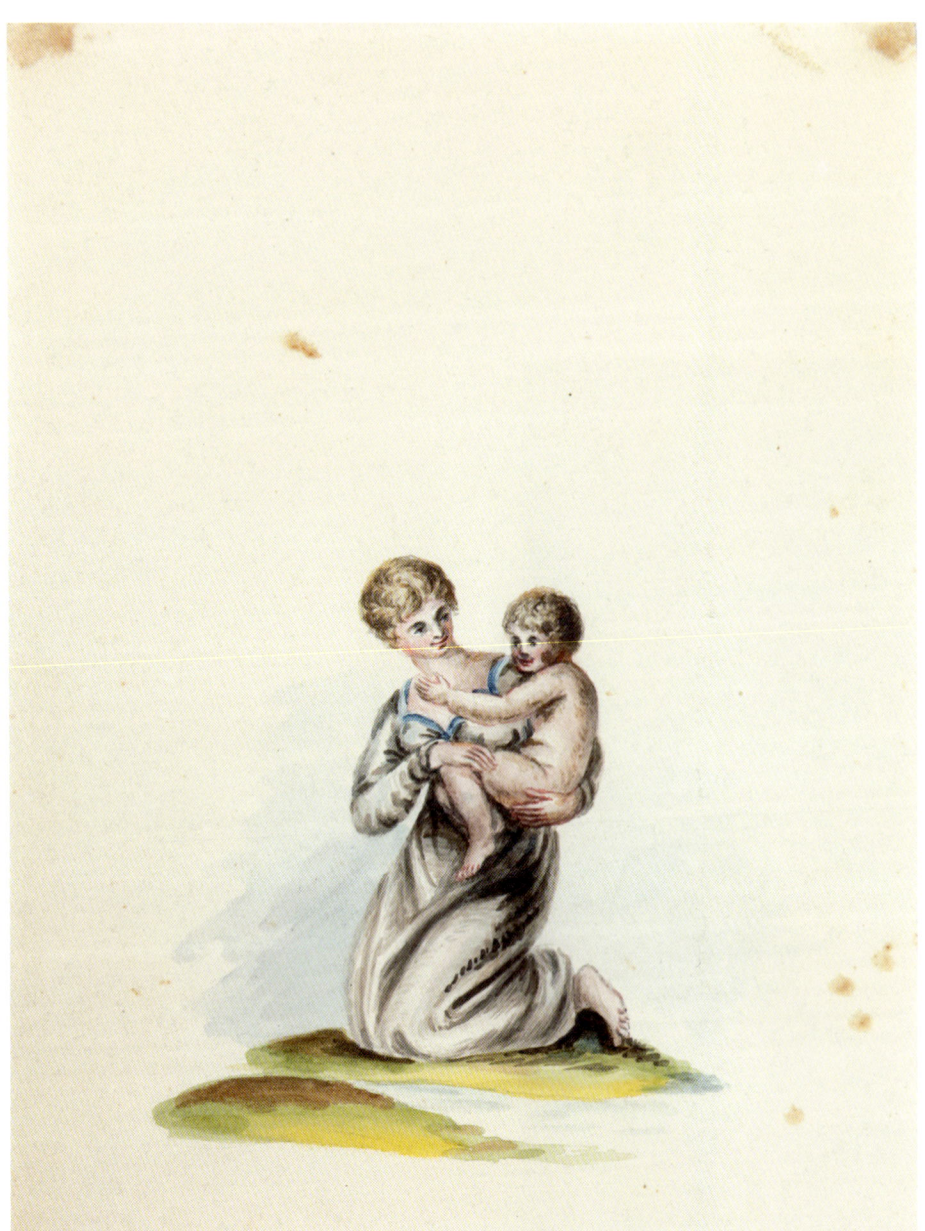

Figure 1 (Book 2)

Woman with child
Watercolor on paper
4⅞" × 6¾"
Unknown date

Figure 2 (Book 2)

Study sheet
Ink on paper
7¼" × 8⅜"
Unknown date

Although lacking in detail, these seven quick sketches are not lacking in energy. Anna Maria hastily recorded everyday scenes of a woman hanging laundry to dry, two people with a dog, children at play, and three figures who appear to be repairing an overturned chair or stool.

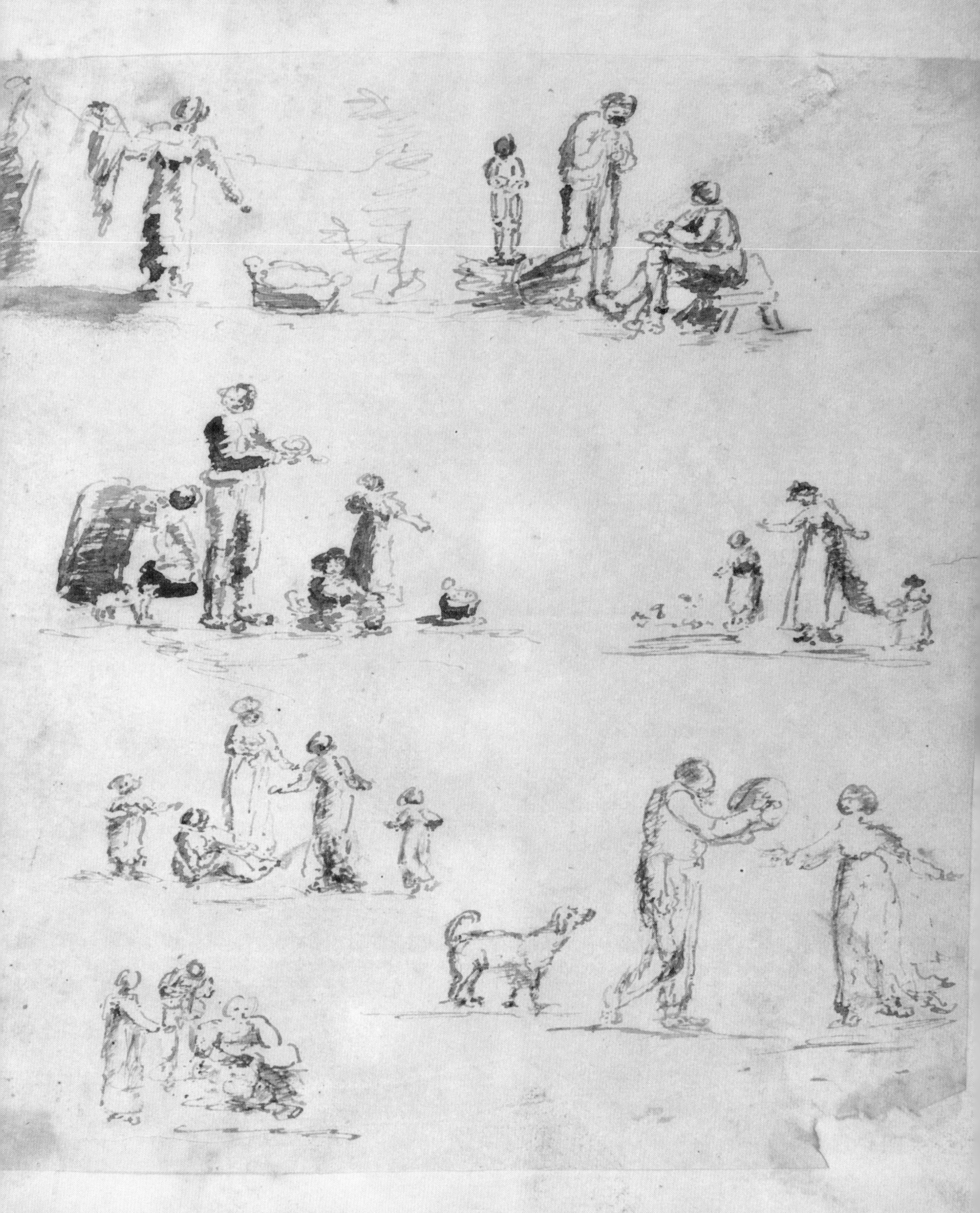

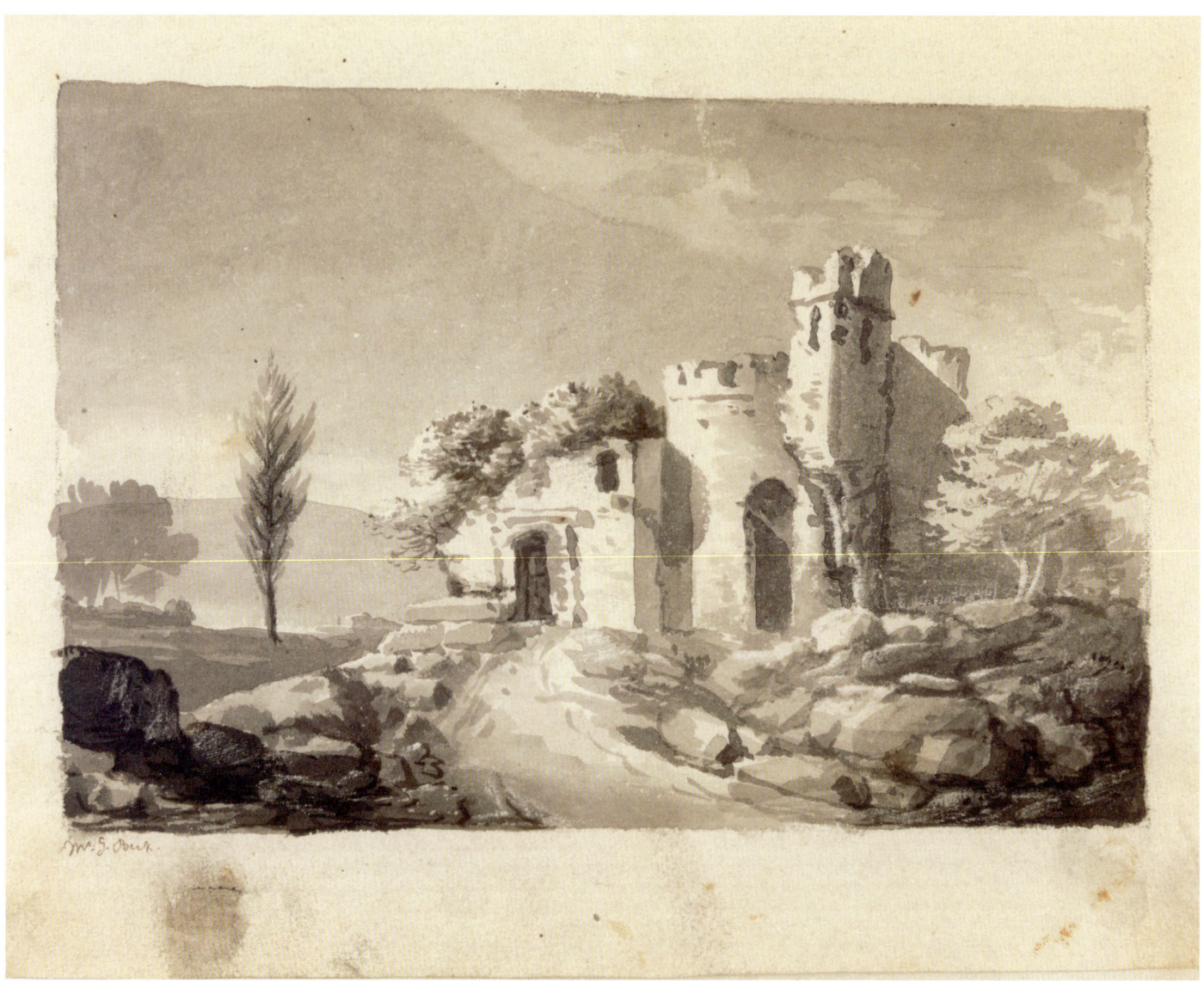

Figure 3 (Book 2)

Penrith Castle, Cumberland, 1785 (copy of a work by George Beck)
Wash and pastel on paper
9⅝" × 7⅛"
Unknown date

While Anna Maria copied from George Beck's collection of prints to improve her abilities, she also translated the painter's own oil landscapes into ink washes or watercolor. In this example—and two others from Book 2—she credits her mentor directly by inscribing it "Mr. G. Beck," rather than signing it herself. Moldering castle ruins from Beck's travels across England and Wales must have seemed a romantic departure from daily life in Kentucky.

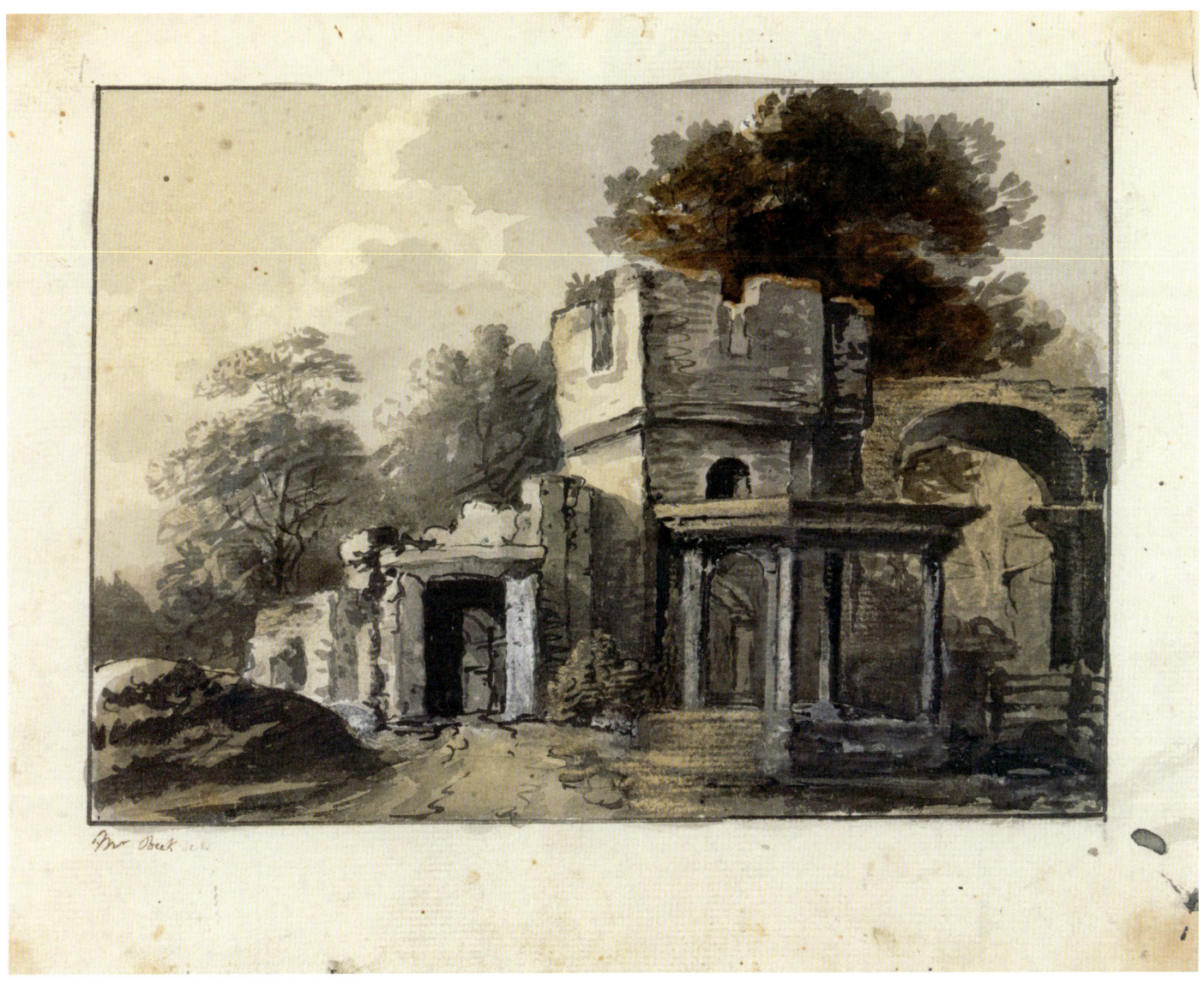

Figure 4 (Book 2)

Copy of a work by George Beck
Watercolor wash and pastel on paper
9⅛" × 7¼"
Unknown date

Inscribed "Mr. Beck."

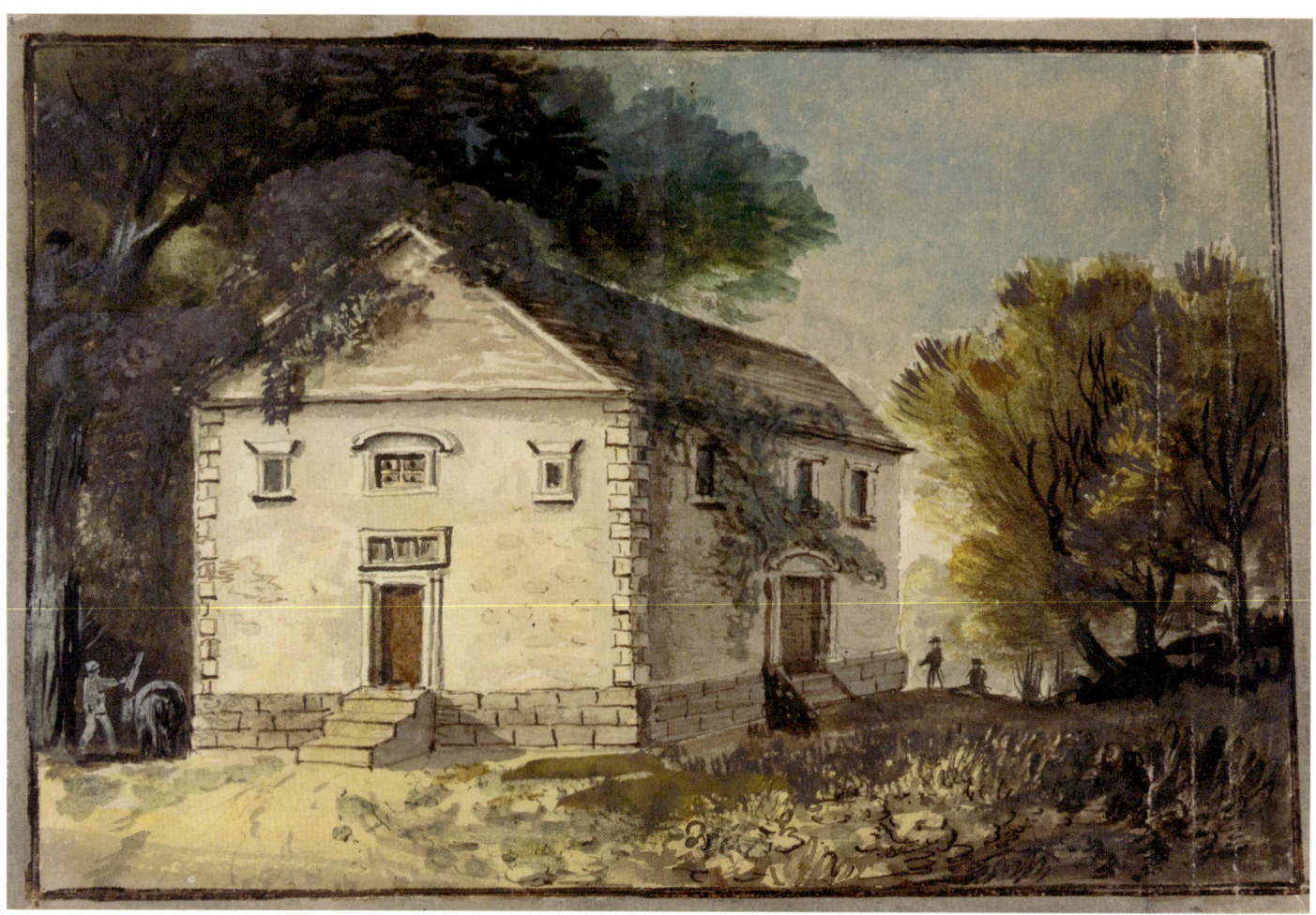

Figure 5 (Book 2)

Landscape with building
Watercolor and gouache on paper
8¼" × 6¼"
Unknown date

Anna Maria's developing style is on display in this landscape depicting an unidentified stone building, likely a site in or around Lexington.

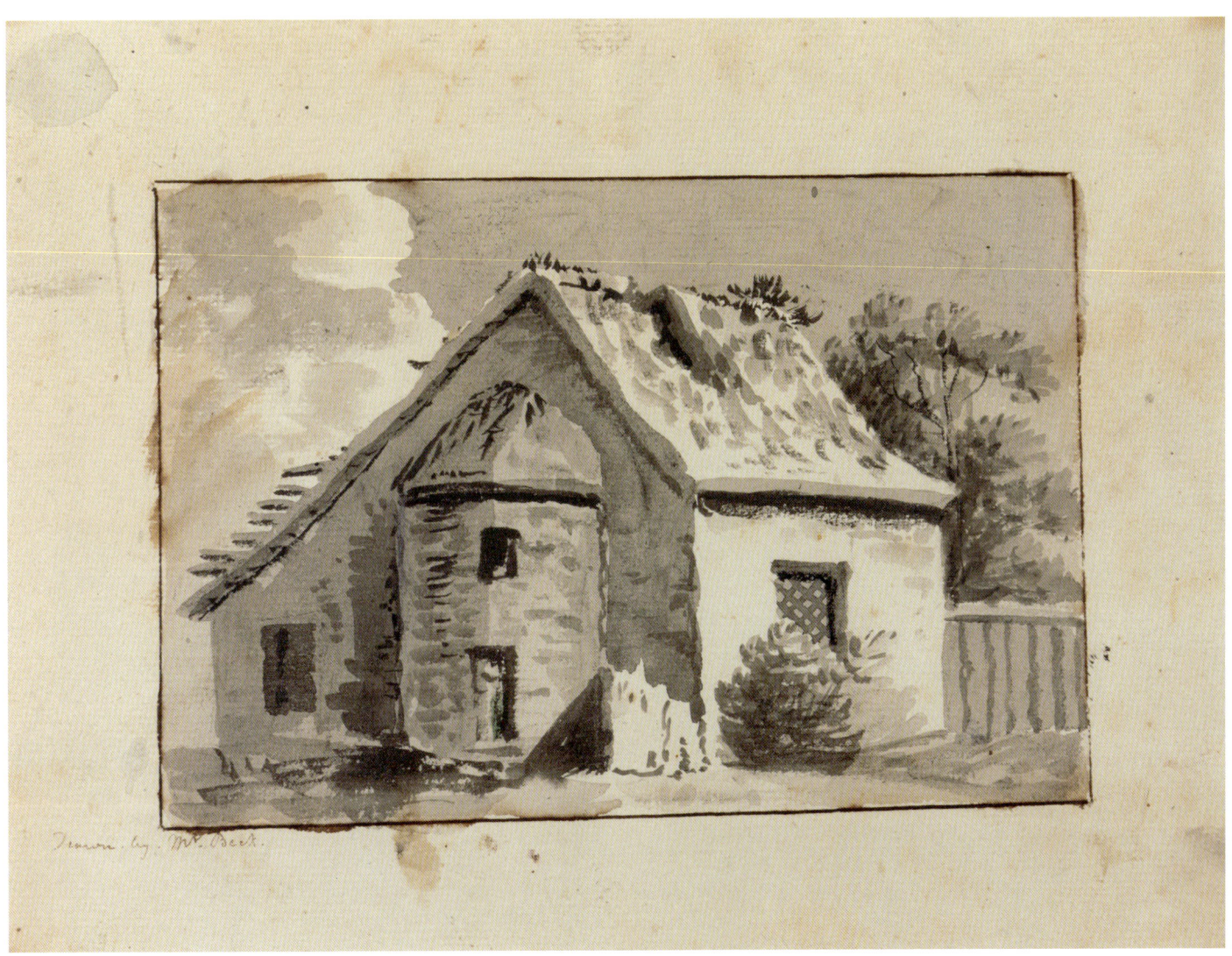

Figure 6 (Book 2)

Copy of a work by George Beck
Watercolor on paper
8⅛" × 6⅝"
Unknown date

Inscribed "Drawn. by. Mr. Beck."

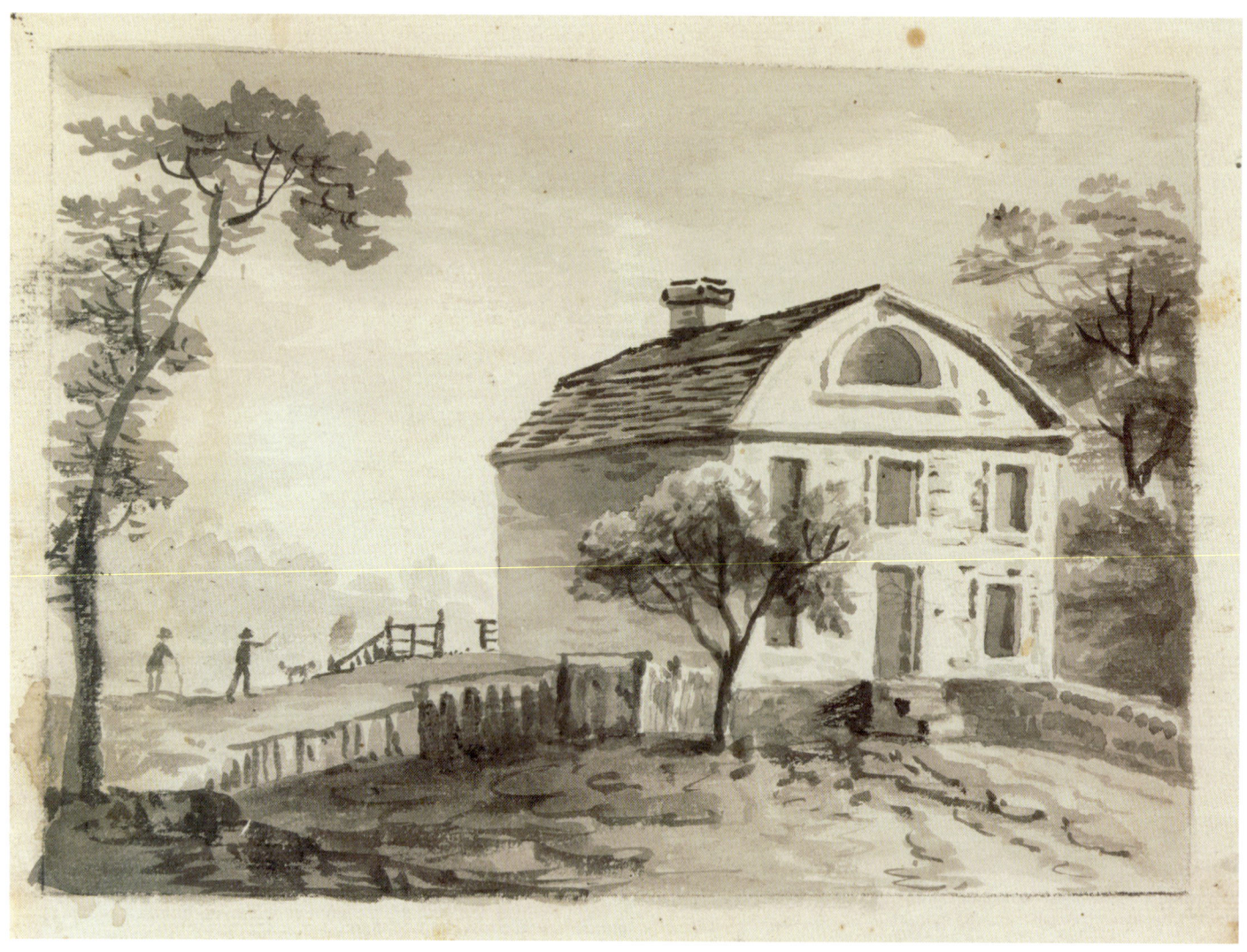

Figure 7 (Book 2)

Landscape with building
Watercolor on paper
8⅛" × 6⅜"
Unknown date

This piece lacks an inscription, but it is likely another copy of George Beck's work.

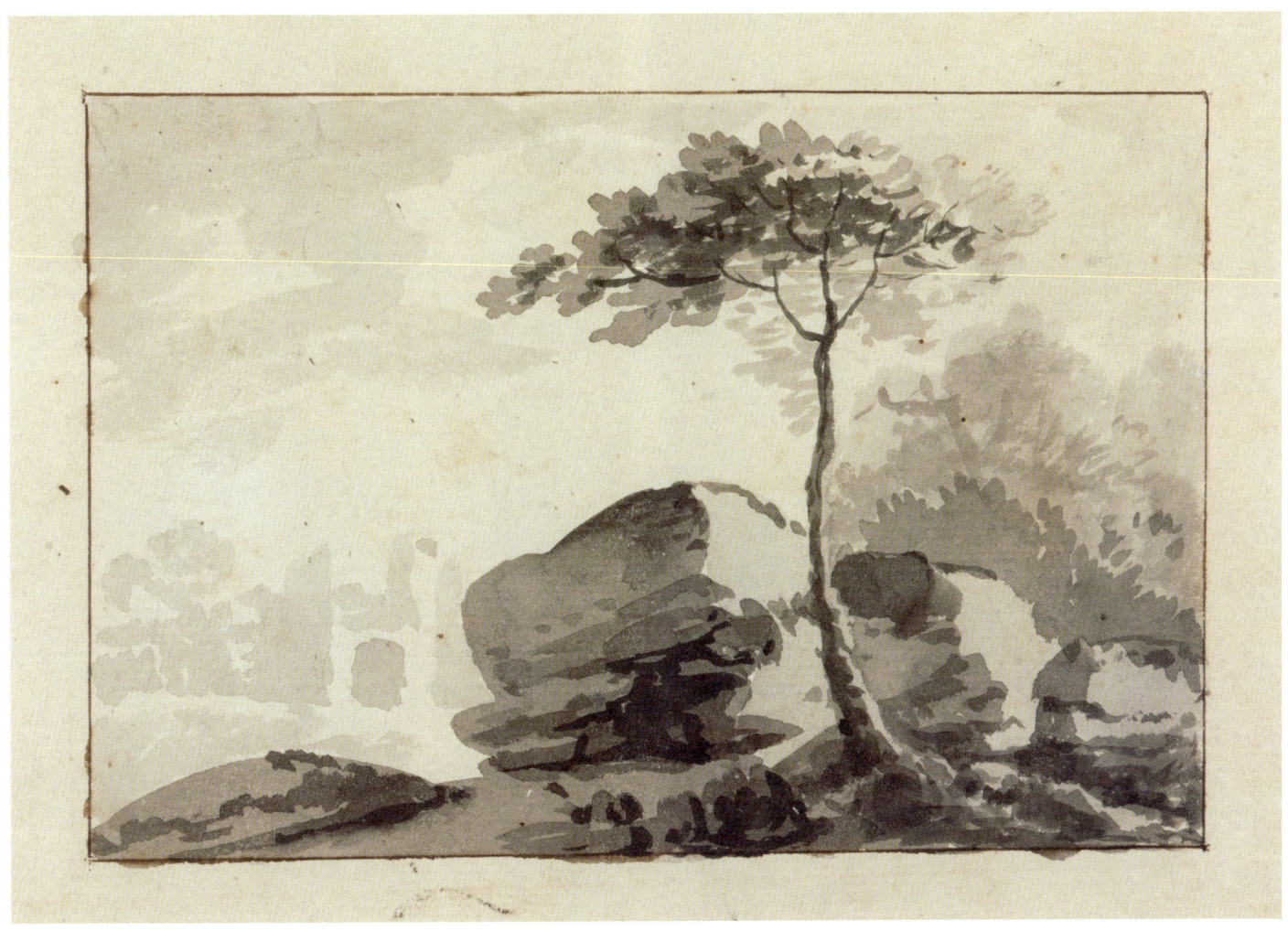

Figure 8 (Book 2)

Landscape
Watercolor on paper
8¼" × 6½"
Unknown date

At first glance this piece is a simple scene of a tree and boulders, but the presence of castle ruins in the background indicate that it's another copy of George Beck's work or perhaps an imagined European landscape.

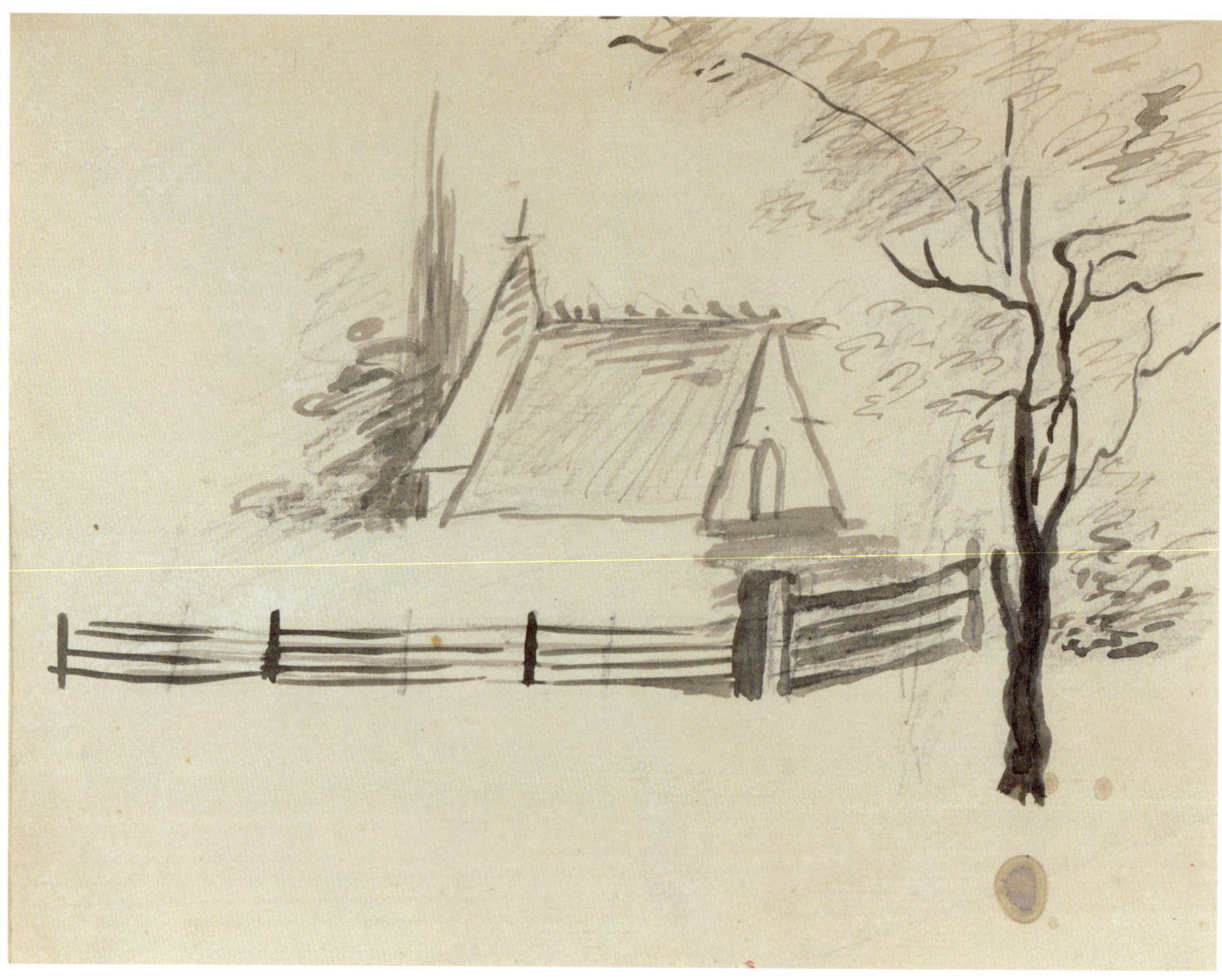

Figure 9 (Book 2)

Building with split-rail fence
Ink and wash on paper
7¾" × 6½"
Unknown date

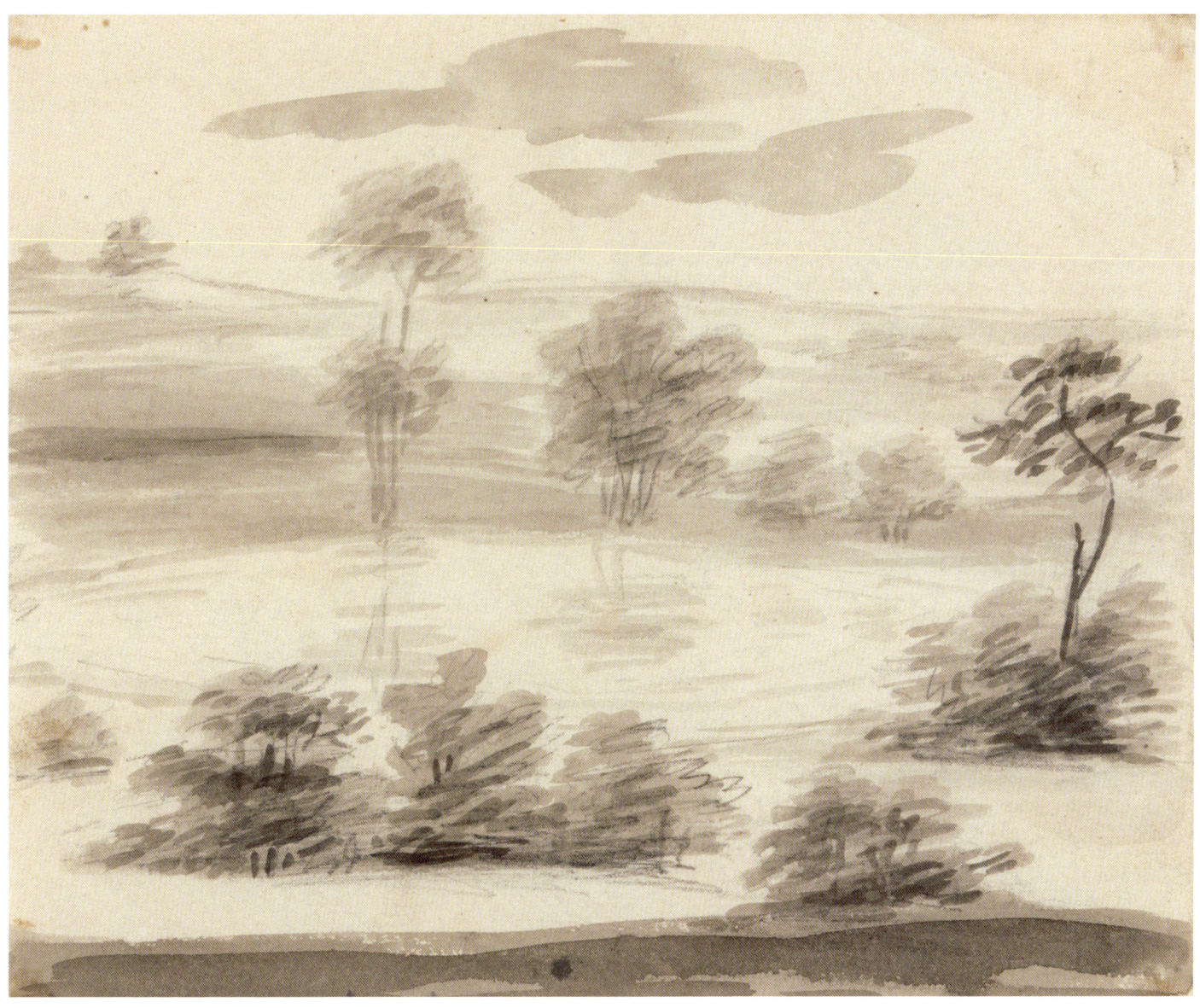

Figure 10 (Book 2)

Landscape
Wash on paper
7⅜" × 6¼"
Unknown date

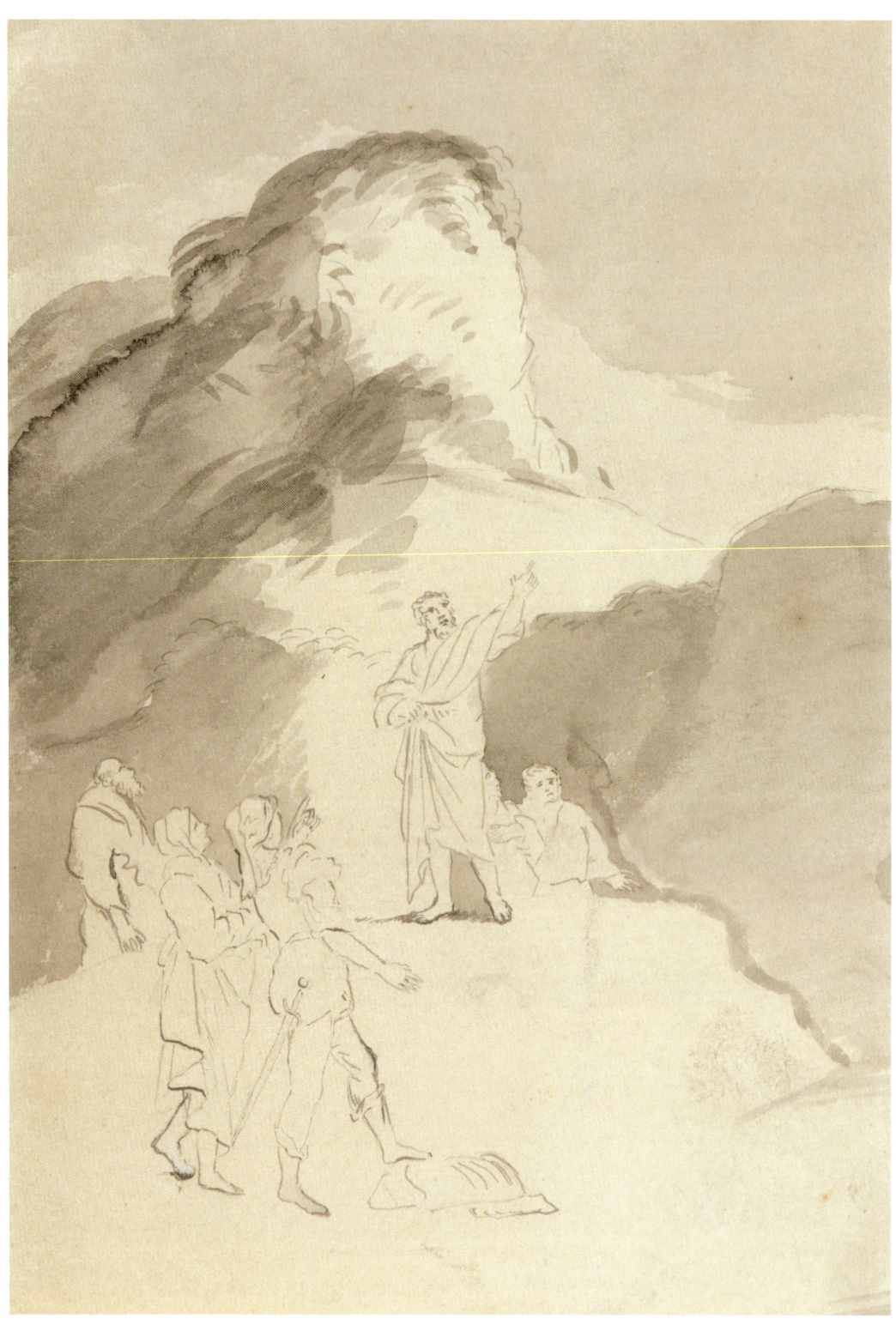

Figure 11 (Book 2)

Study of figures on a mountain
Wash and graphite on paper
5½" × 7¾"
Unknown date

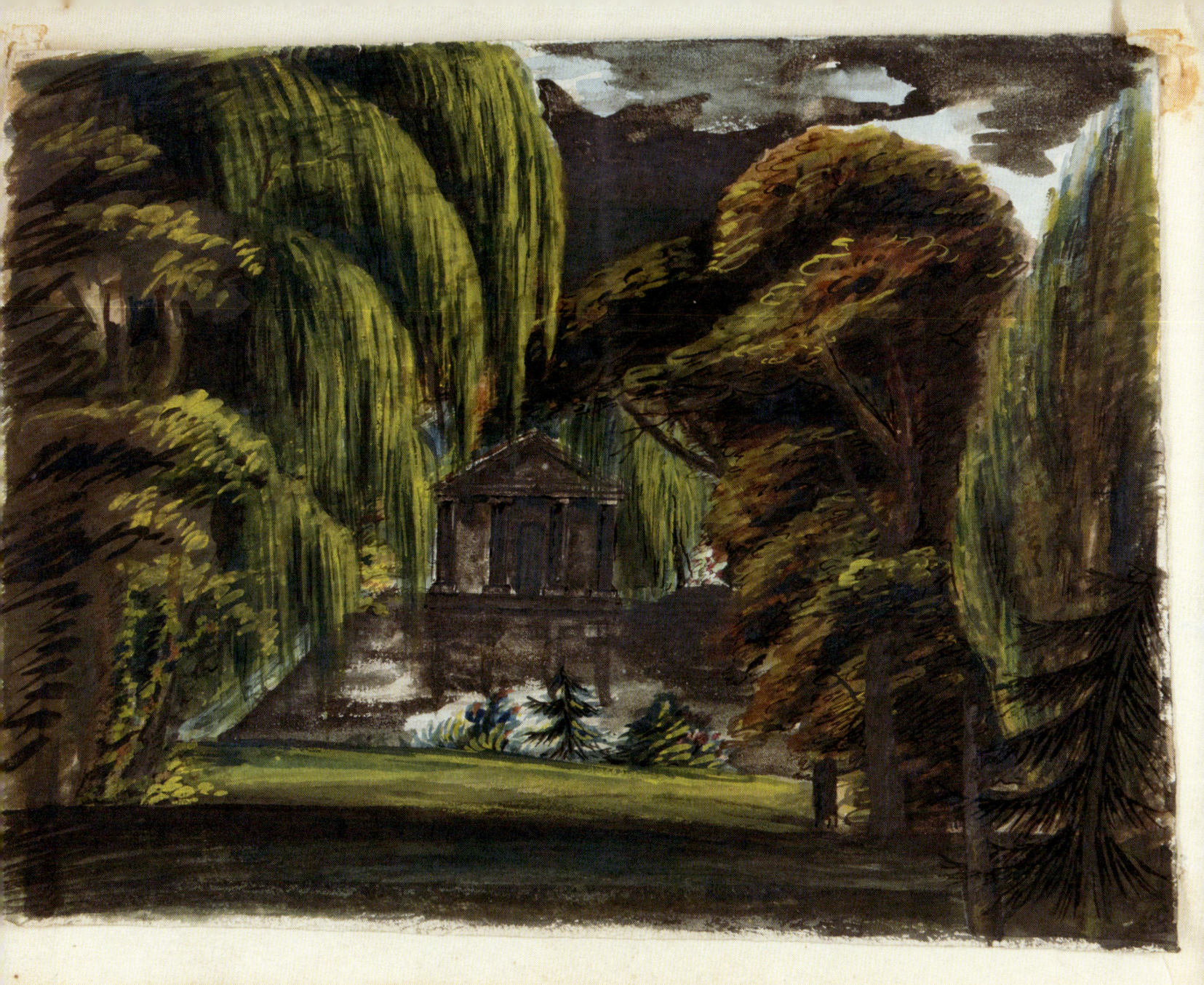

Figure 12 (Book 2)

Greek portico at Chaumiere du Prairie
Gouache and watercolor on paper
8½" × 6⅝"
Unknown date

This landscape is one of several from Anna Maria's books thought to depict Chaumiere du Prairie, David Meade's Kentucky estate. She mentioned the grounds and a Grecian-inspired structure in a letter to her brother Henry dated May 12, 1821: "There is a beautiful white temple built near the lake in front is a pediment supported by 4 columns. The walk around the garden is over one mile. . . ."

MORE THAN ORDINARY | 43

Figure 13 (Book 2)

Flower
Watercolor on paper
7⅝" × 9⅞"
April 29, 1817

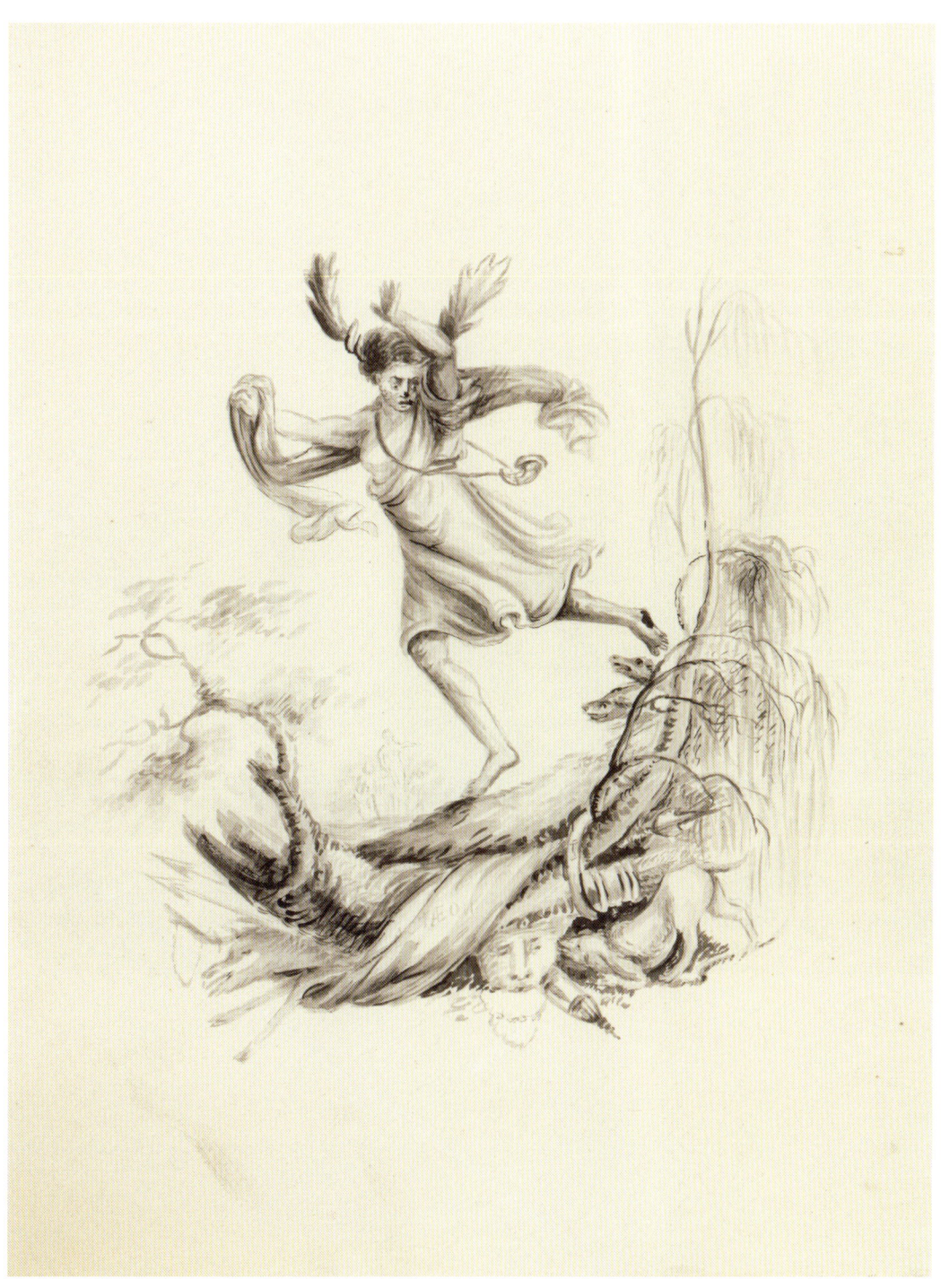

Figure 14 (Book 2)

Actaeon
Ink on paper
7¼" × 8⅞"
Unknown date

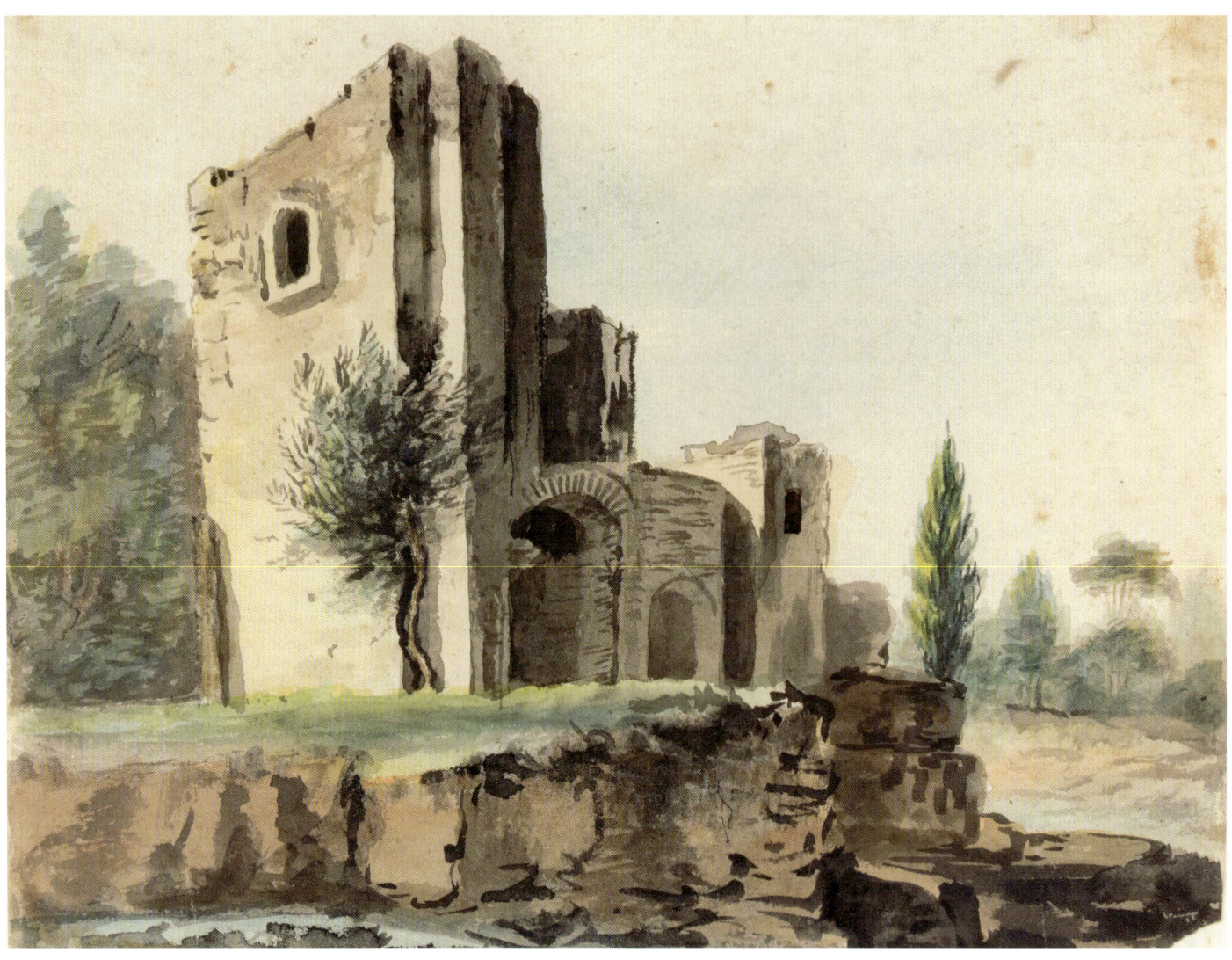

Figure 15 (Book 2)

Castle ruins
Watercolor on paper
8⅝" × 7"
Unknown date

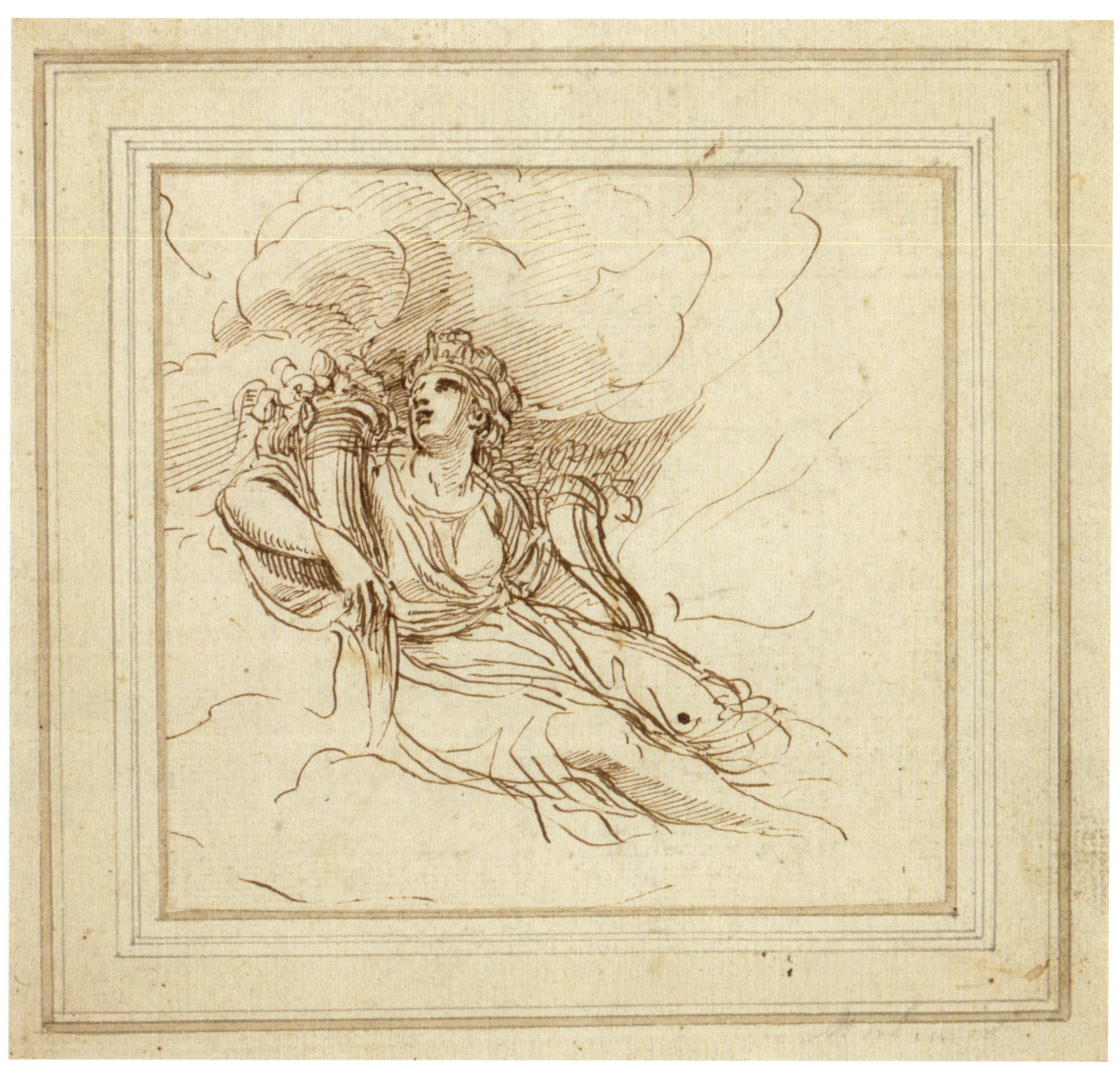

Figure 16 (Book 2)

Classical figure study
Ink on paper
6¾" × 6⅜"
Unknown date

MORE THAN ORDINARY | 47

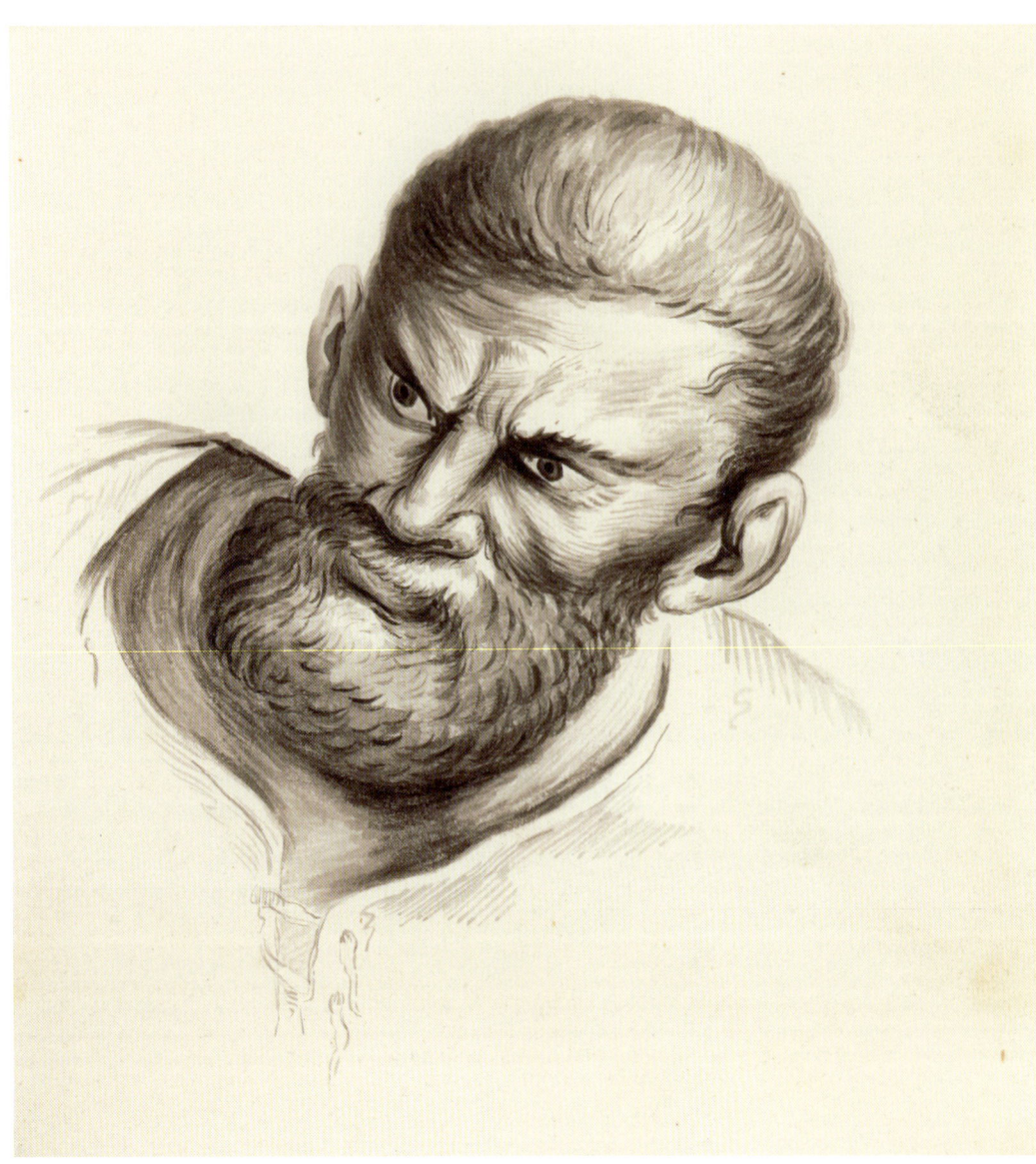

Figure 17 (Book 2)

Study of a head
Ink on paper
6⅝" × 8¼"
Unknown date

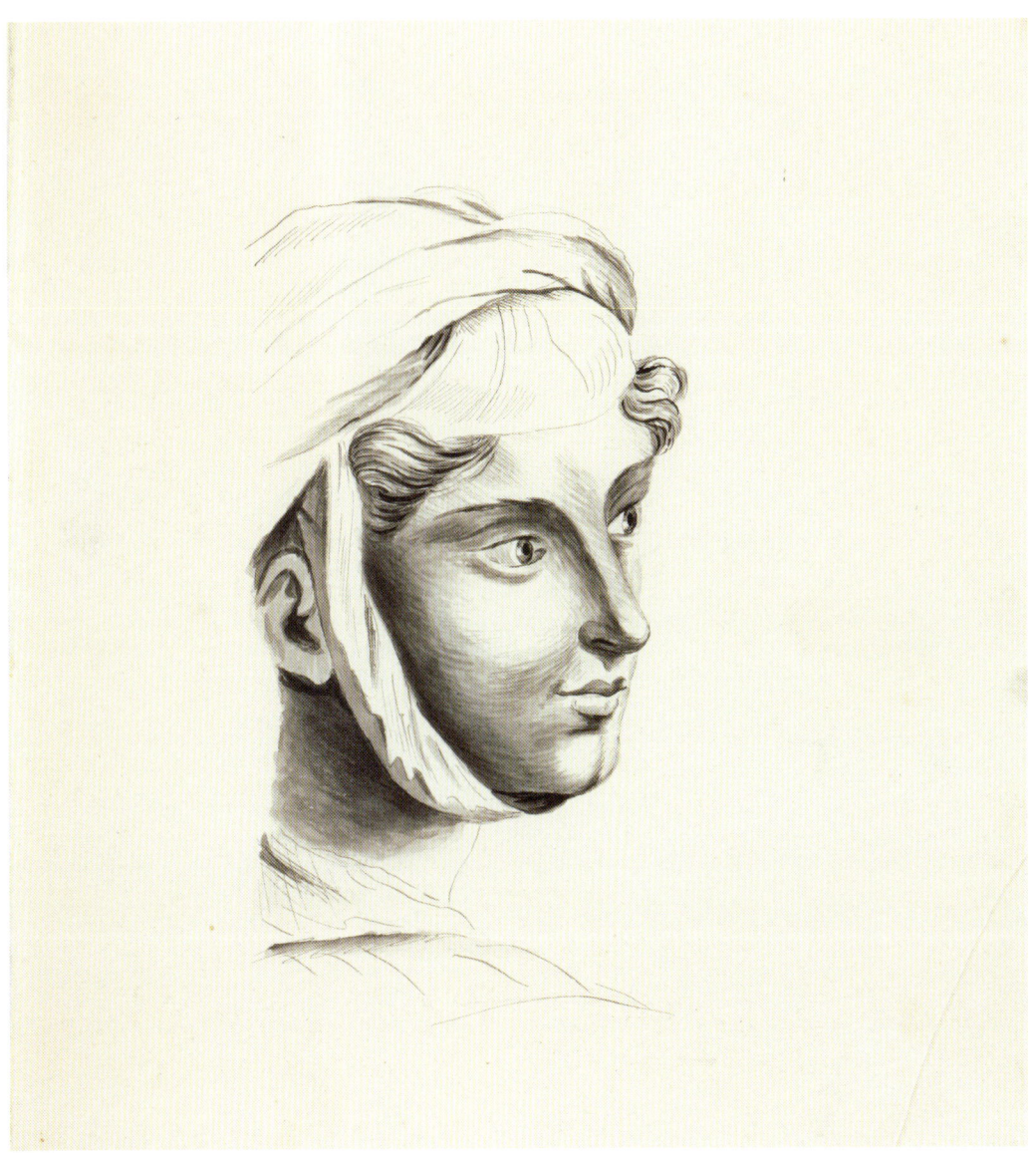

Figure 18 (Book 2)

Study of a head
Ink on paper
6⅝" × 8¼"
Unknown date

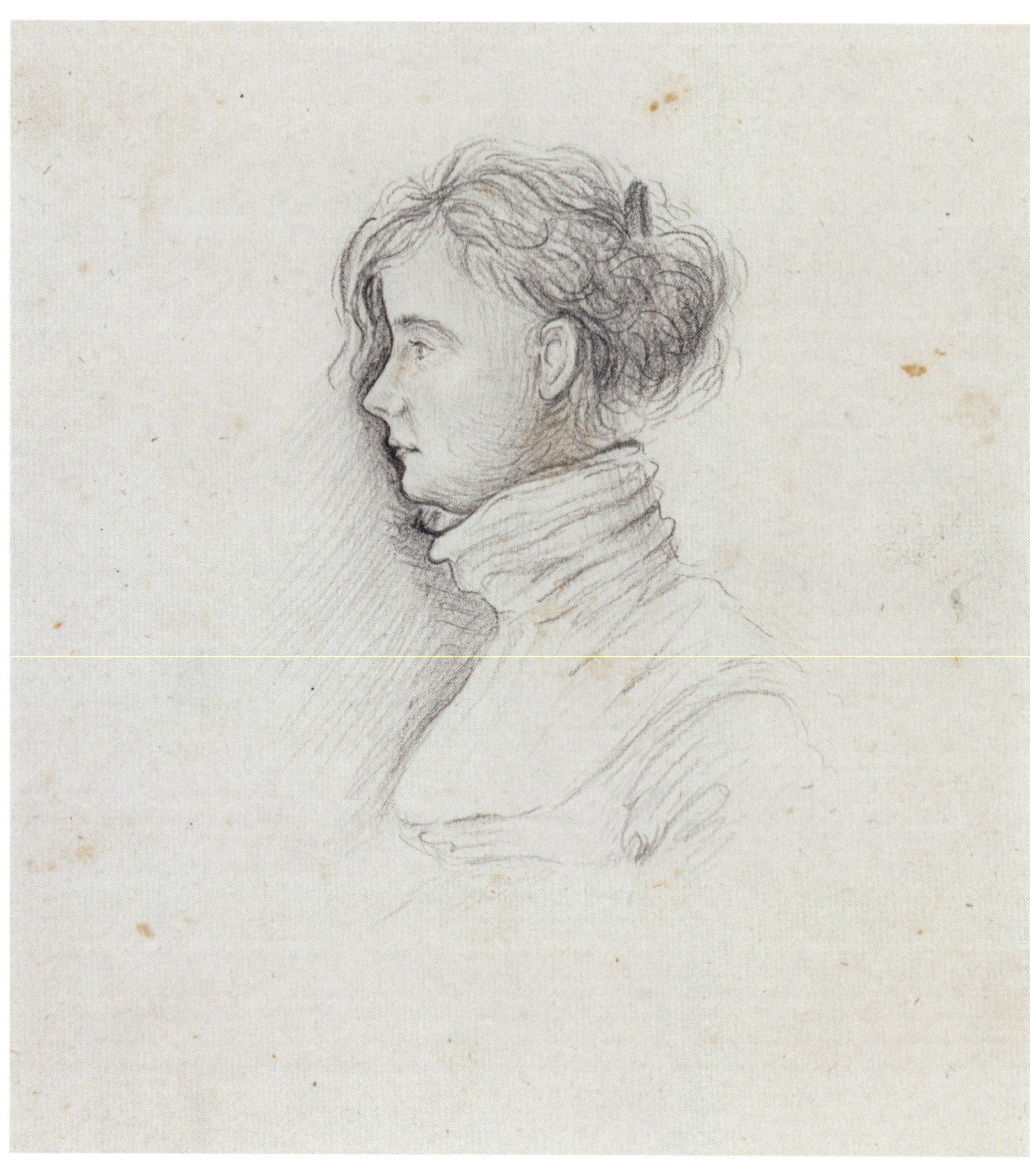

Figure 19 (Book 2)

Woman in profile
Graphite on paper
7⅜" × 9¼"
Unknown date

Inscribed "Lexington" on reverse.

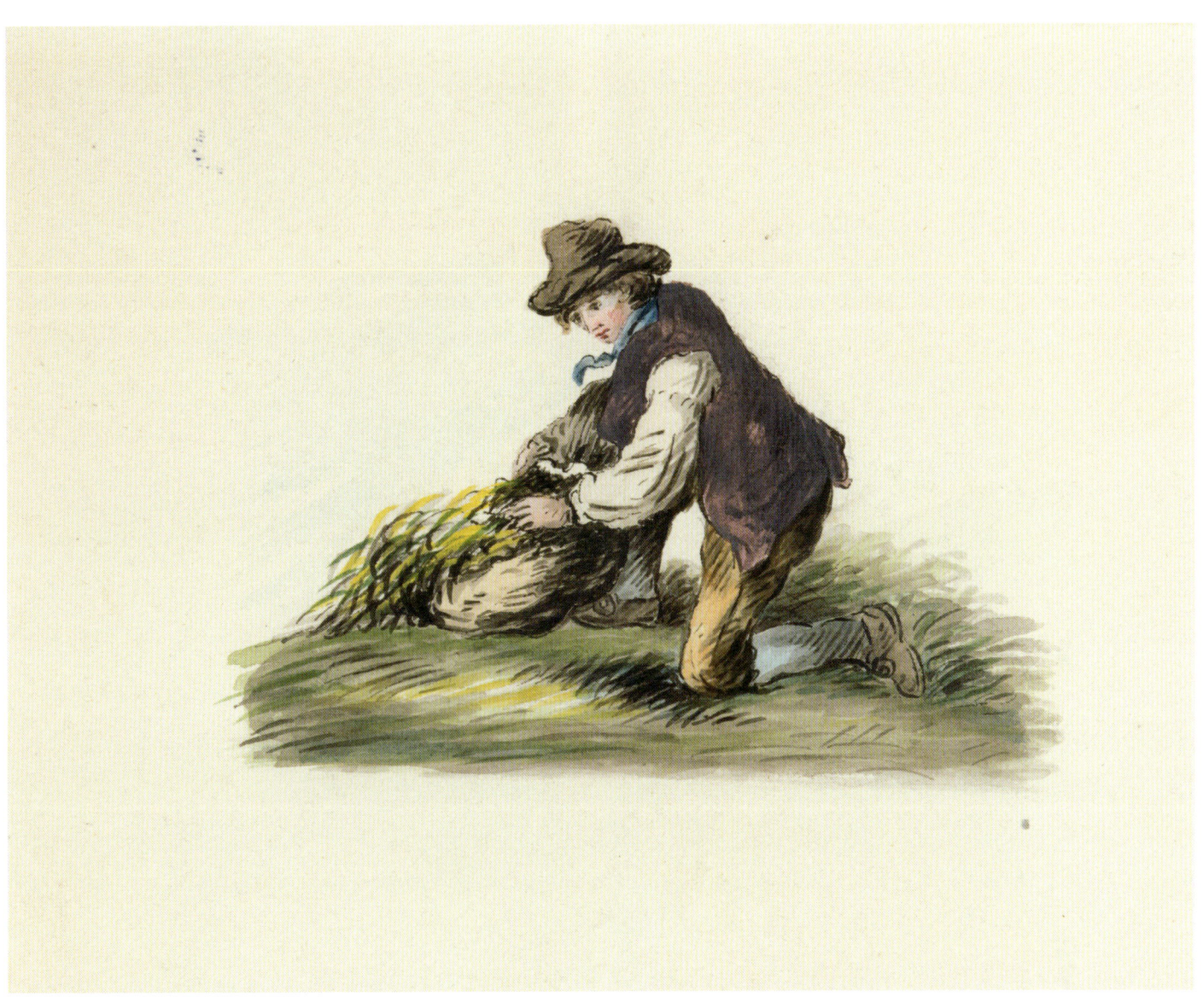

Figure 20 (Book 2)

Boy with bag
Ink and watercolor on paper
6⅝" × 4⅛"
Unknown date

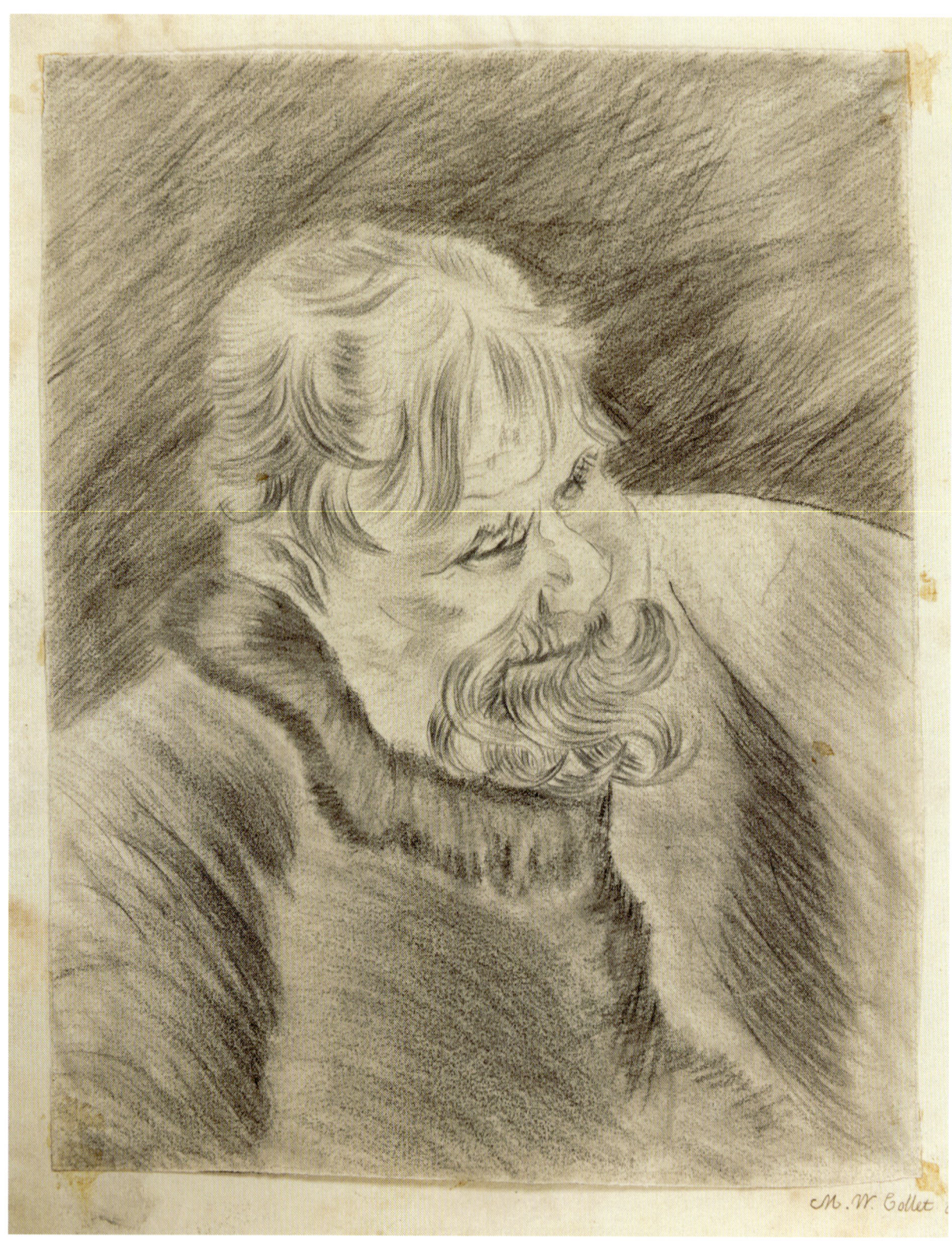

Figure 21 (Book 2)

Portrait of a man
Charcoal on paper
5¾" × 7¼"
Unknown date

Inscribed "M. W. Collet del."

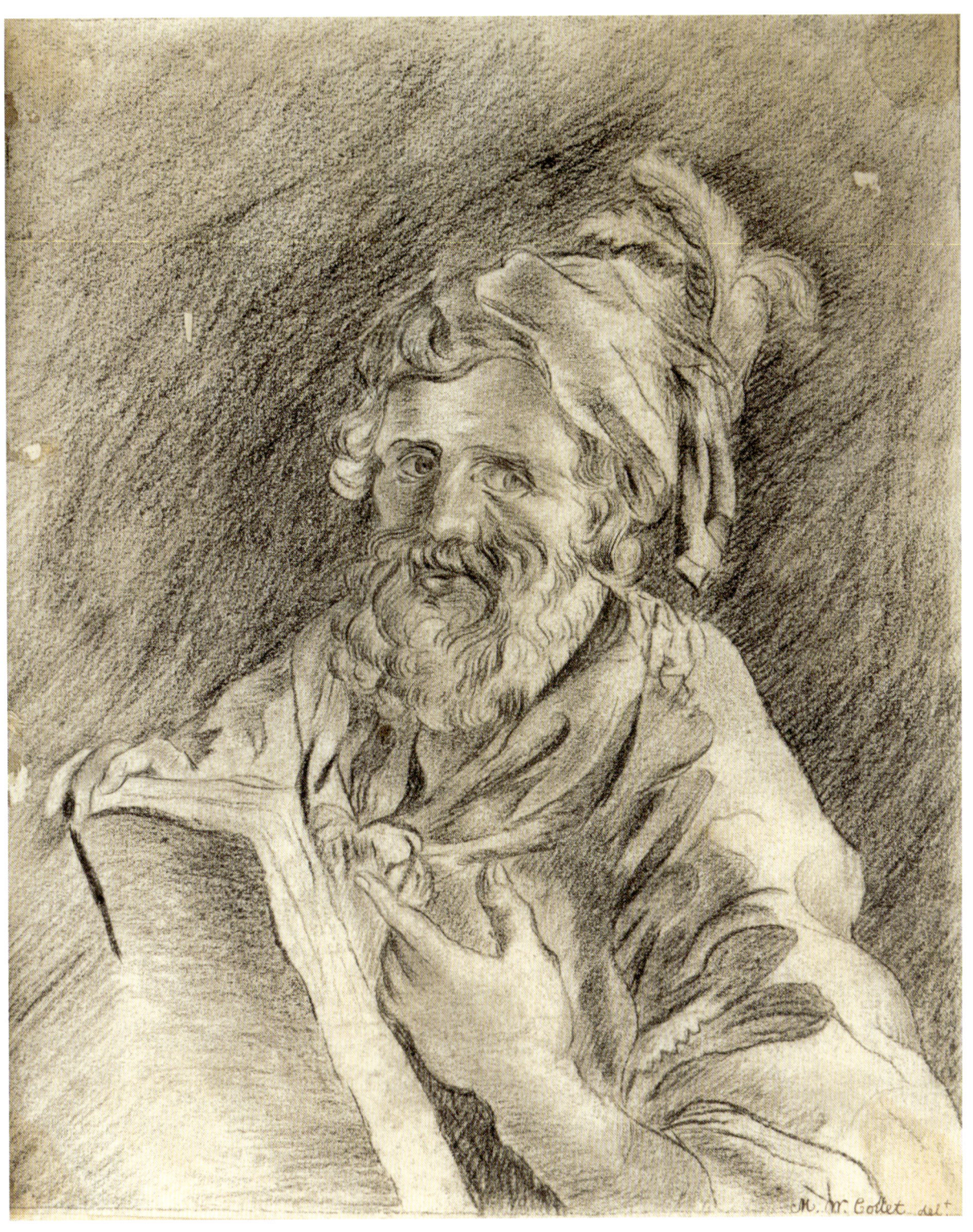

Figure 22 (Book 2)

Portrait of a man with book
Charcoal on paper
7½" × 9¼"
Unknown date

Inscribed "M. W. Collet del."

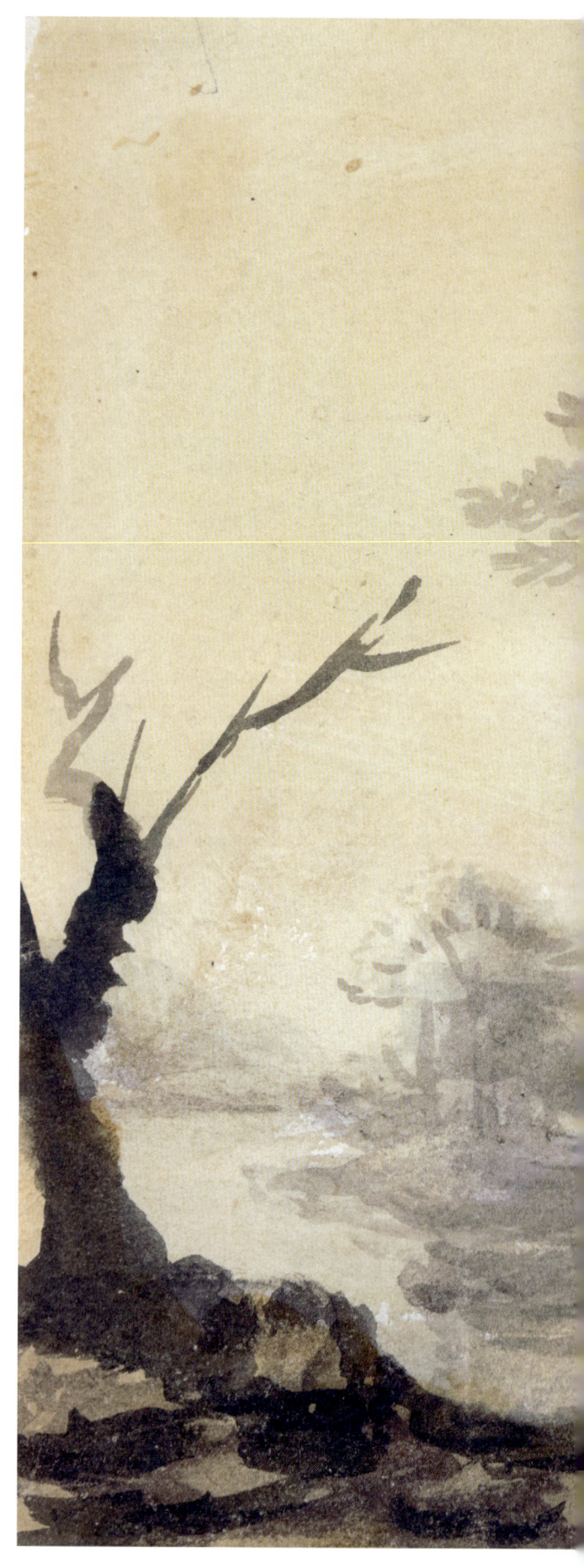

Figure 23 (Book 2)

Landscape
Ink and watercolor on paper
9¾" × 7½"
Unknown date

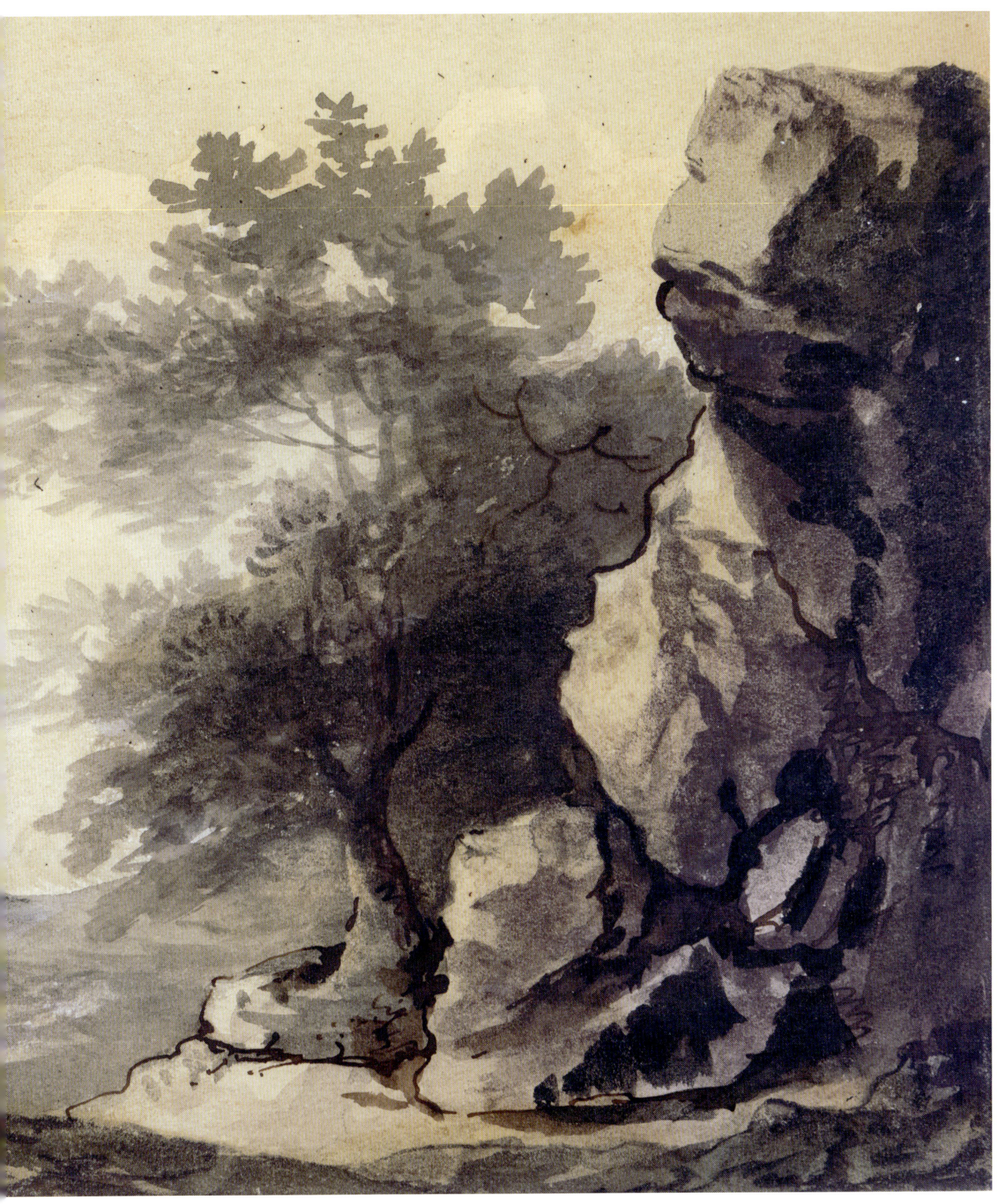

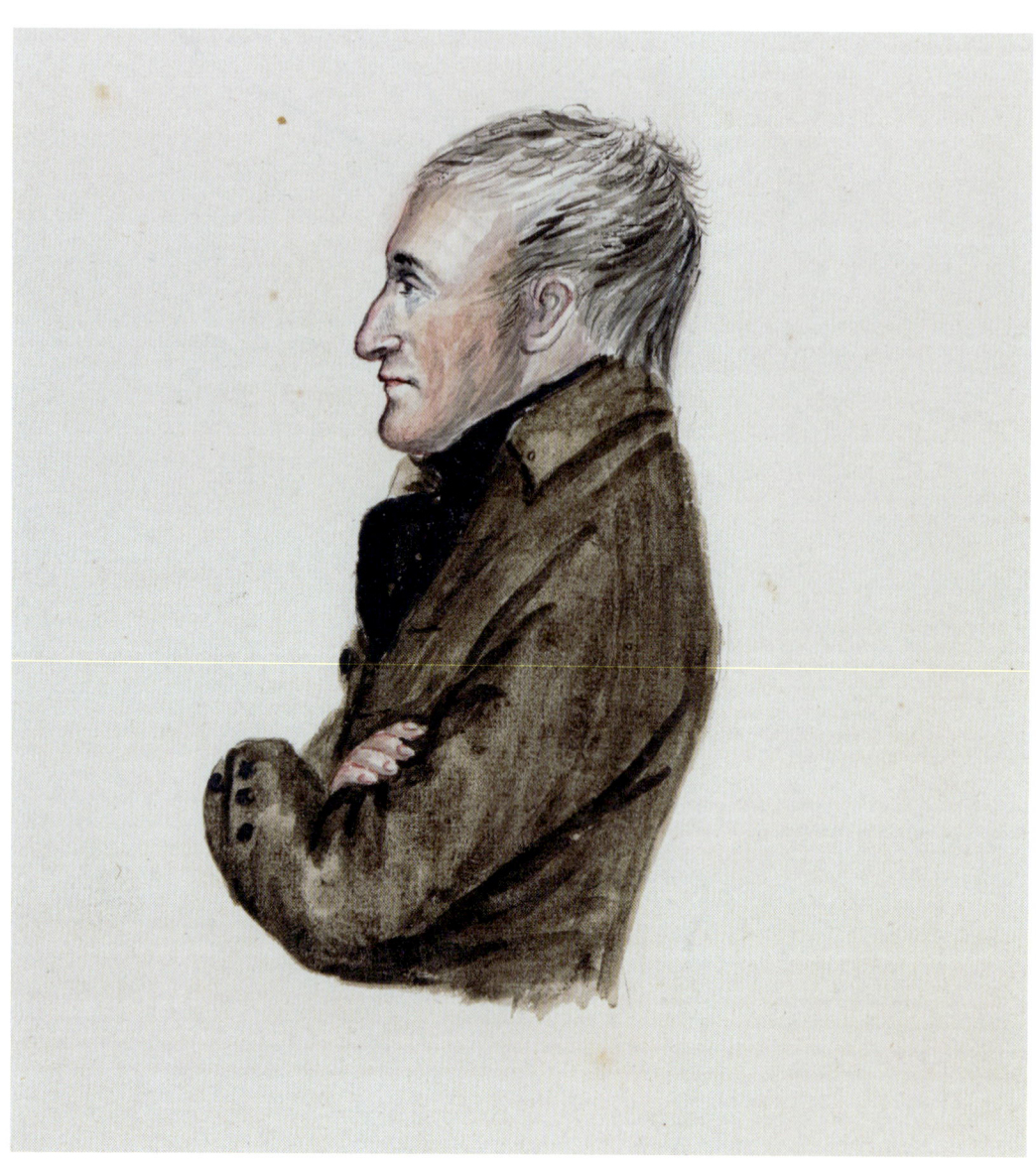

Figure 24 (Book 2)

Portrait of a man in profile
Ink and watercolor on paper
5" × 7⅞"
Unknown date

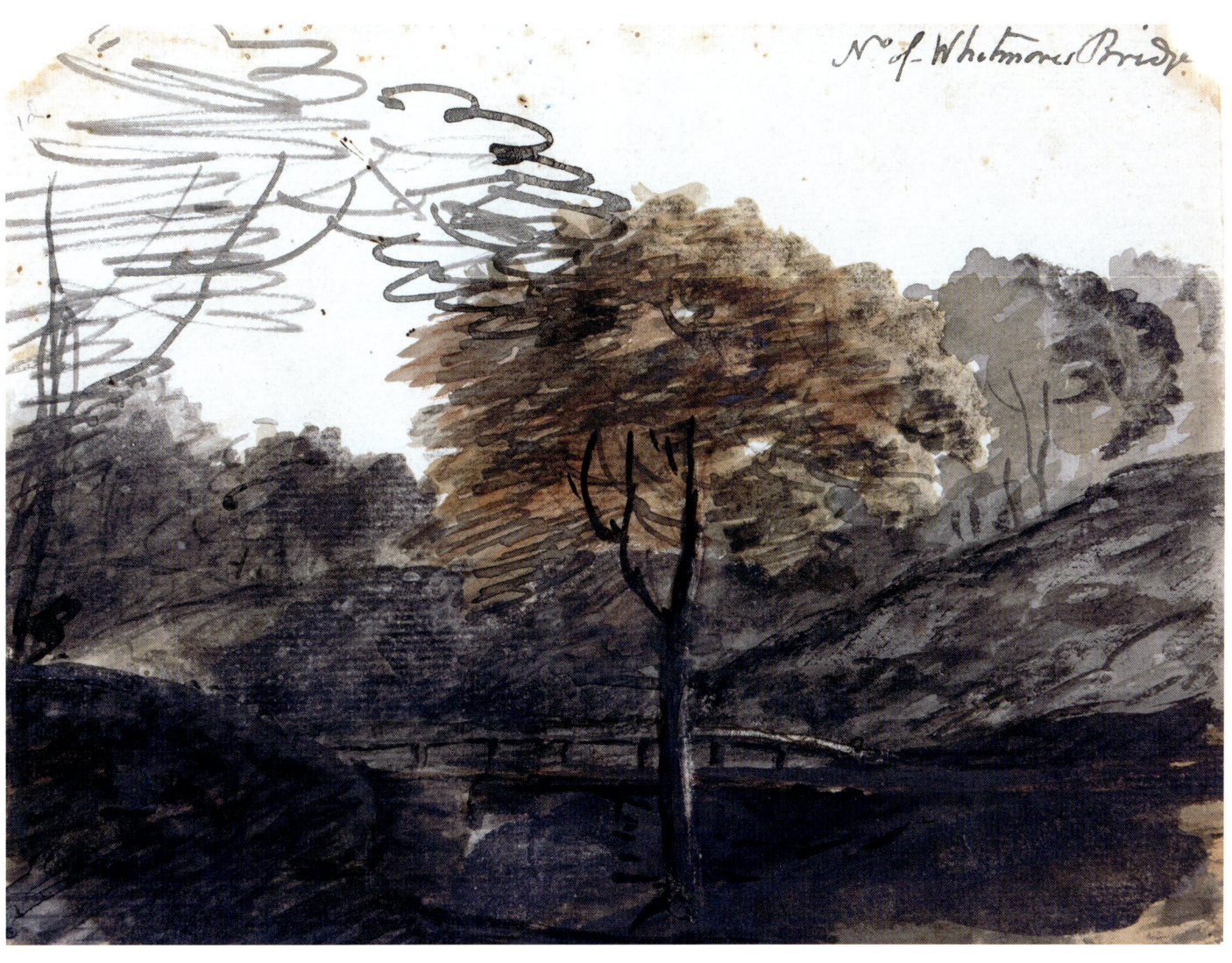

Figure 25 (Book 2)

Nº of Whitmores Bridge
Watercolor on paper
7⅝" × 6"
Unknown date

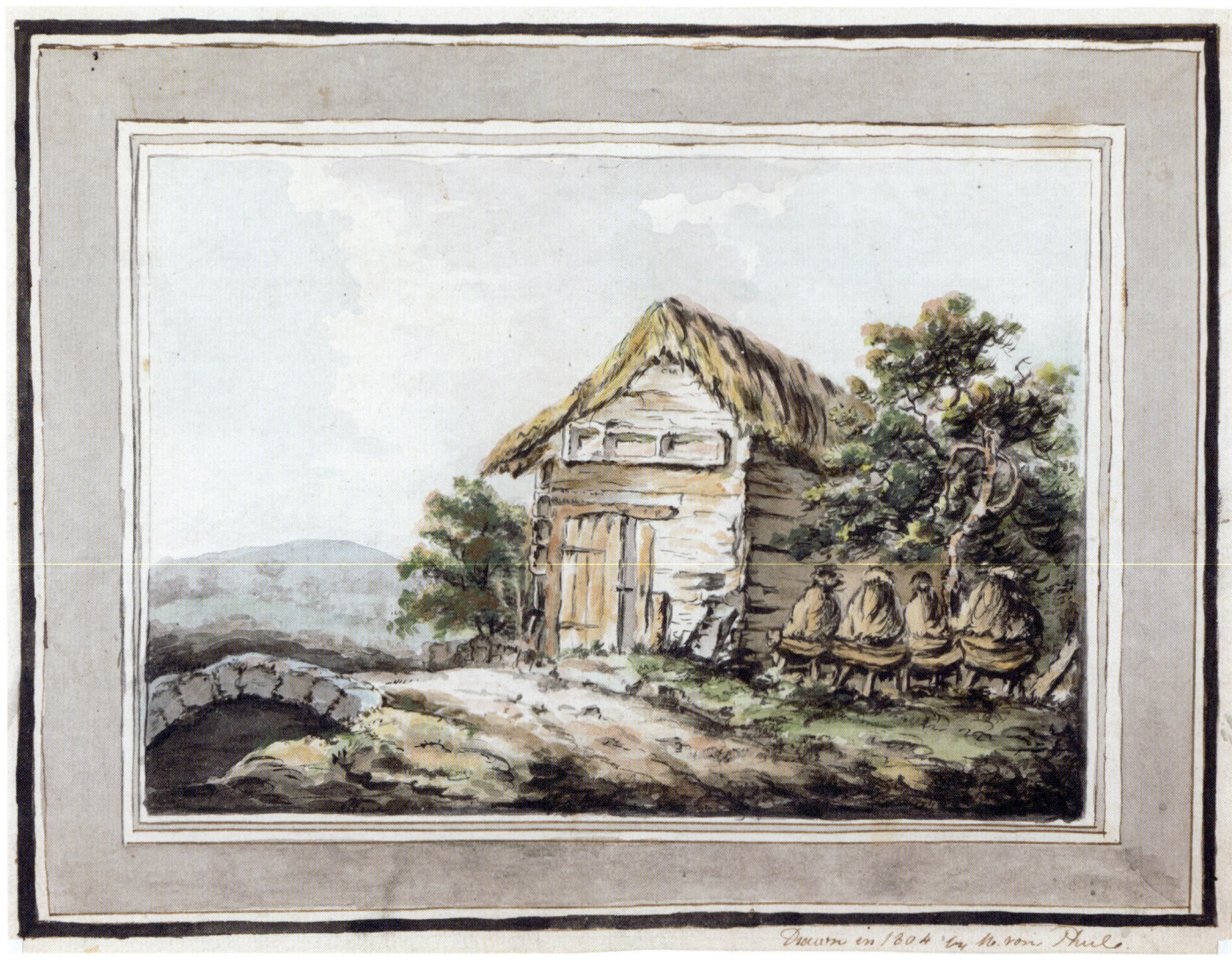

Figure 26 (Book 4)

Copy of a European scene
Watercolor and ink on paper
8⅝" × 6⅜"
1804

Inscribed "Drawn in 1804 by M. von Phul." This work, likely a copy, is Anna Maria's earliest dated painting. Although it seems she hadn't yet begun studying with George or Mary Beck when she painted it, the piece reveals the 18-year-old was already competent in watercolor.

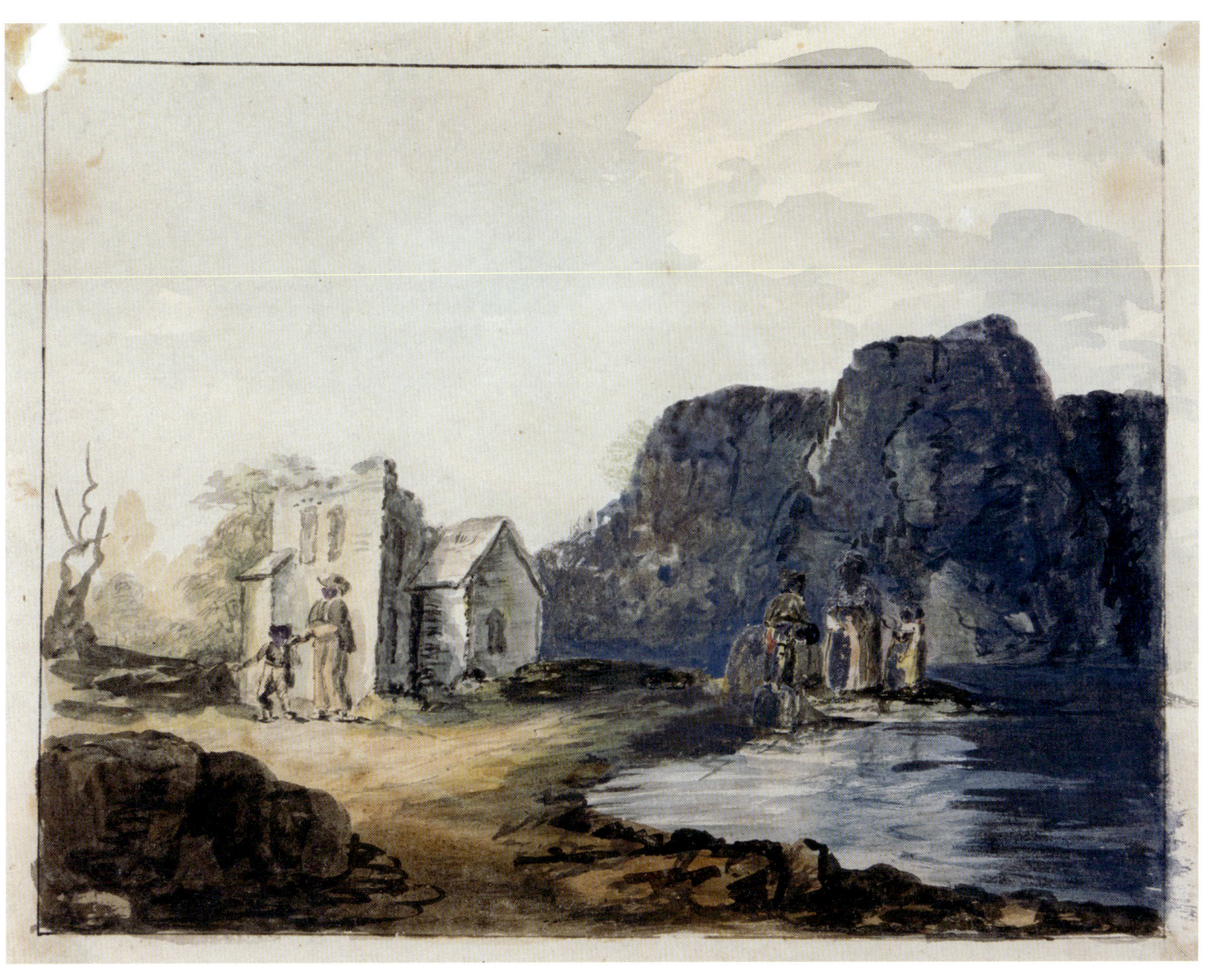

Figure 27 (Book 4)

Landscape with figures
Watercolor and ink on paper
10" × 8"
Unknown date

MORE THAN ORDINARY | 59

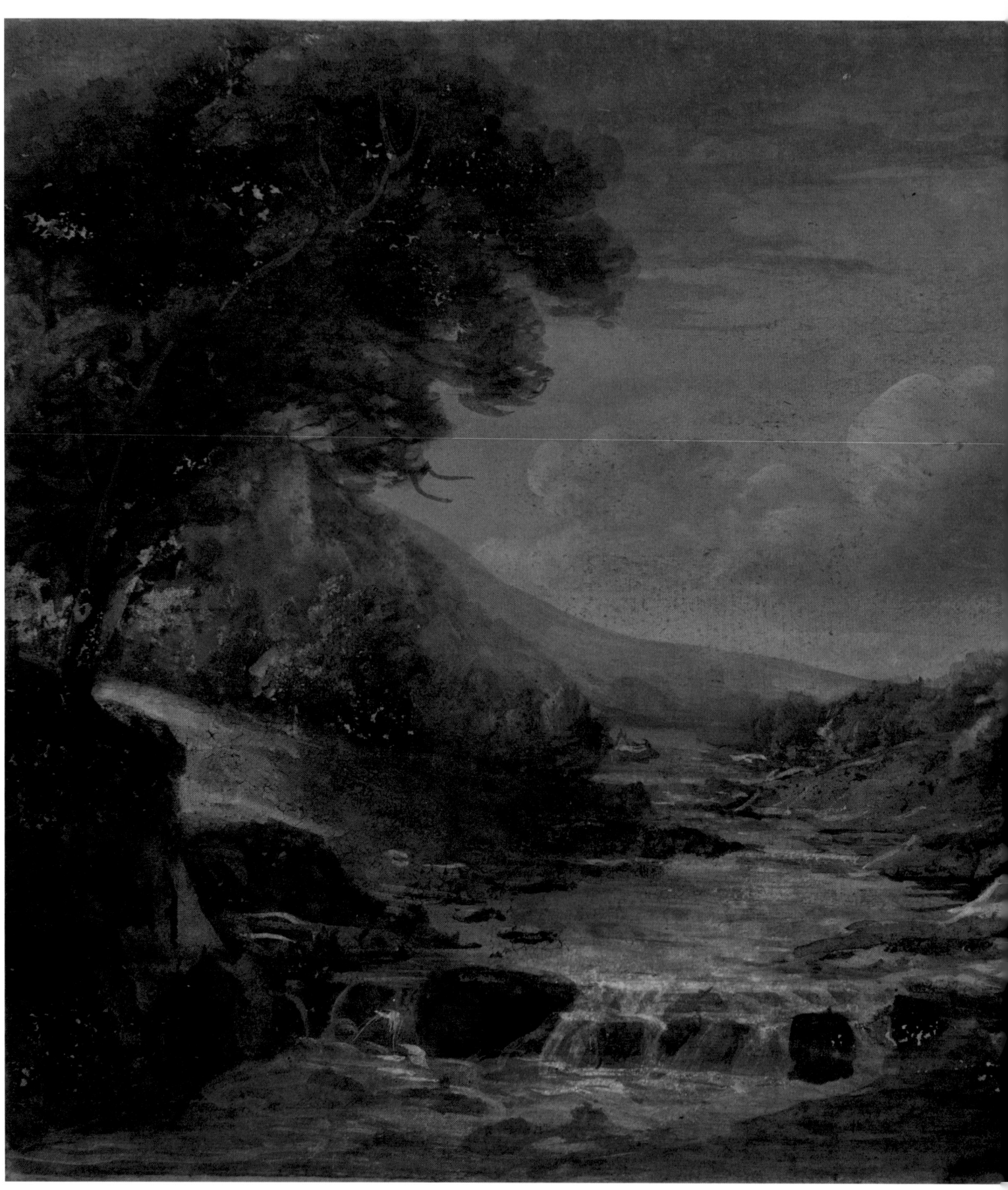

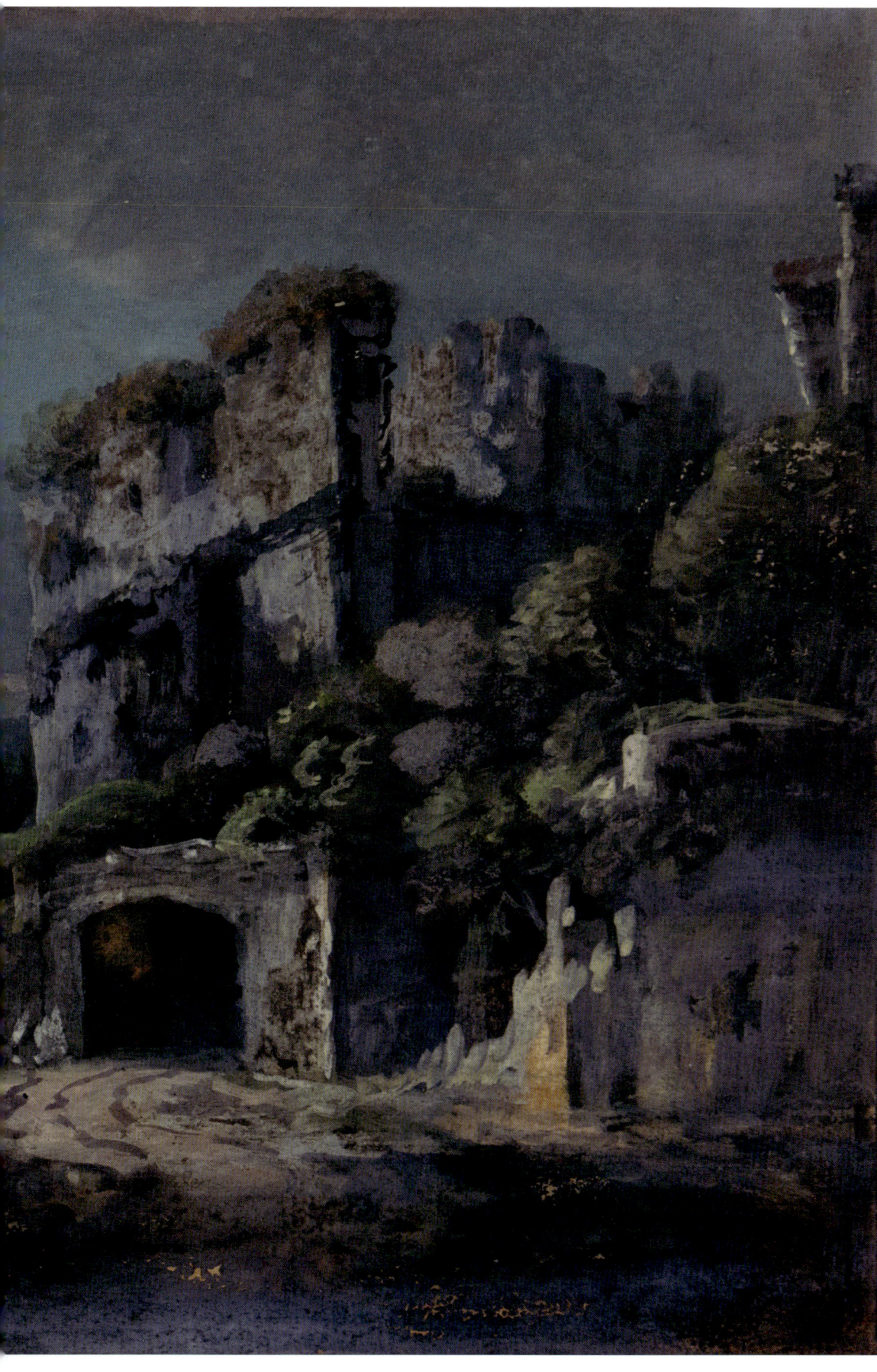

Figure 28 (Book 4)

Landscape with stream and castle ruins
Watercolor and gouache on paper
10" × 7"
Unknown date

In this atmospheric European landscape, Anna Maria's capabilities as a watercolorist are on display. The command of perspective and color harmony make it one of her more ambitious paintings.

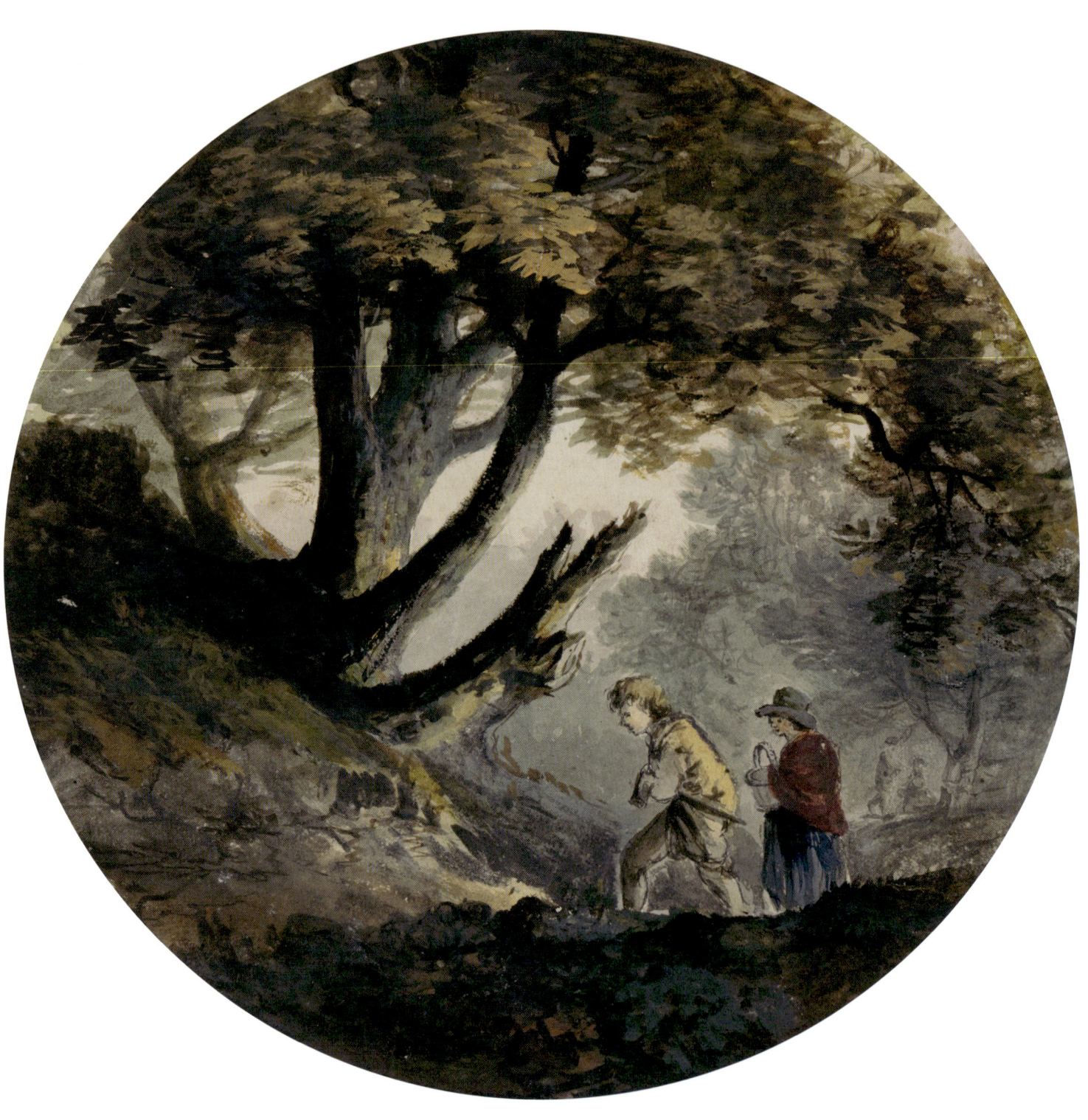

Figure 29 (Book 4)
Landscape with man and woman
Watercolor on paper
8½" × 8½"
Unknown date

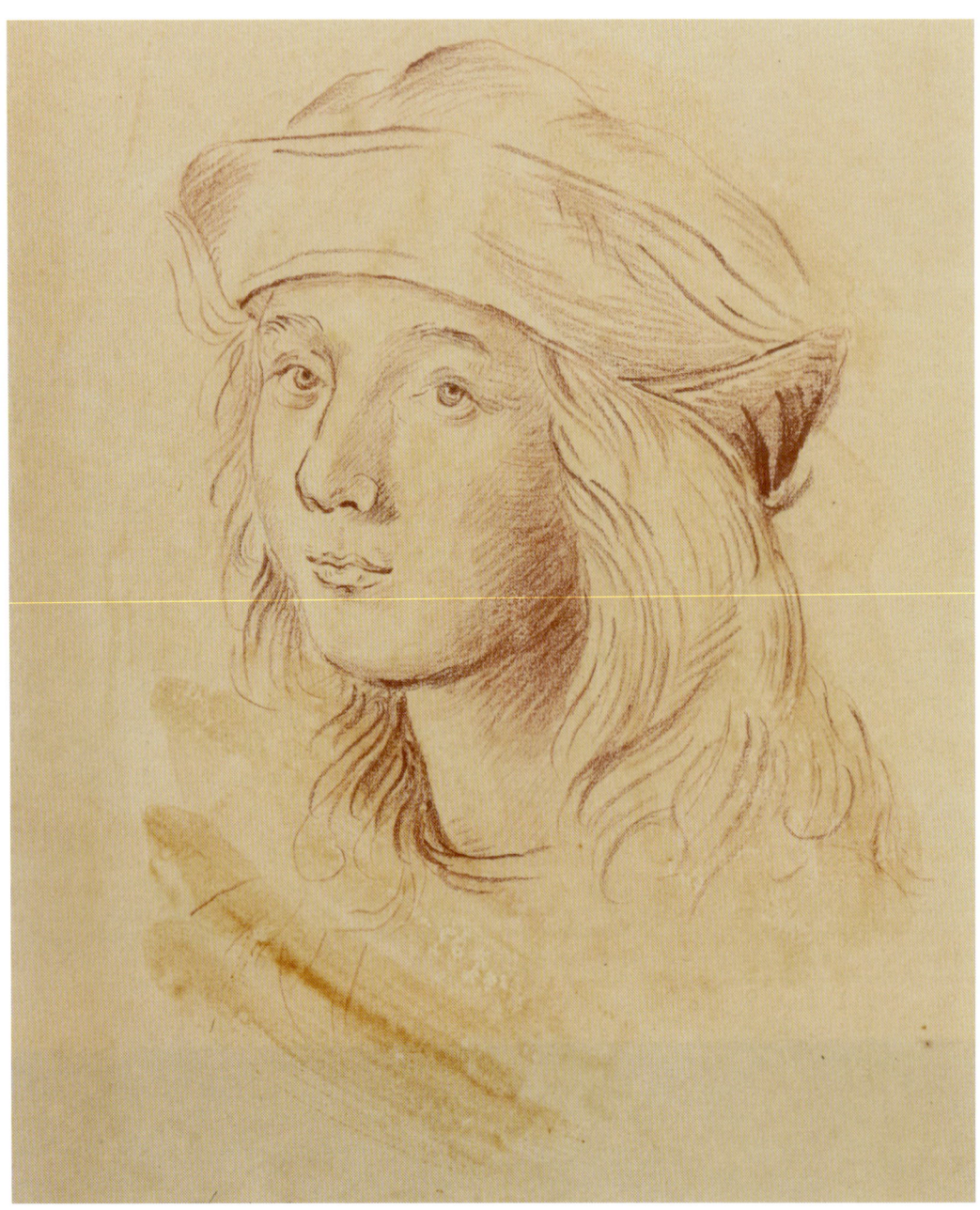

Figure 30 (Book 4)

Raffaello D'Urbino
Chalk on paper
Unknown date

SECTION 2: BOOK 1 AND BOOK 5

Book 1 and Book 5 contain the known entirety of Anna Maria's work done while visiting the Missouri and Illinois territories during the winter, spring, and summer of 1818. Totaling 65 sketches and drawings, the books include endearing portraits, studies of trees and flowers, and some of the earliest depictions of St. Louis and the surrounding areas.

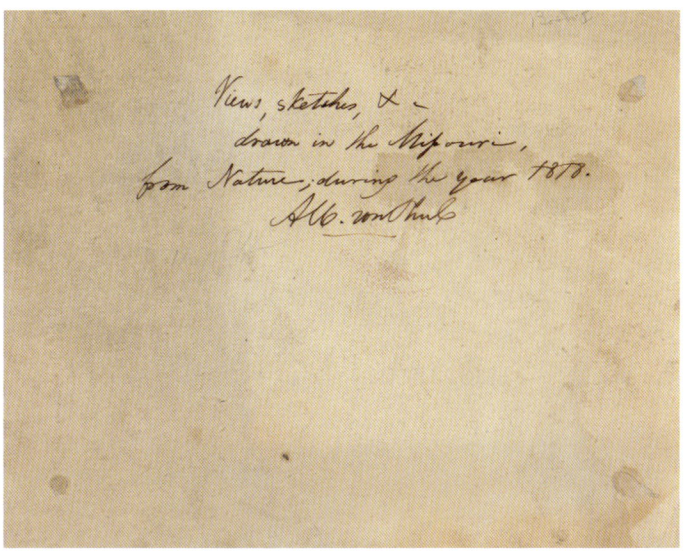

Cover of Book 1

Views, sketches, [etc.] drawn in the Missouri, from Nature, during the year 1818. AM. von Phul
7¾" × 6¼"
1818

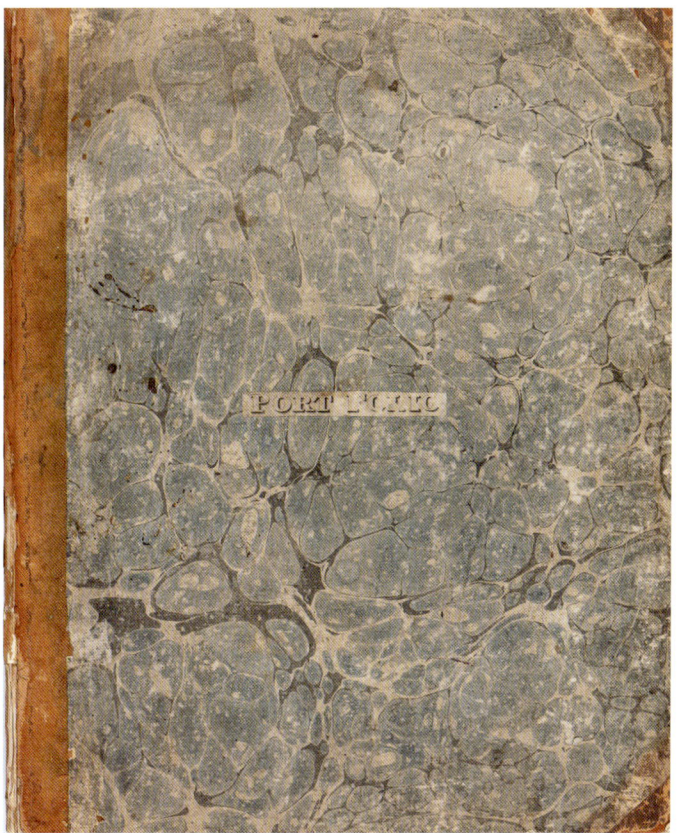

Cover of Book 5

Portfolio
11" × 13¾"
1818

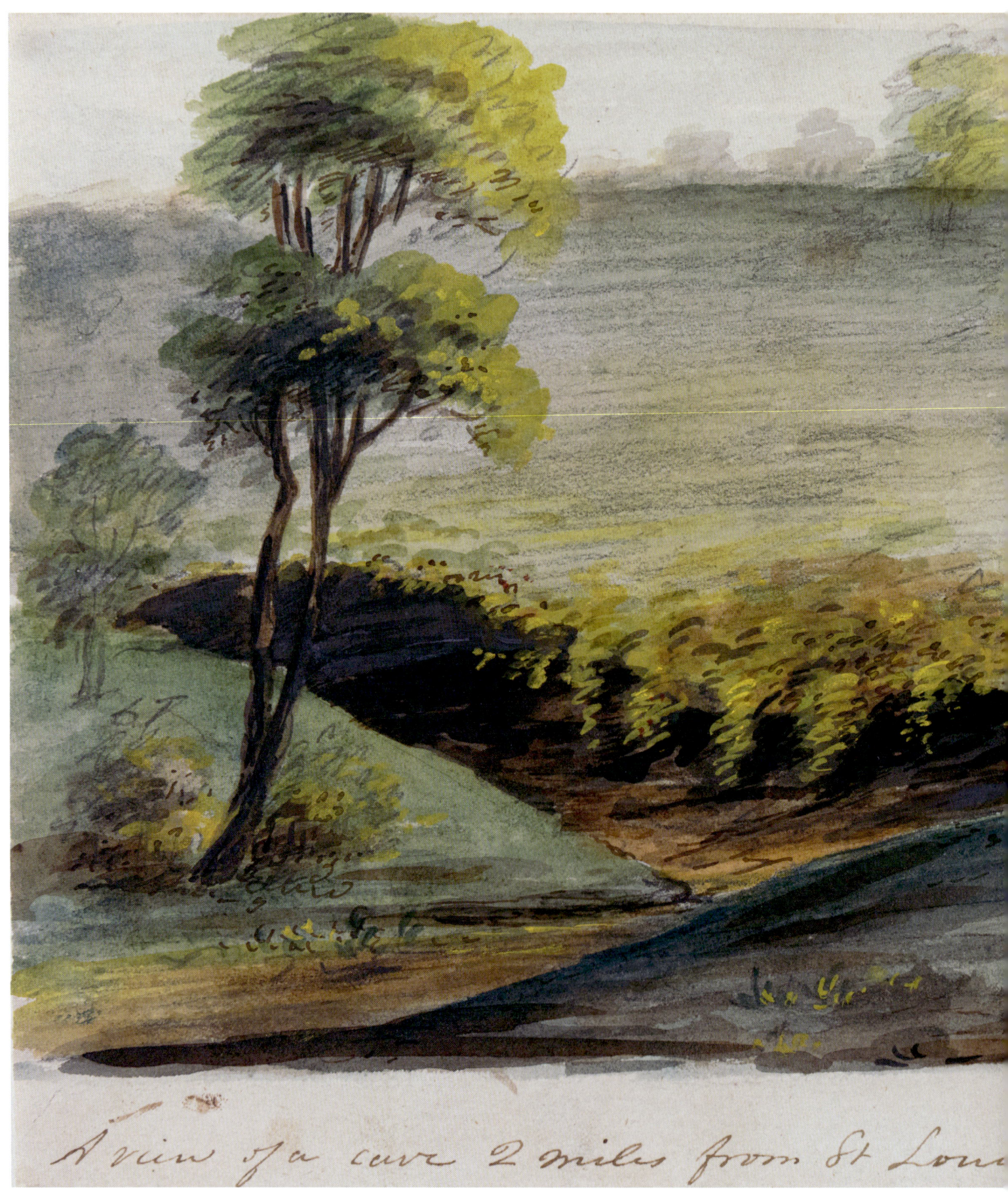

A view of a cave 2 miles from St Louis

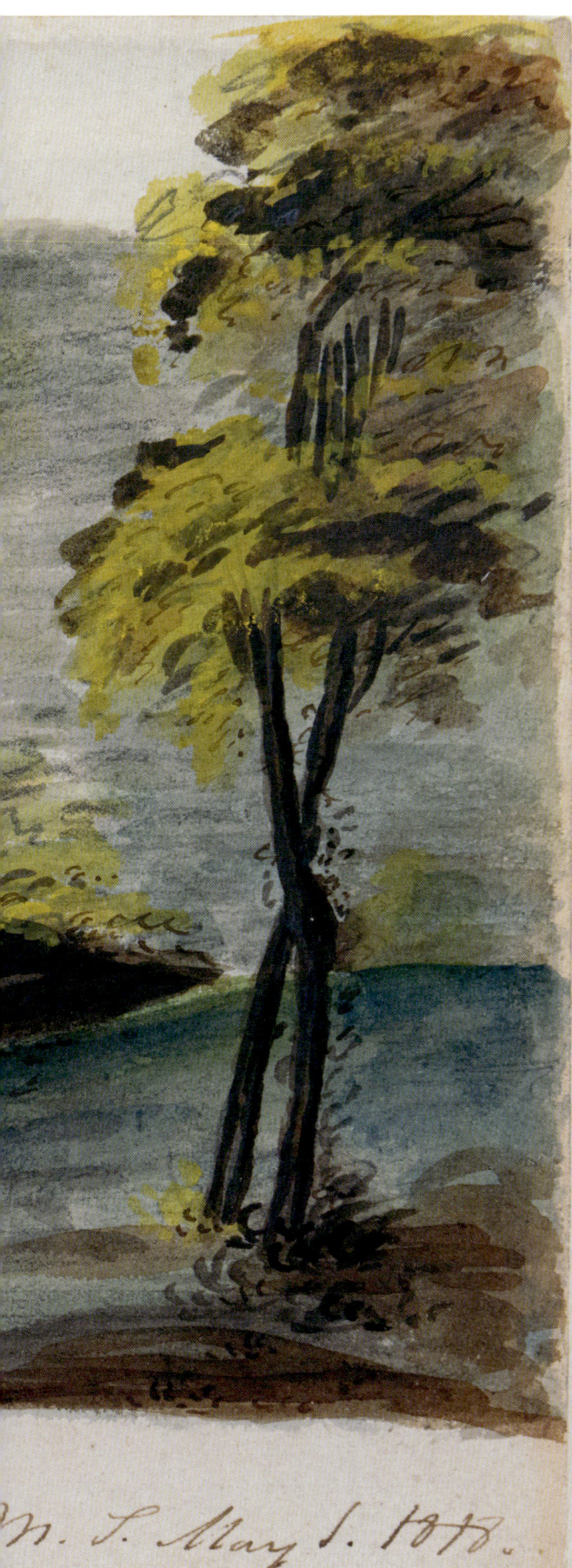

Figure 31 (Book 1)

**A view of a cave 2 miles
from St Louis M. T. May 1, 1818**
Graphite, ink,
and wash on paper
7½" × 6¼"
1818

Inscribed "A view of a cave 2 miles from St Louis M. T. May 1. 1818." The topography of the St. Louis region is riddled with natural caves. Though Anna Maria identified this cave only by its proximity to St. Louis, the entrance and surrounding landscape resemble that of English's Cave. Named for Ezra English, who operated a brewery and subterranean beer garden there, English's Cave was one of many caves repurposed for use in the city's growing beer industry during the mid-19th century.

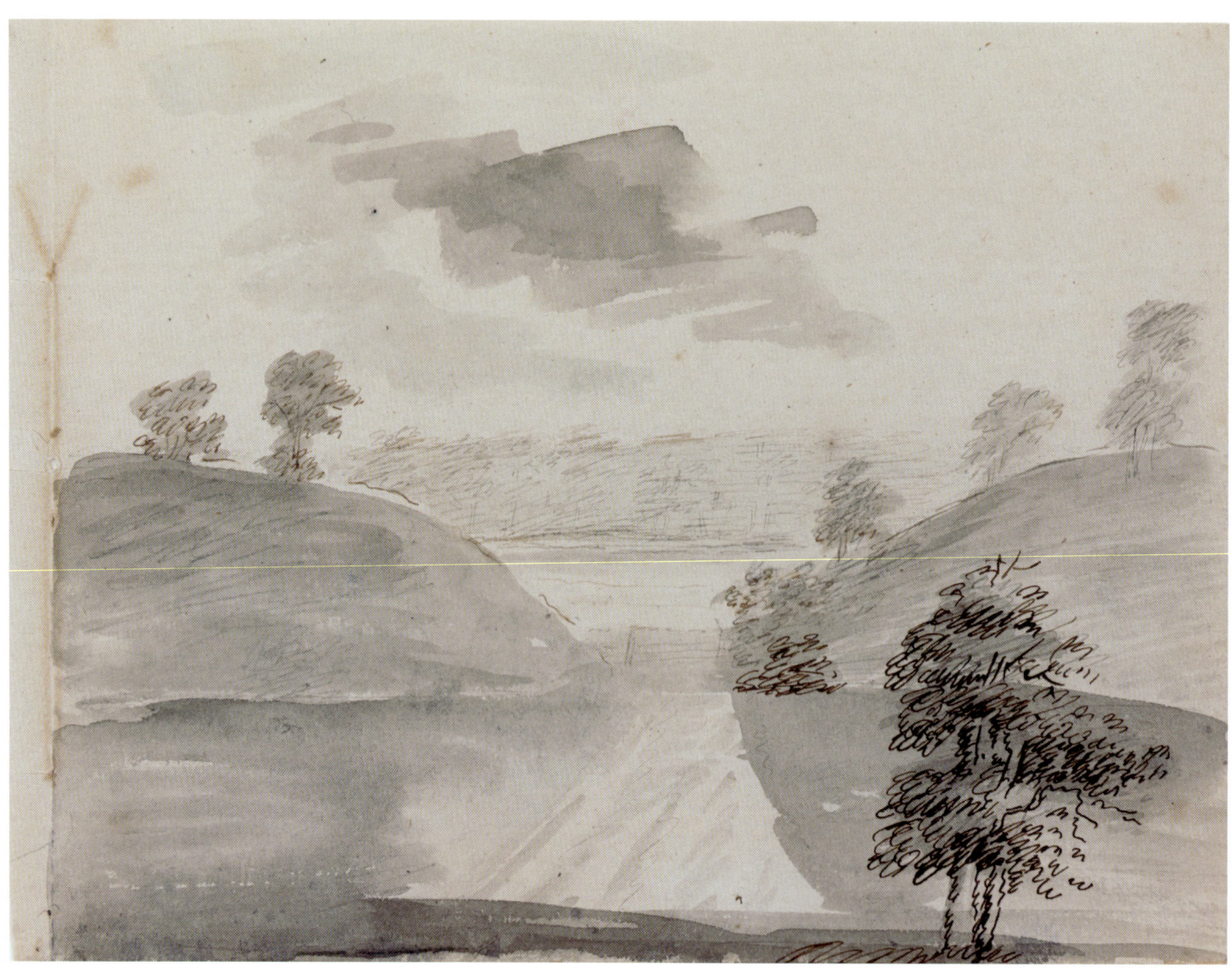

Figure 32 (Book 1)

Landscape with two hills
Wash and ink on paper
8" × 6⅛"
1818

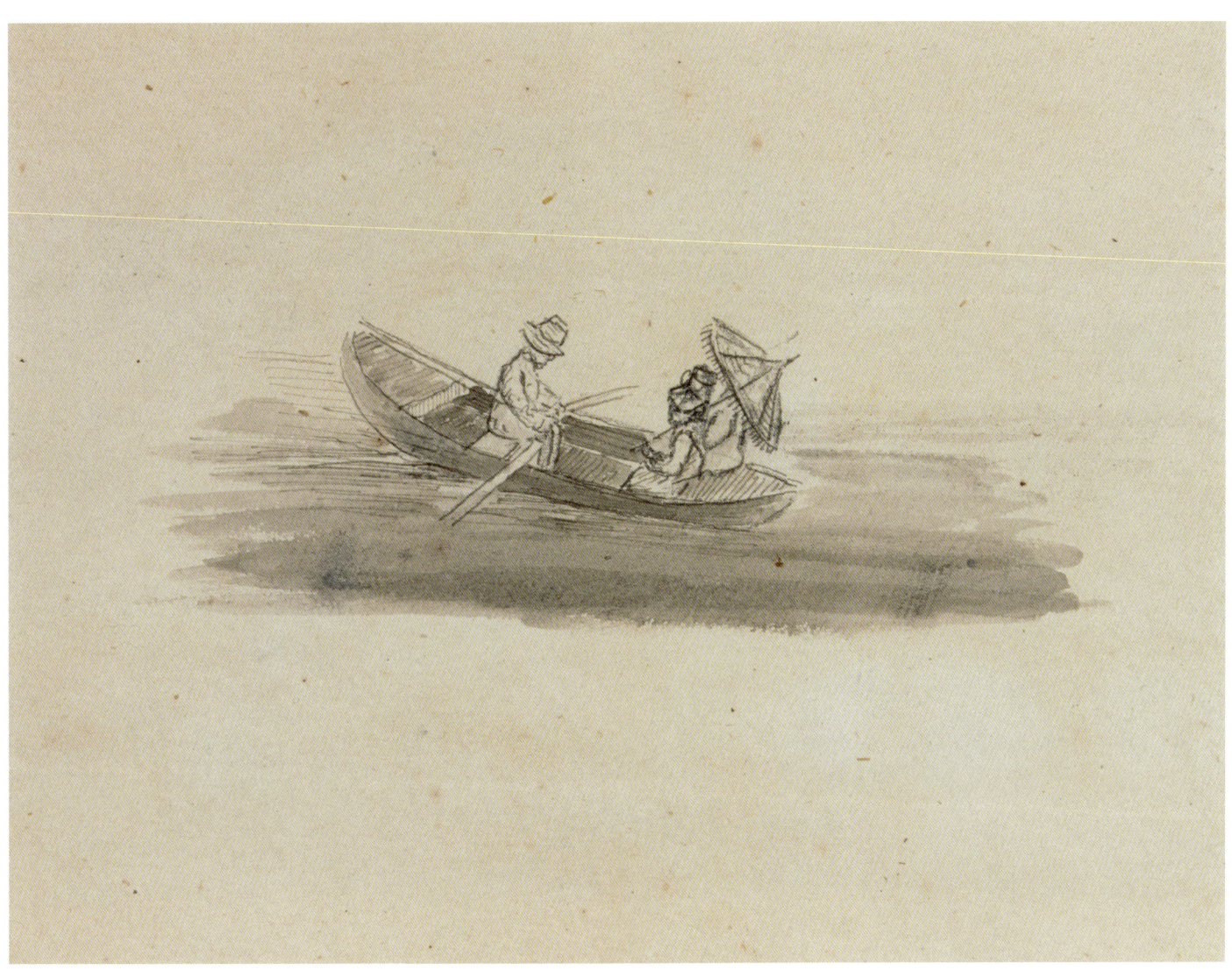

Figure 34 (Book 1)

Couple in a rowboat
Graphite, ink, and wash on paper
7¼" × 6¼"
1818

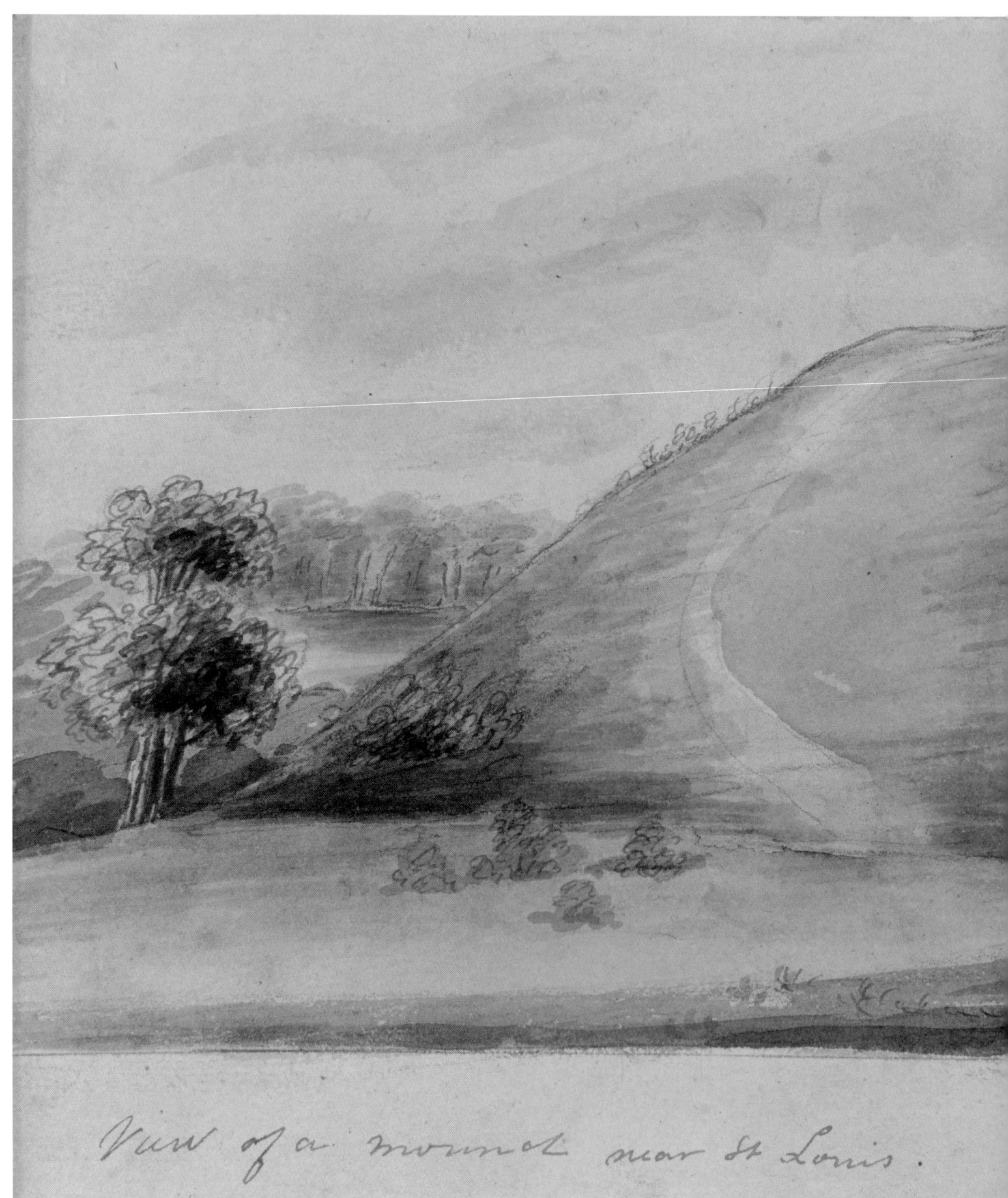

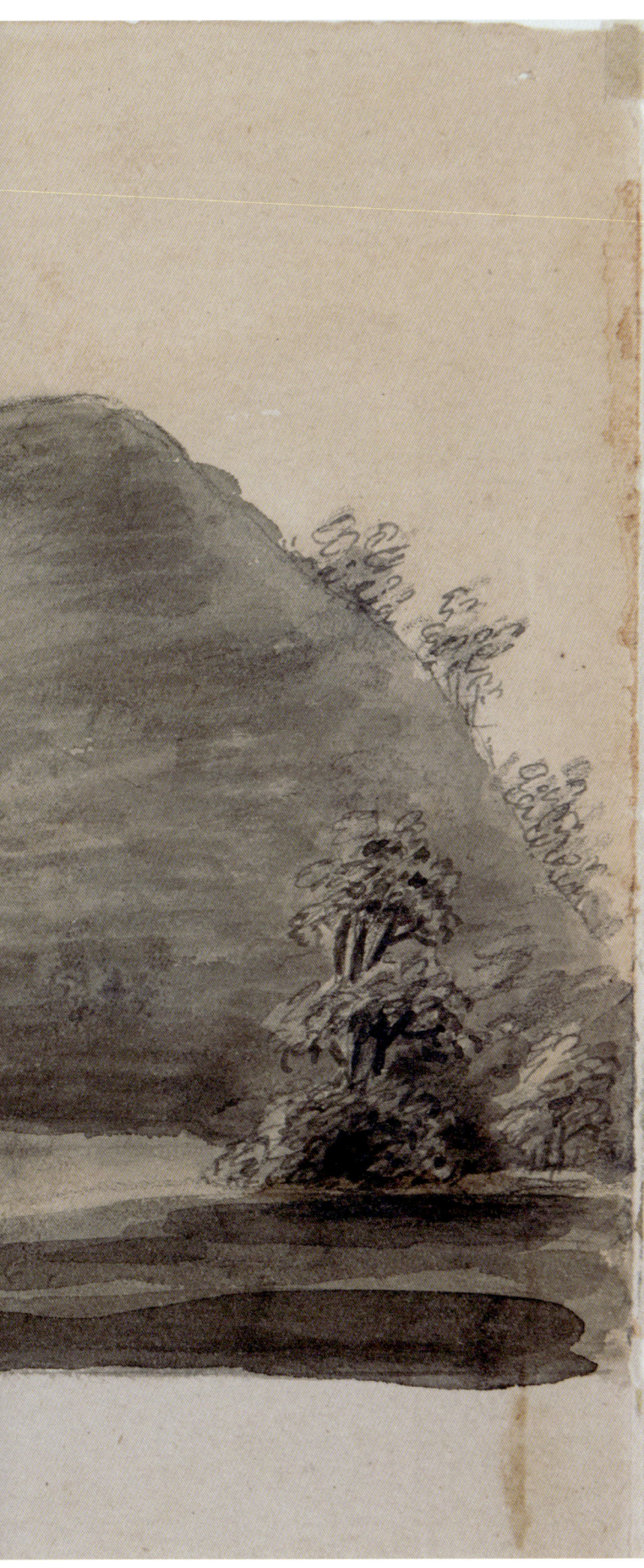

Figure 33 (Book 1)

View of a mound near St Louis
Graphite, ink, and wash on paper
7¼" × 6¼"
1818

Inscribed "View of a mound near St Louis."

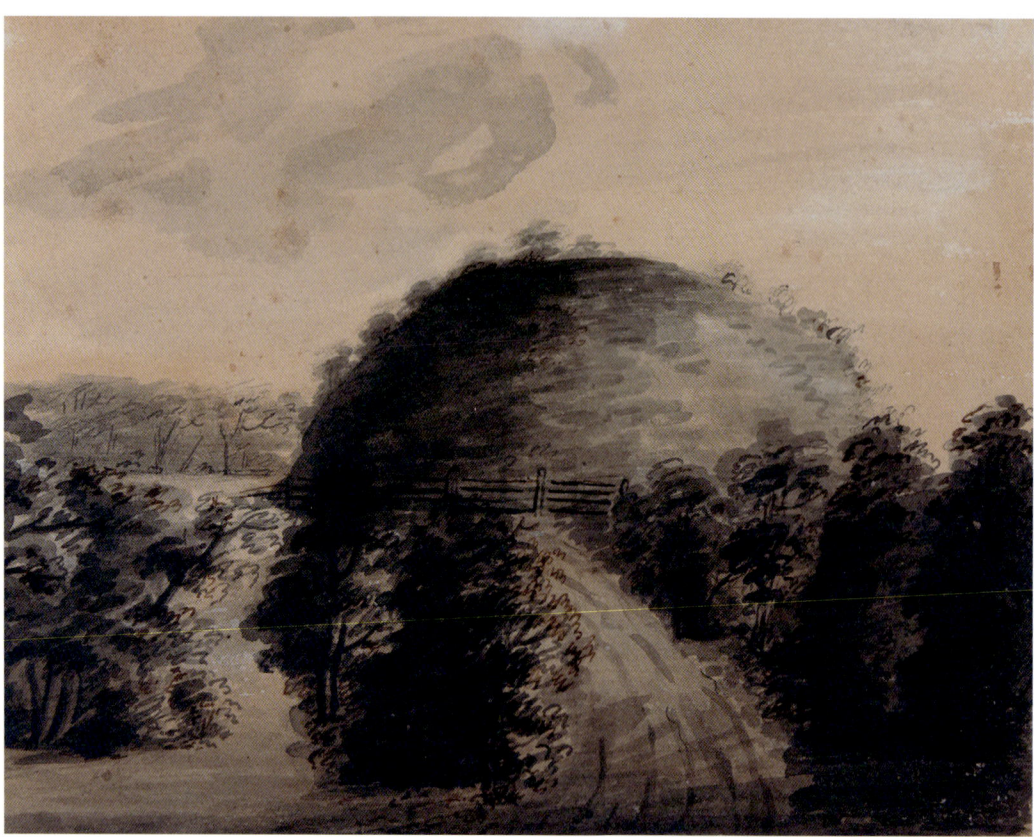

Figure 35 (Book 1)

Landscape with Native American mound
Graphite, ink, and wash on paper
7¾" × 6⅛"
1818

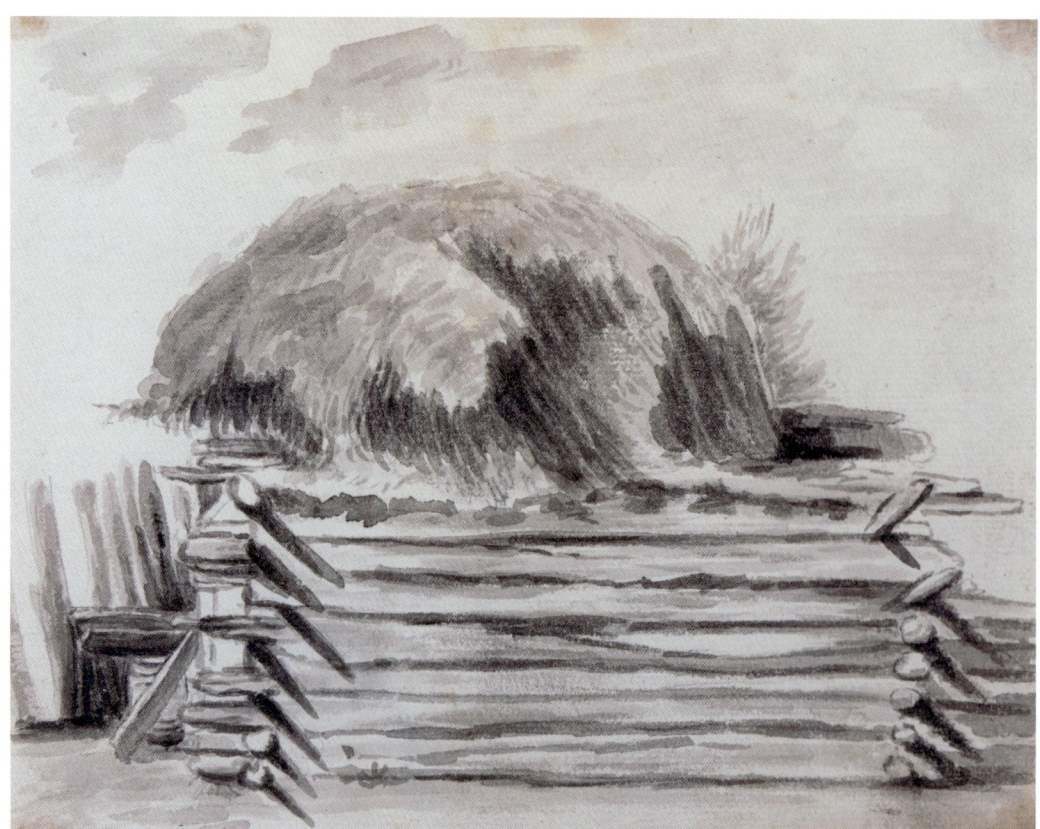

Figure 37 (Book 1)

Haystack and split-rail fence
Graphite, ink, and wash on paper
7¾" × 6⅛"
1818

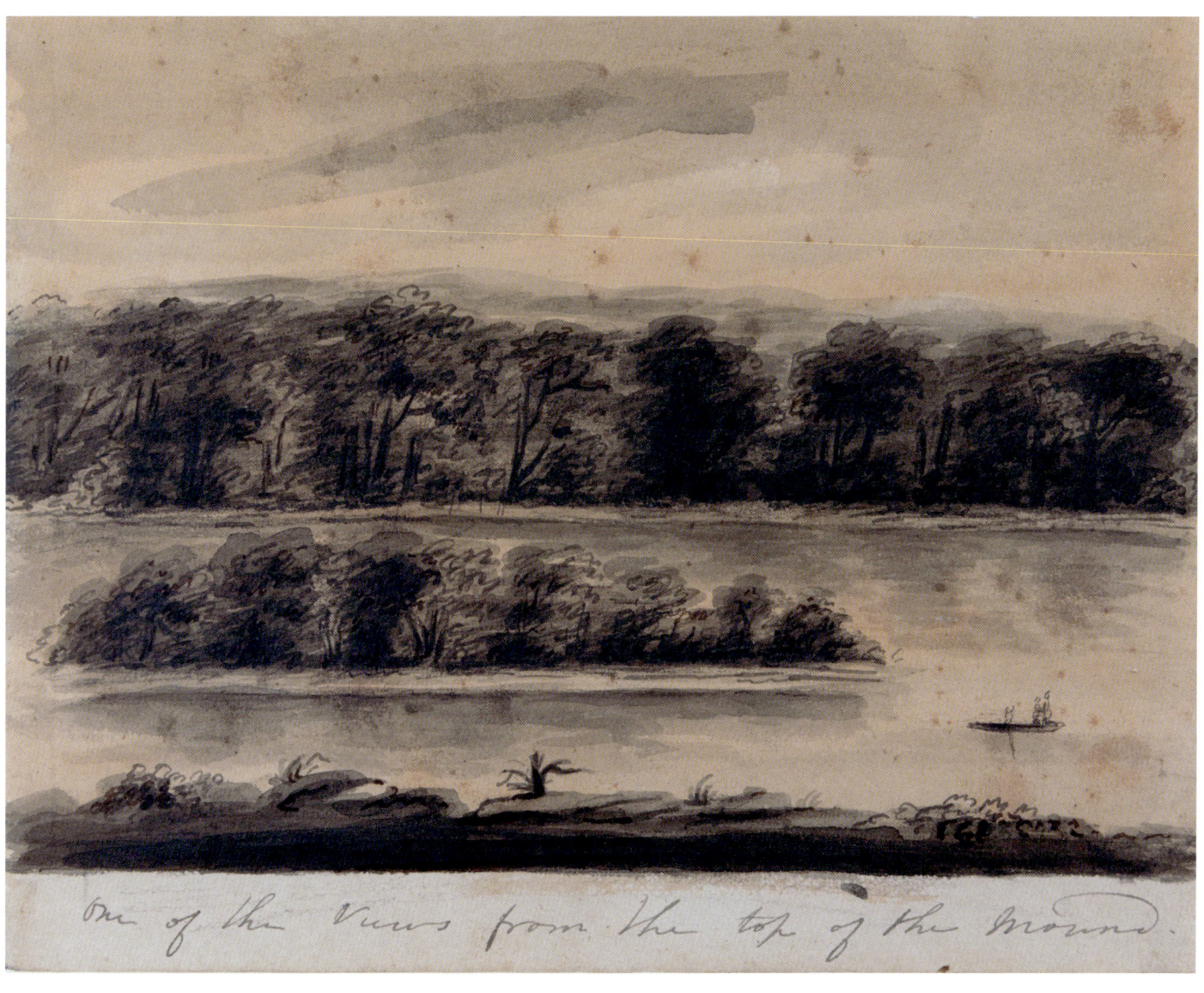

Figure 36 (Book 1)

One of the Views from the top of the Mound
Graphite, ink, and wash on paper
7¾" × 6⅛"
1818

Inscribed "One of the Views from the top of the Mound."

Figure 38 (Book 1)

Two St. Louis homes
Ink and wash on paper
7⅝" × 6⅛"
1818

Positioned along the Mississippi River, these two St. Louis homes are thought to be the Carr Residence (foreground) and the Marcheteau Desnoyers Residence, built in 1815 and 1766, respectively. In this work, Anna Maria captured the city's transition from Creole to American as reflected through its architecture.

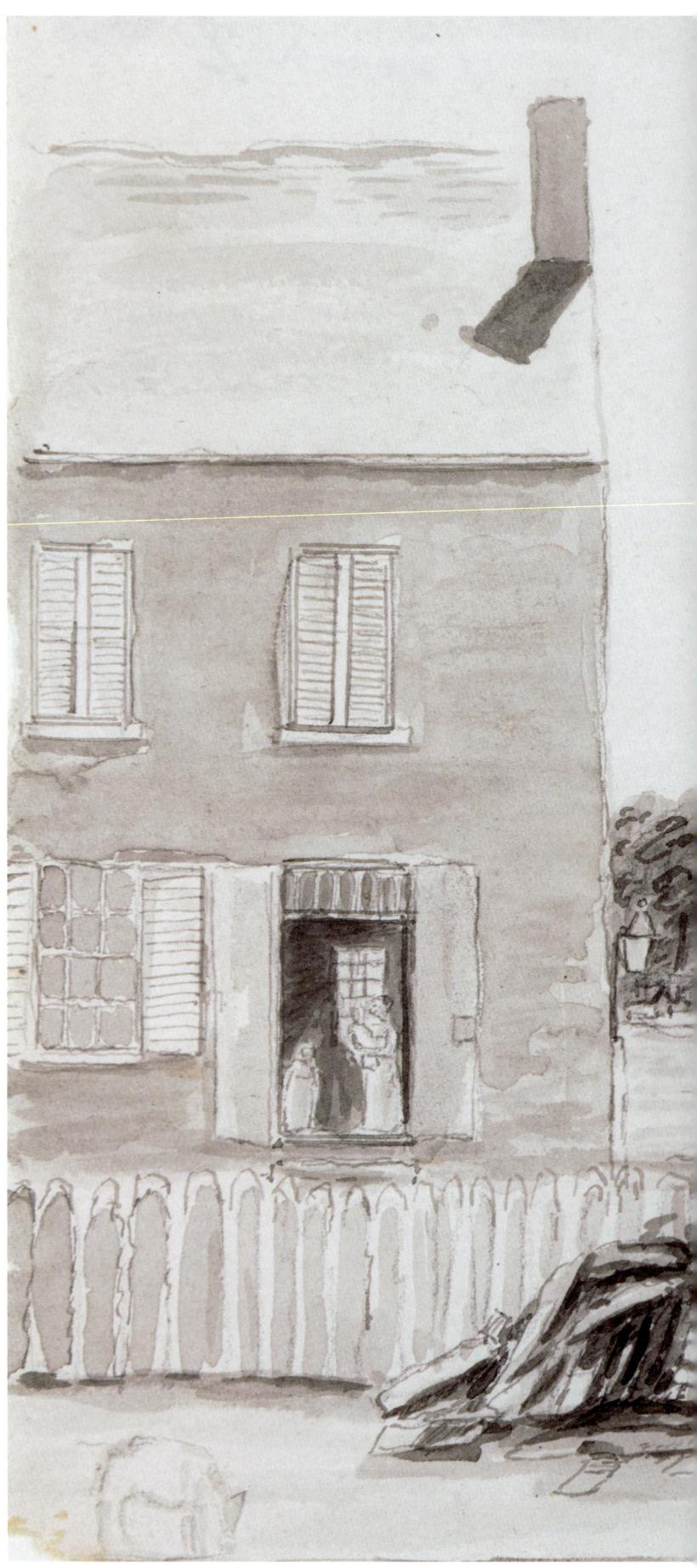

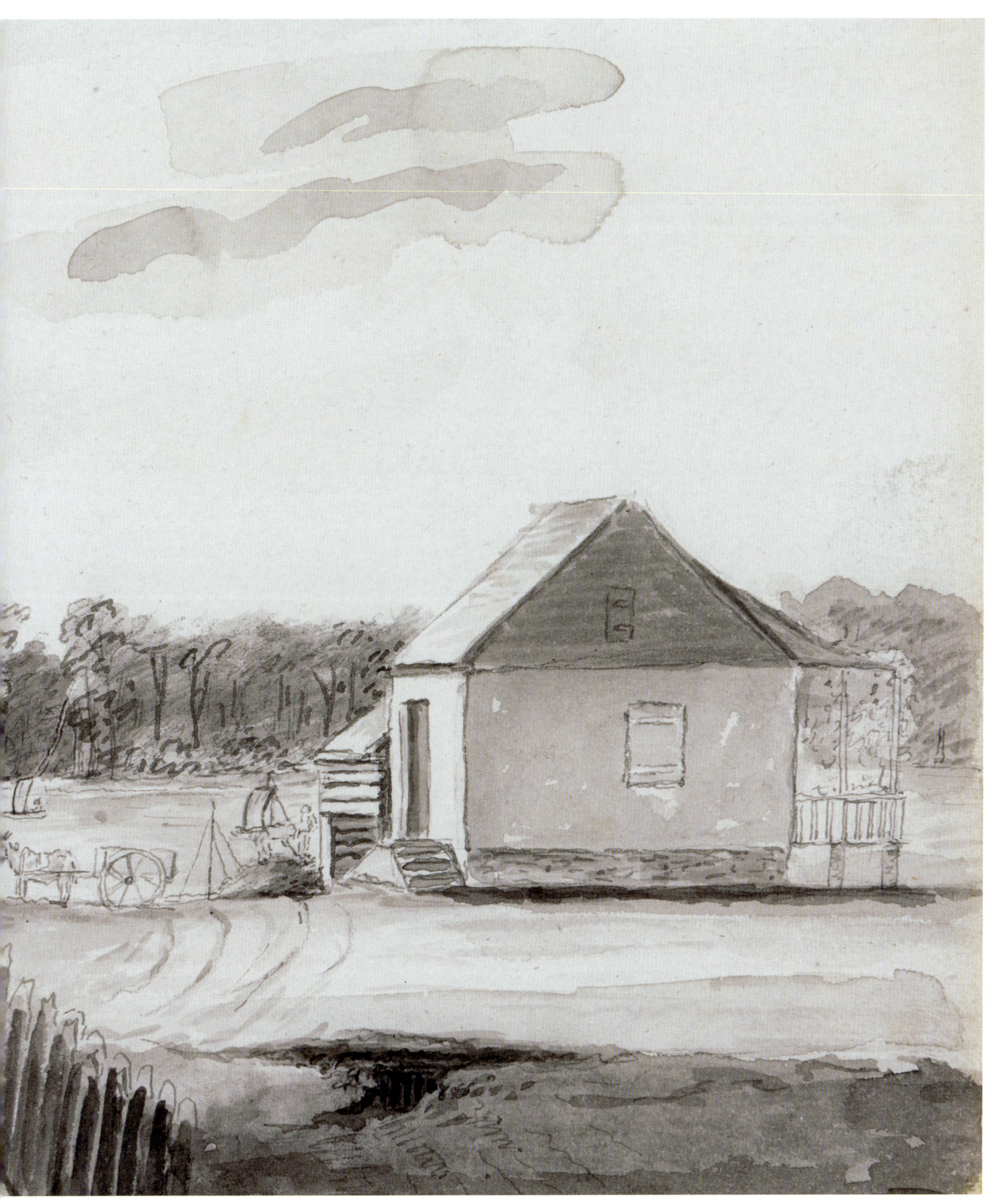

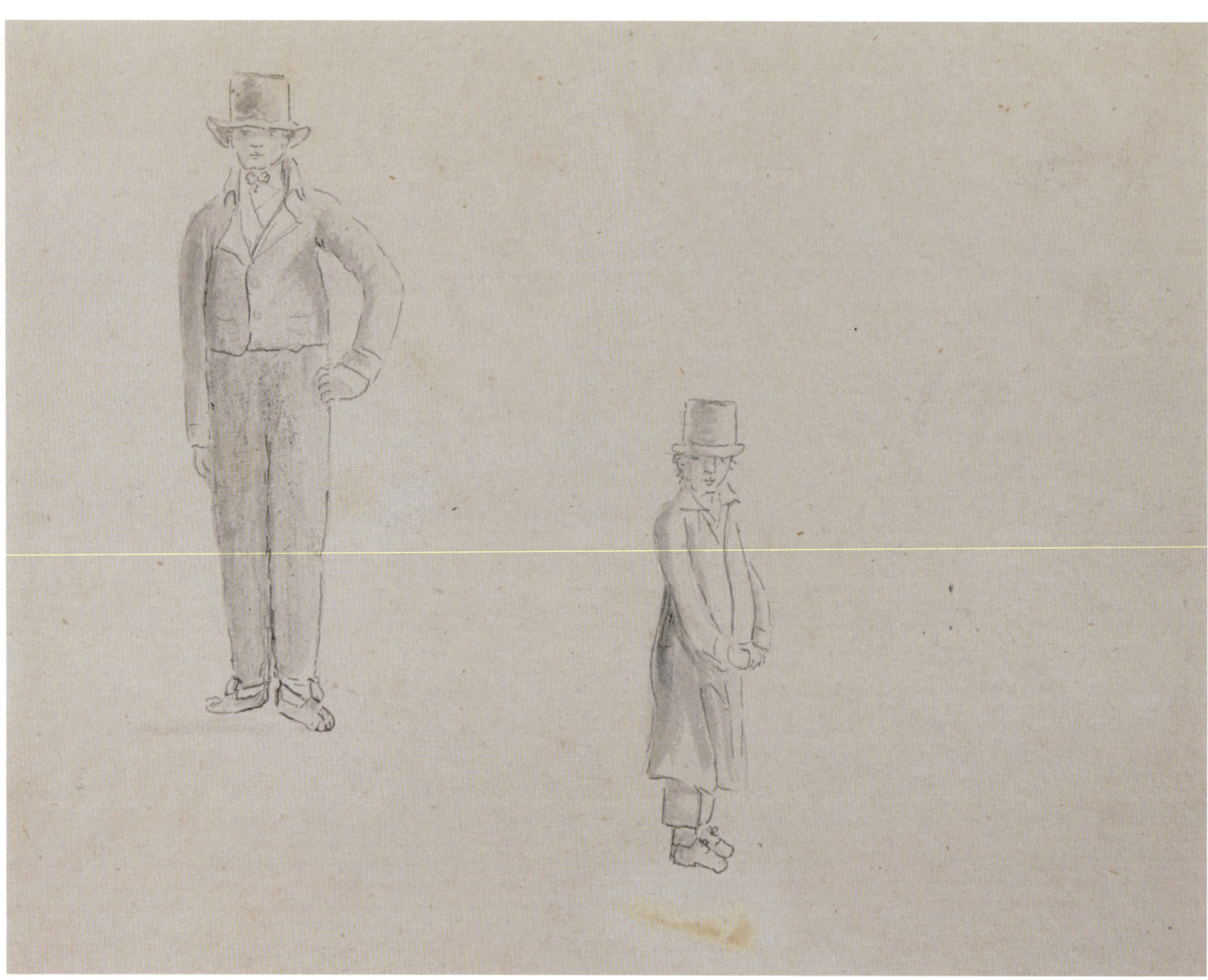

Figure 39 (Book 1)

Two studies of a man wearing a hat
Graphite and wash on paper
7⅝" × 6⅛"
1818

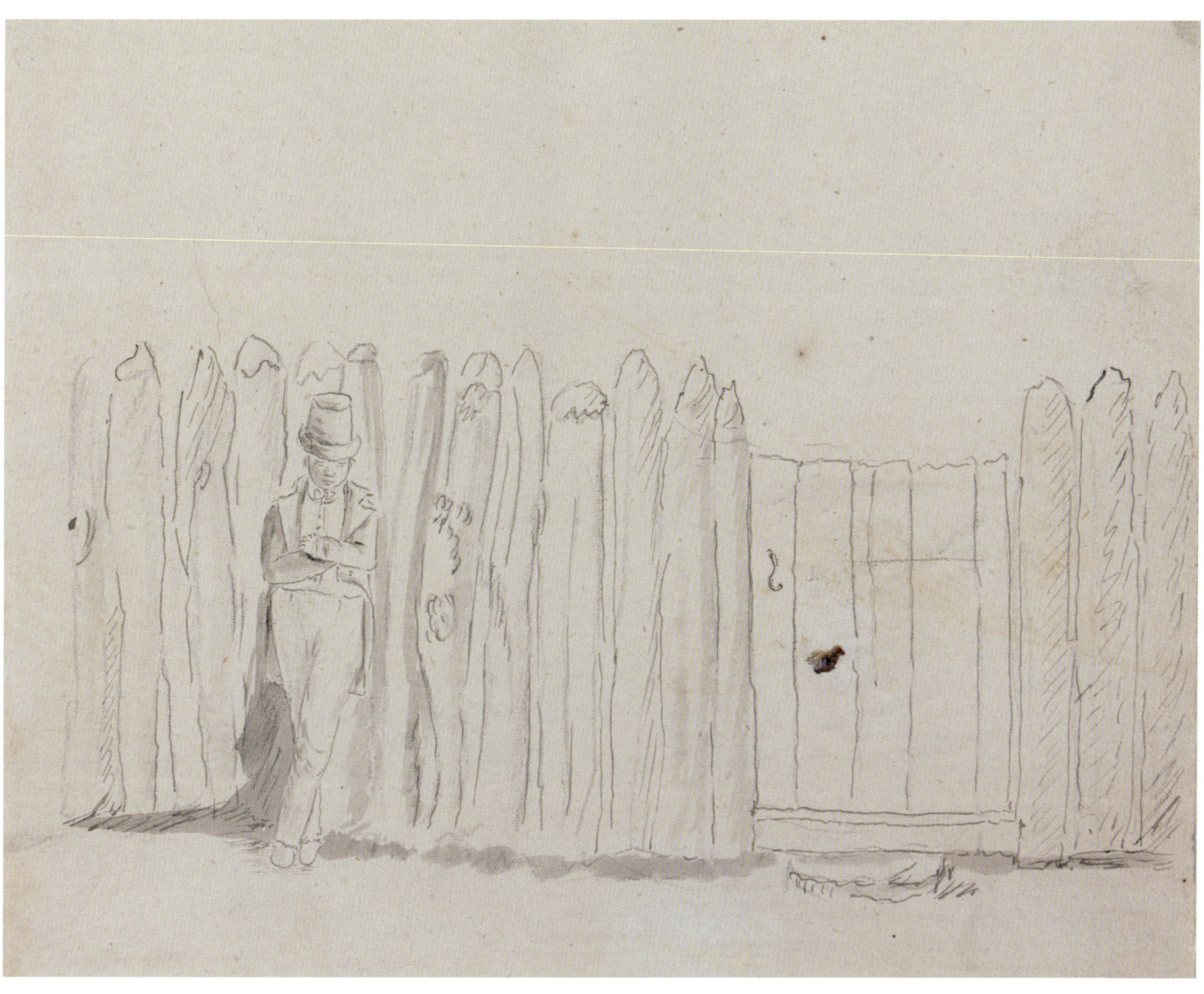

Figure 40 (Book 1)

Man leaning on a post fence
Graphite and wash on paper
7⅝" × 6⅛"
1818

Tall post fences, like the one depicted here, surrounded nearly every home in early St. Louis. The structures offered security and privacy while limiting the number of domestic animals that could run free on the streets. A requirement during the city's colonial era, this style of fencing endured into the late territorial period, as Anna Maria's sketches document.

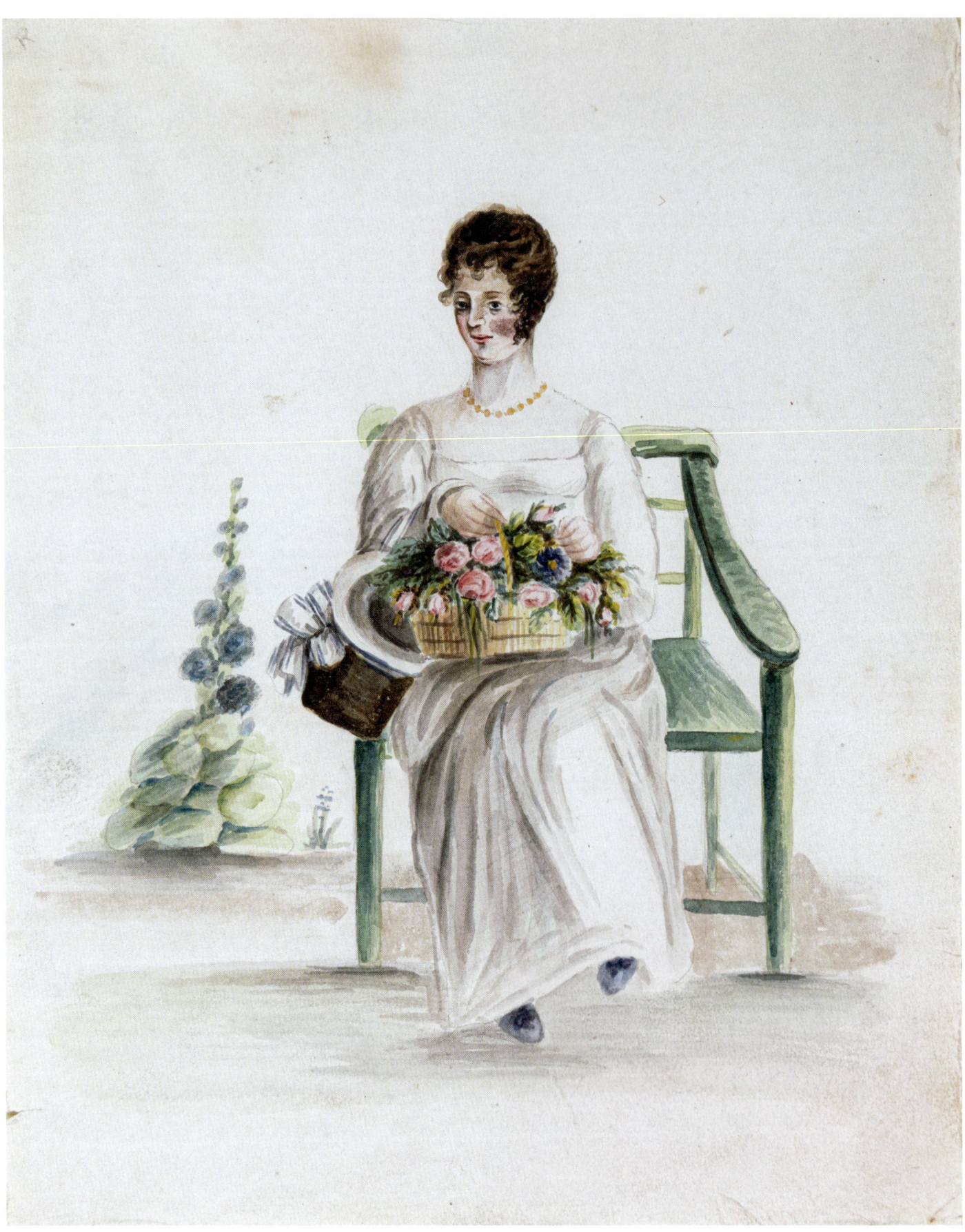

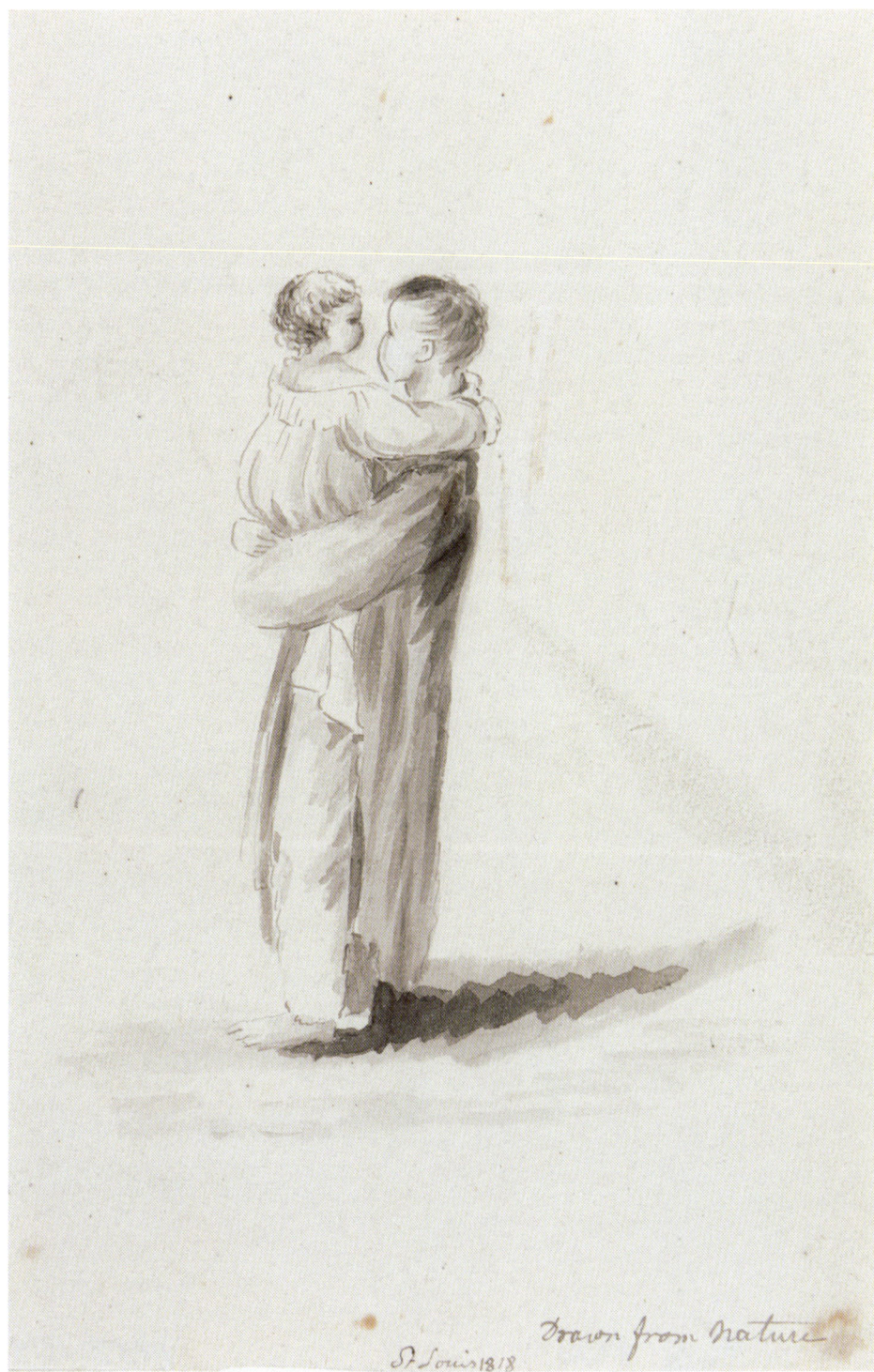

Figure 42 (Book 1)

Boy holding a baby
Graphite and wash on paper
7⅜" × 7¼"
1818

Inscribed "Drawn from nature, St. Louis 1818."

Figure 41 (Book 1)

Woman with basket of flowers
Watercolor and graphite on paper
6⅛" × 7⅝"
1818

MORE THAN ORDINARY | 79

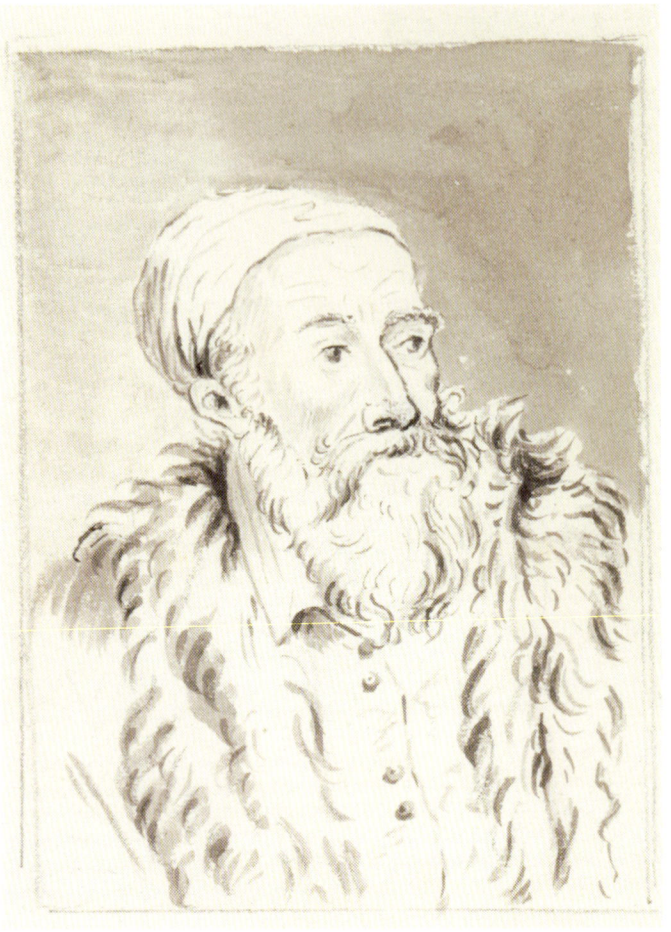 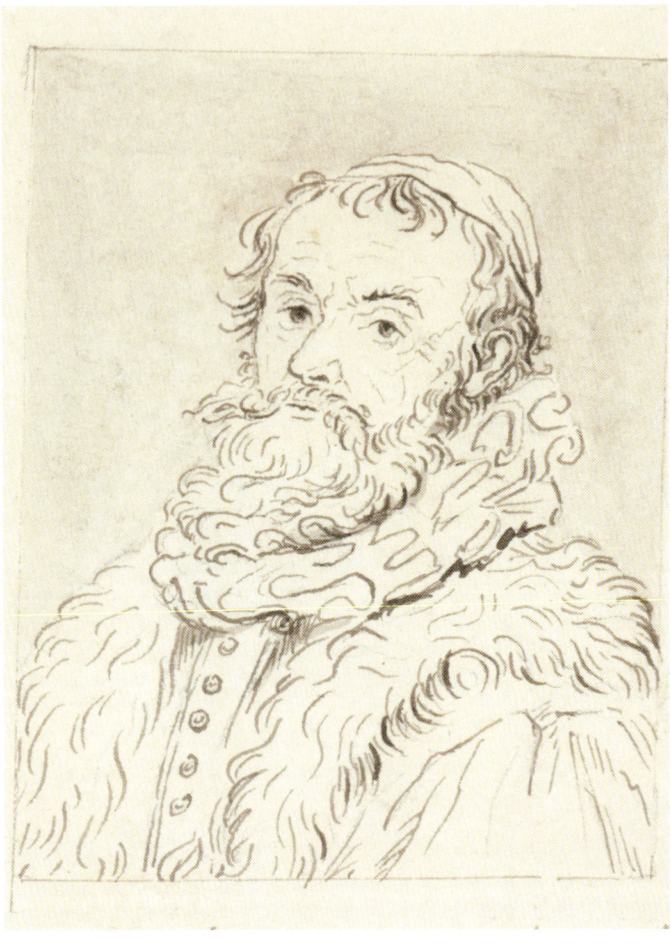

Figure 43 (Book 1)

Titian
Graphite, ink, and wash on paper
2¾" × 4½"
1818

Inscribed "Titian born in 1480 died 1576." The placement of these small portrait studies of historic artists within Anna Maria's sketchbook from her 1818 trip may indicate that they were copied from paintings or prints in St. Louis collections—perhaps those of Auguste Chouteau or Bishop William DuBourg.

Figure 44 (Book 1)

Goltzius
Graphite, ink, and wash on paper
3¼" × 4"
1818

Inscribed "Goltzius born at Muebrecht 1588 died at Harlem 1617."

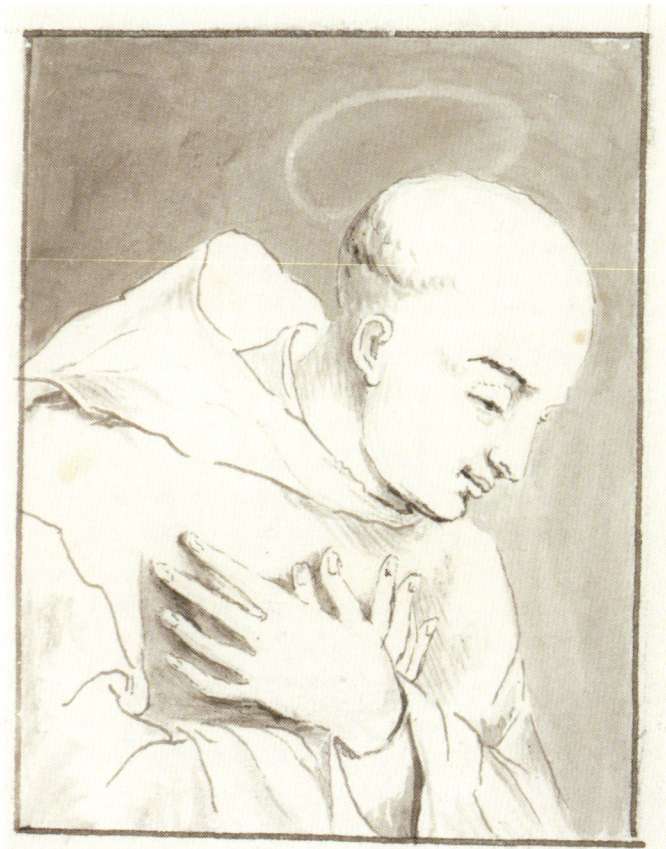

Figure 45 (Book 1)

Unidentified man
Ink and wash on paper
2⅜" × 4⅜"
1818

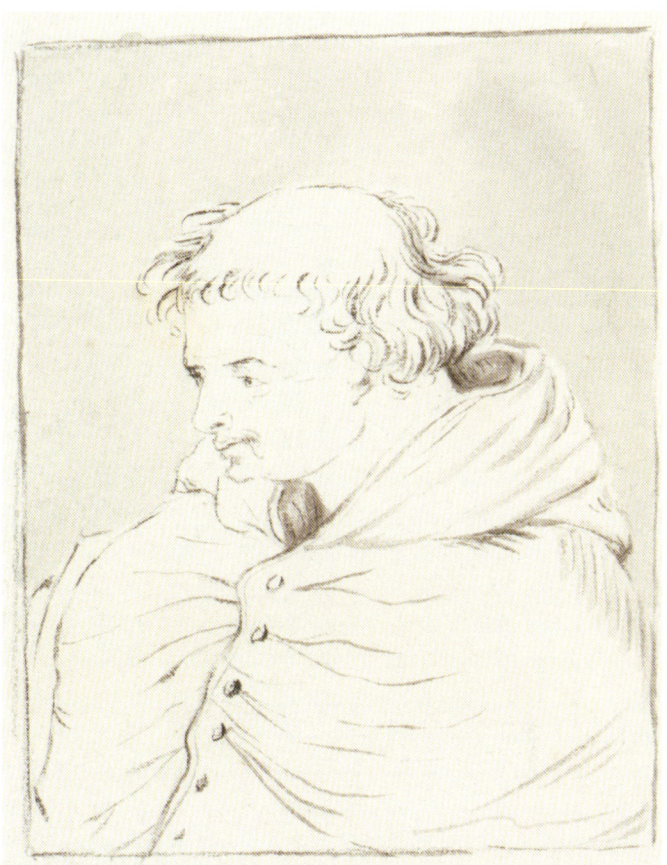

Figure 46 (Book 1)

Bramante
Graphite, ink, and wash on paper
2½" × 4"
1818

Inscribed "Bramante 1444 died at Rome at the age of 70 and buried at St Peter's."

MORE THAN ORDINARY | 81

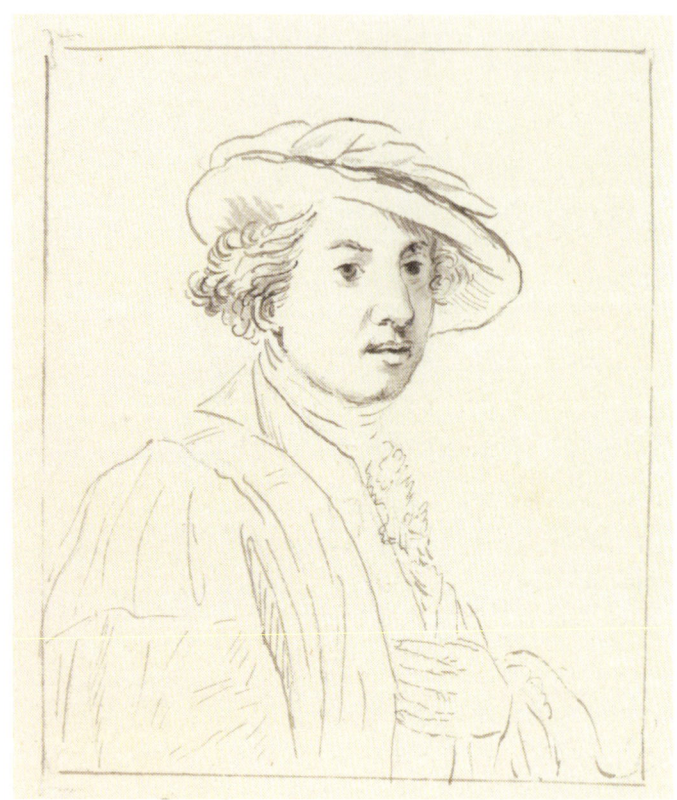

Figure 47 (Book 1)

Sir Joshua
Graphite, ink, and wash on paper
3¼" × 4⅛"
1818

Inscribed "Sir Joshua painted by himself born at [illegible] 16 July 1723 died 23 Febr 1792."

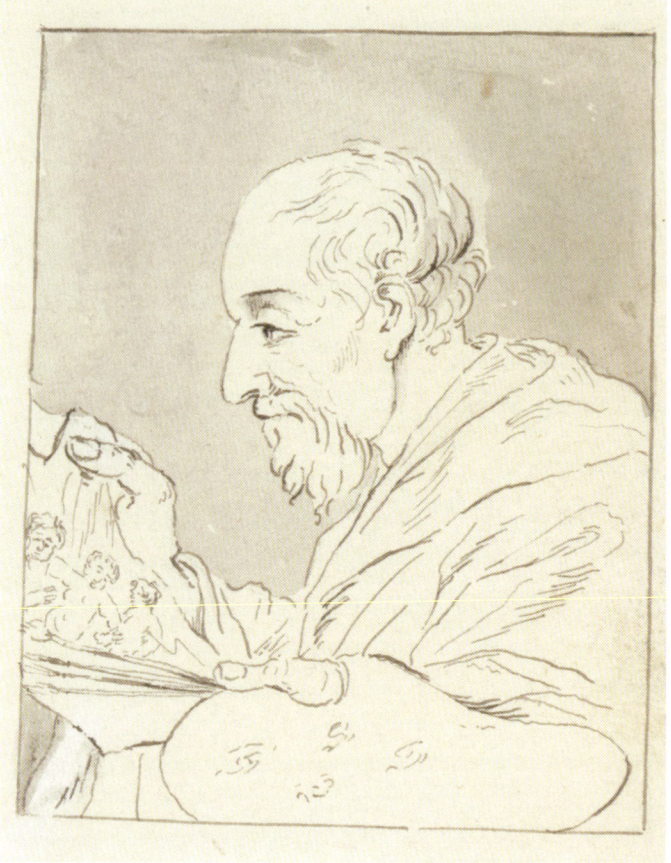

Figure 48 (Book 1)

Unidentified portrait of an artist with palette
Ink and wash on paper
3⅜" × 4⅛"
1818

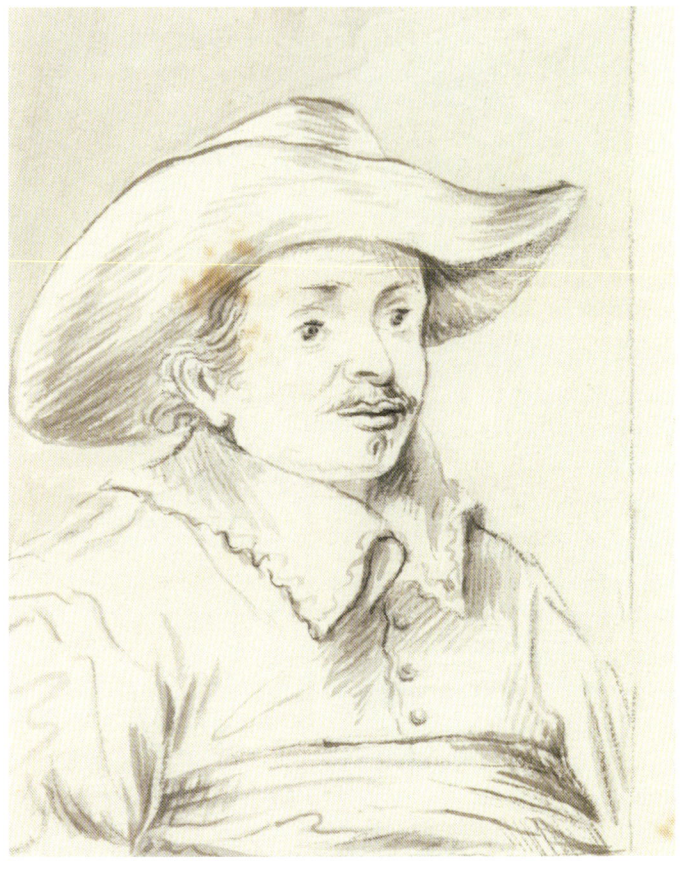 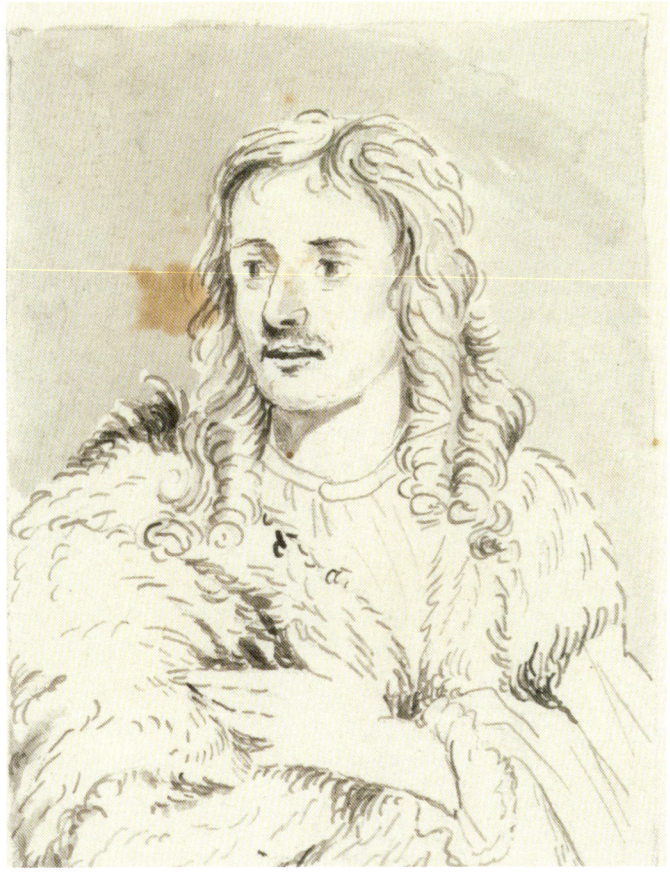

Figure 49 (Book 1)

Van Ostade
Graphite, ink, and wash on paper
3" × 4⅜"
1818

Inscribed "Van Ostade born at Lubeck 1610 died aged 75."

Figure 50 (Book 1)

Du Fresnoy
Graphite, ink, and wash on paper
3¼" × 4⅛"
1818

Inscribed "Du Fresnoy born at Paris 1611 died 1665."

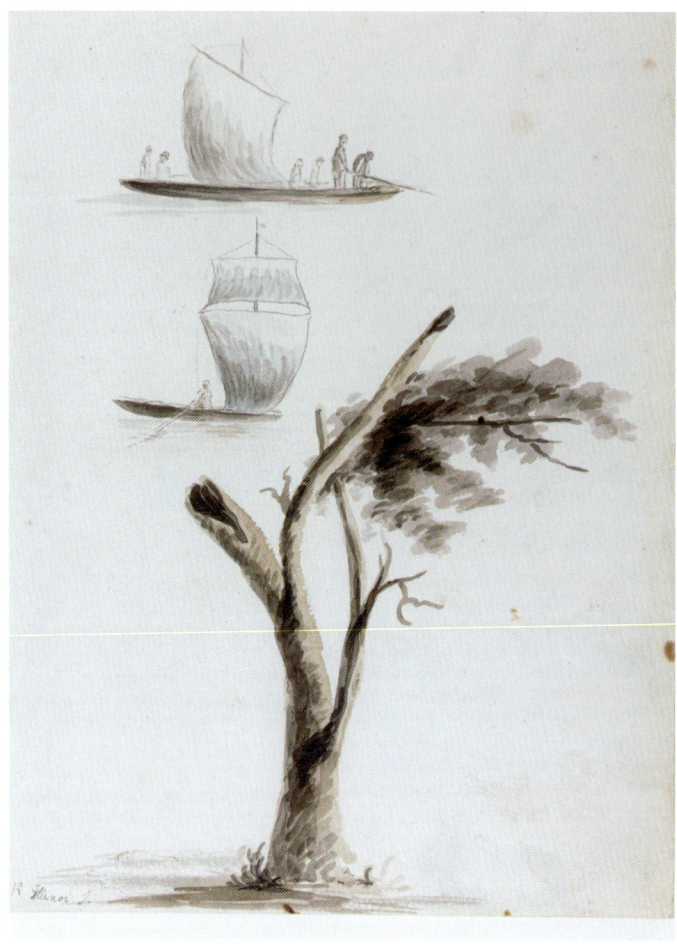
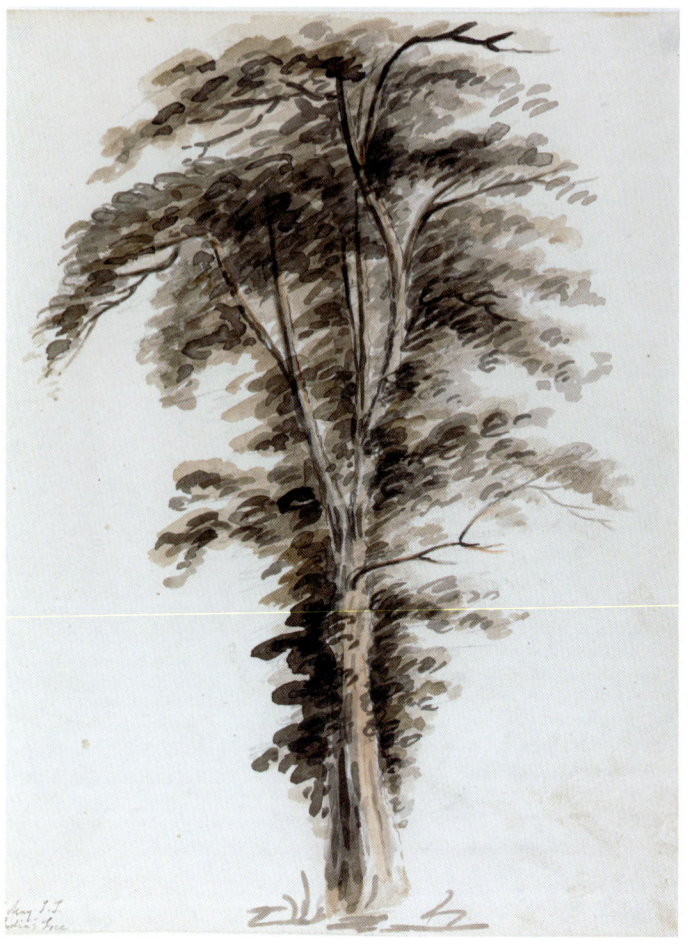

Figure 51 (Book 5)

Study of two keelboats and a tree
Ink and watercolor on paper
7¾" × 9¾"
May 19, 1818

Inscribed "19 May 1818 Illinoi. T."

Figure 52 (Book 5)

Lydia's Tree
Graphite and watercolor on paper
7⅞" × 9⅞"
May 19, 1818

Inscribed "19 May I. T. Lydia's Tree." In these studies of trees, I. T. stands for Illinois Territory.

84 | MORE THAN ORDINARY

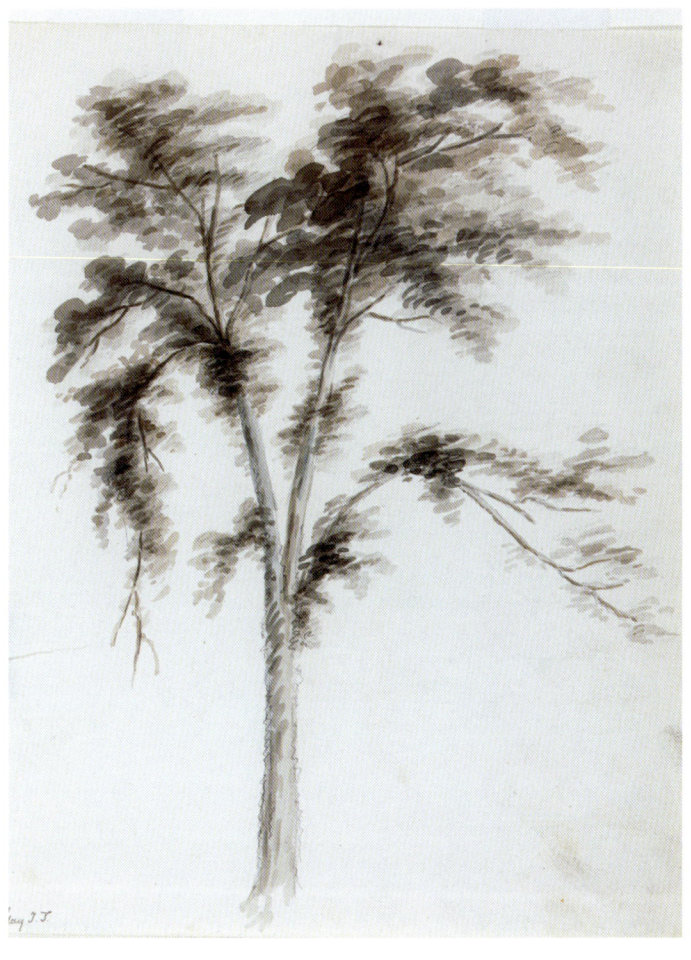

Figure 53 (Book 5)

Study of a tree
Graphite and watercolor on paper
7¾" × 9⅞"
May 19, 1818

Inscribed "19 May I. T."

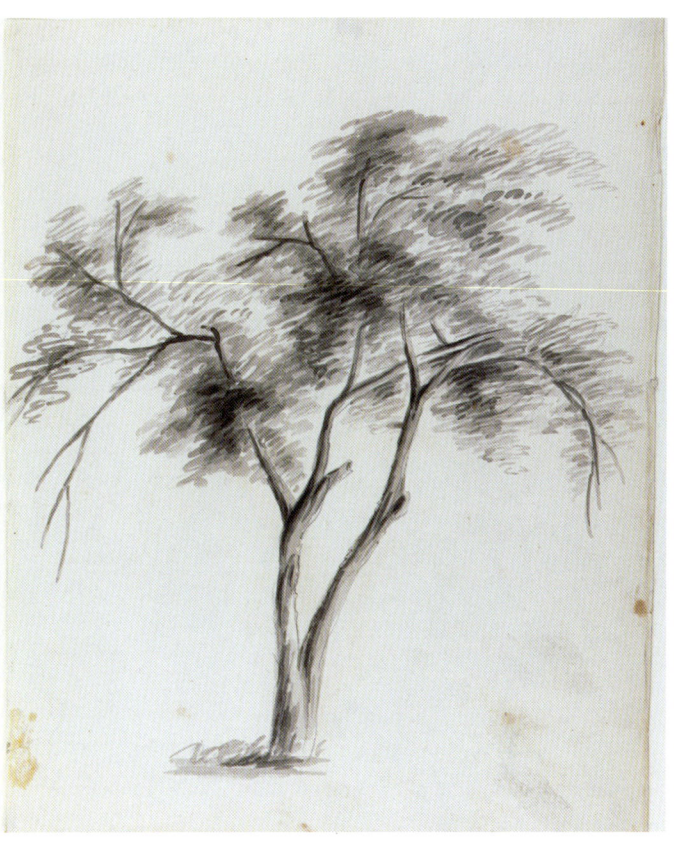

Figure 54 (Book 5)

Study of a tree
Graphite, ink, and wash on paper
7¾" × 9⅞"
1818

MORE THAN ORDINARY | 85

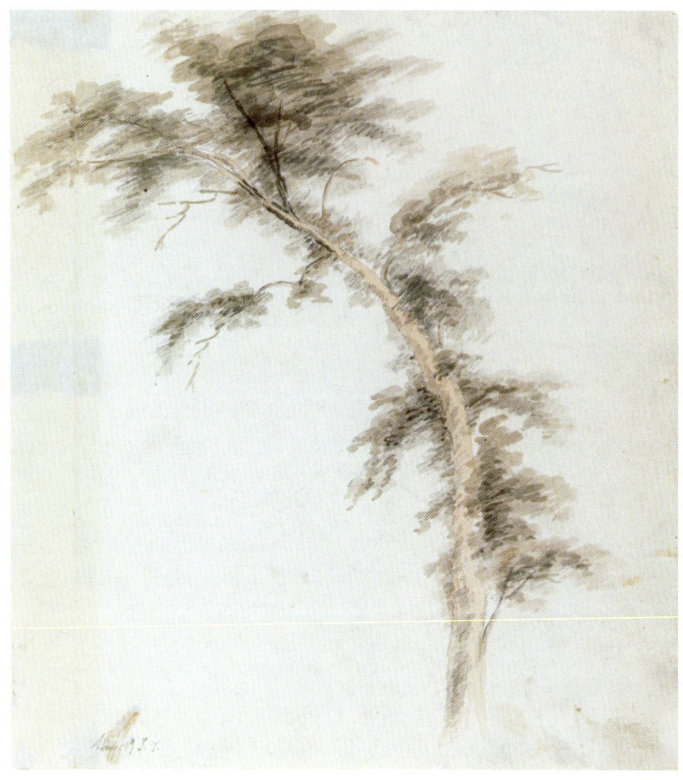
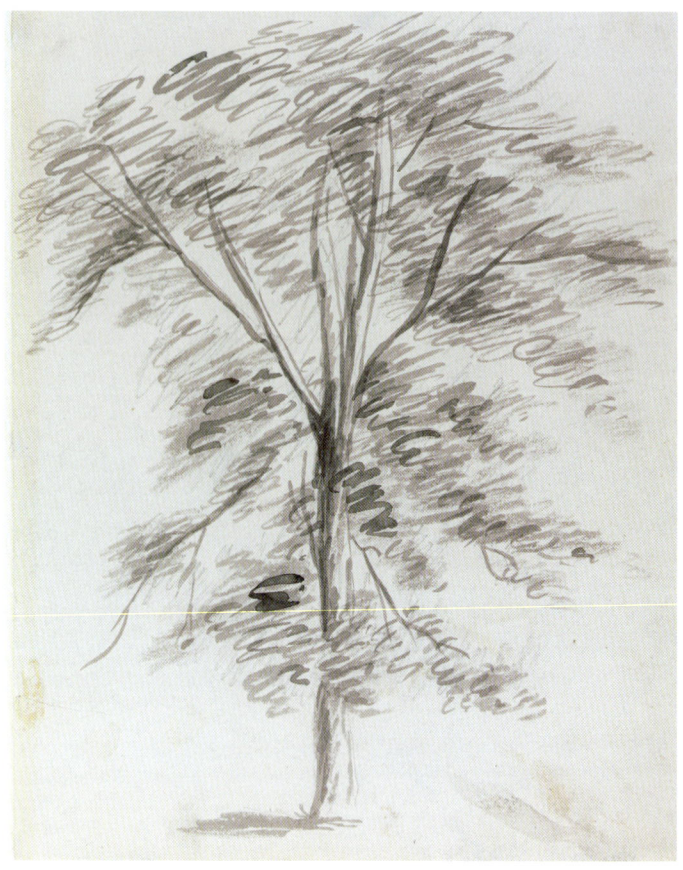

Figure 55 (Book 5)

Study of a tree
Ink and watercolor on paper
8¾" × 9⅞"
May 19, 1818

Inscribed "May 19 I. T."

Figure 56 (Book 5)

Study of a tree
Graphite and ink on paper
7¾" × 9¾"
1818

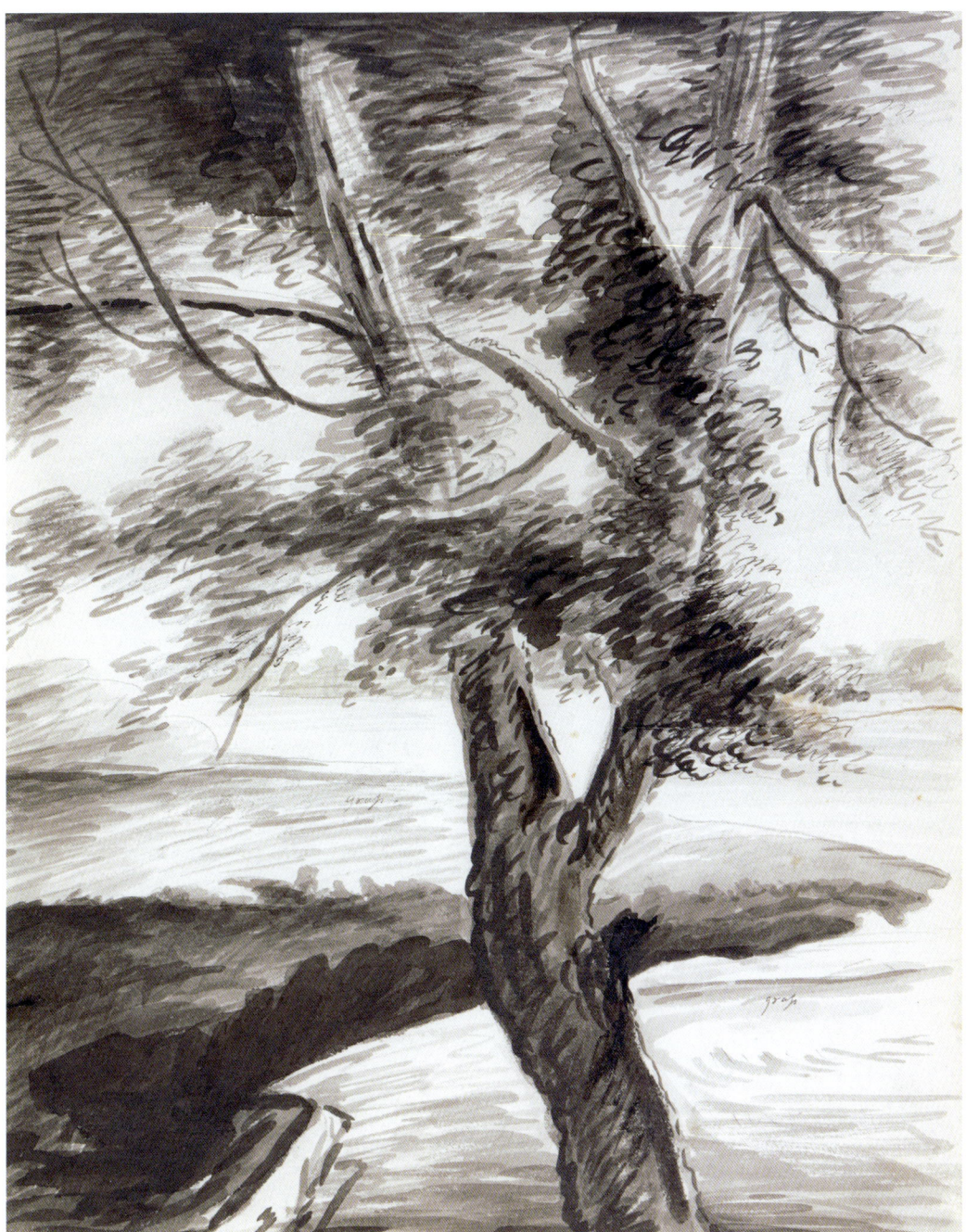

Figure 57 (Book 5)

Study of a landscape with tree
Ink and wash on paper
7¾" × 9⅞"
1818

In this study, Anna Maria has labeled two areas as "grass," denoting this piece as a preparatory sketch for a future painting.

Figure 58 (Book 5)

Town along a river (possibly St. Charles)
Watercolor on paper
10" × 8"
1818

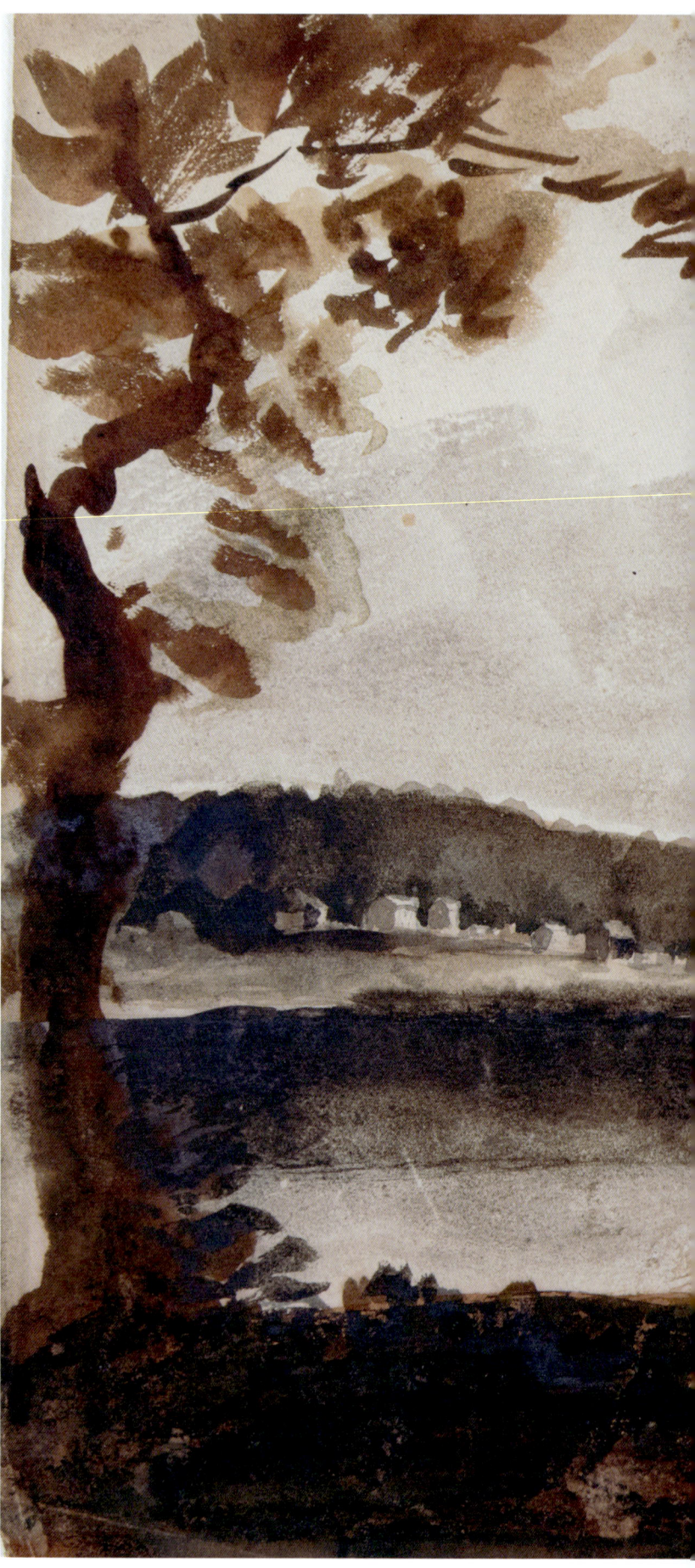

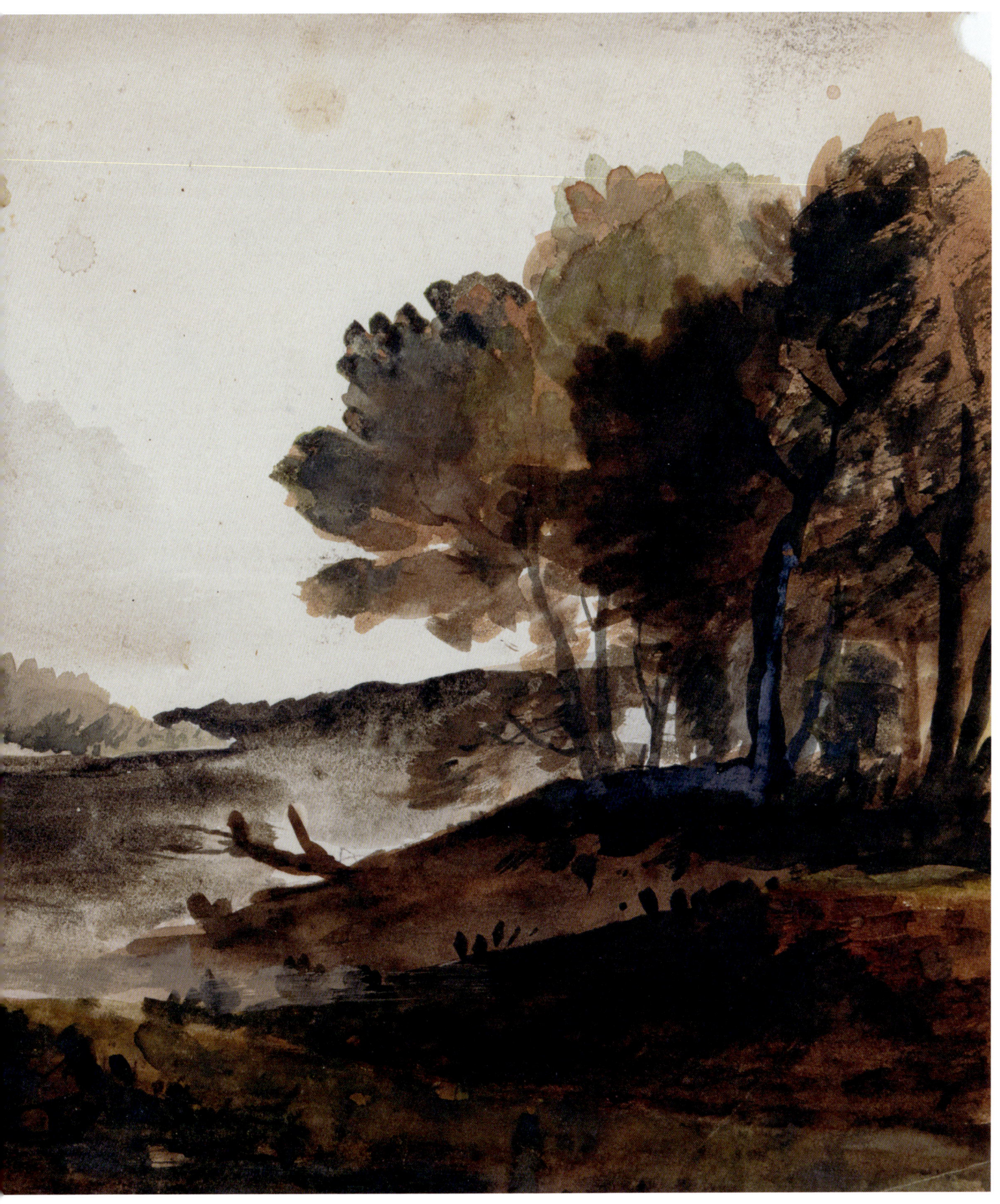

Figure 59 (Book 5)

A view from St. Charles
Watercolor on paper
8½" × 6¾"
1818

Inscribed "A view from St. Charles 9 [month illegible] 1818 M T."

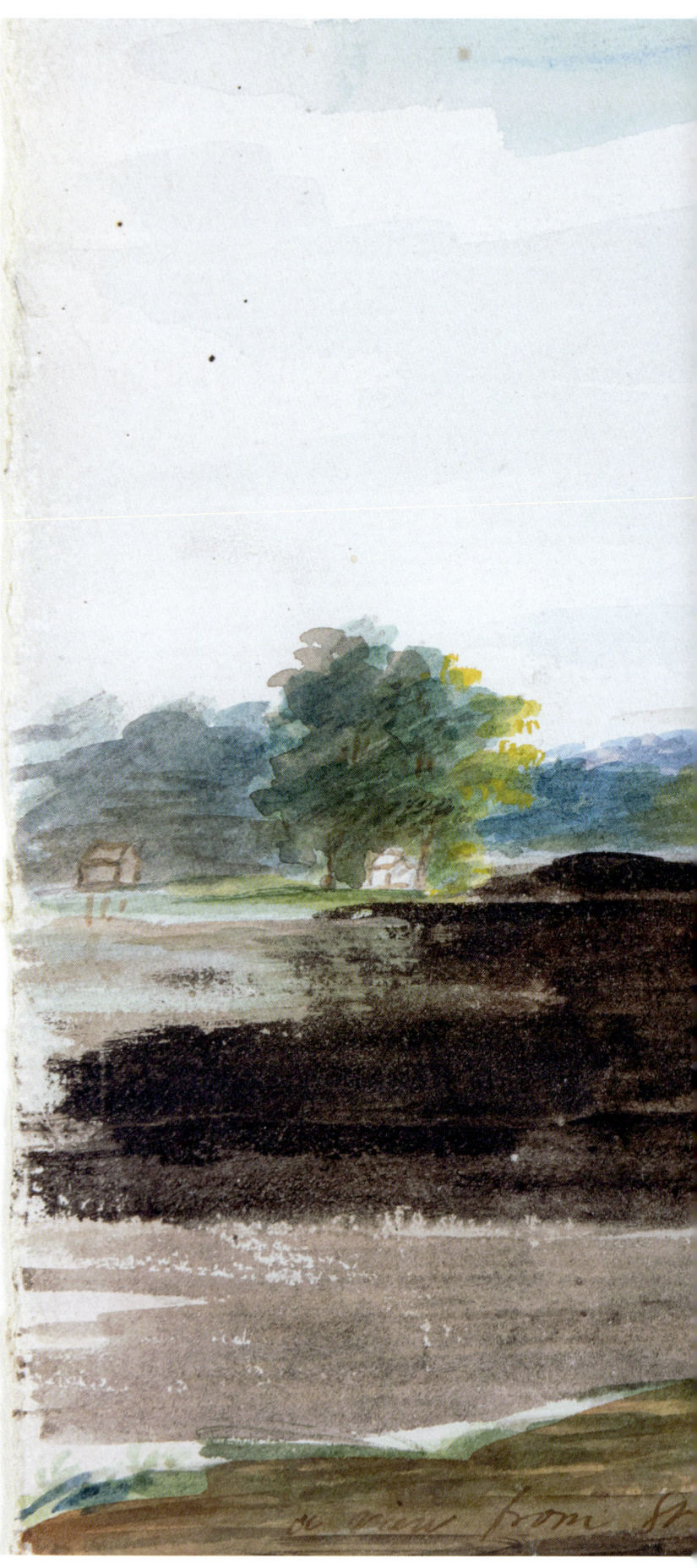

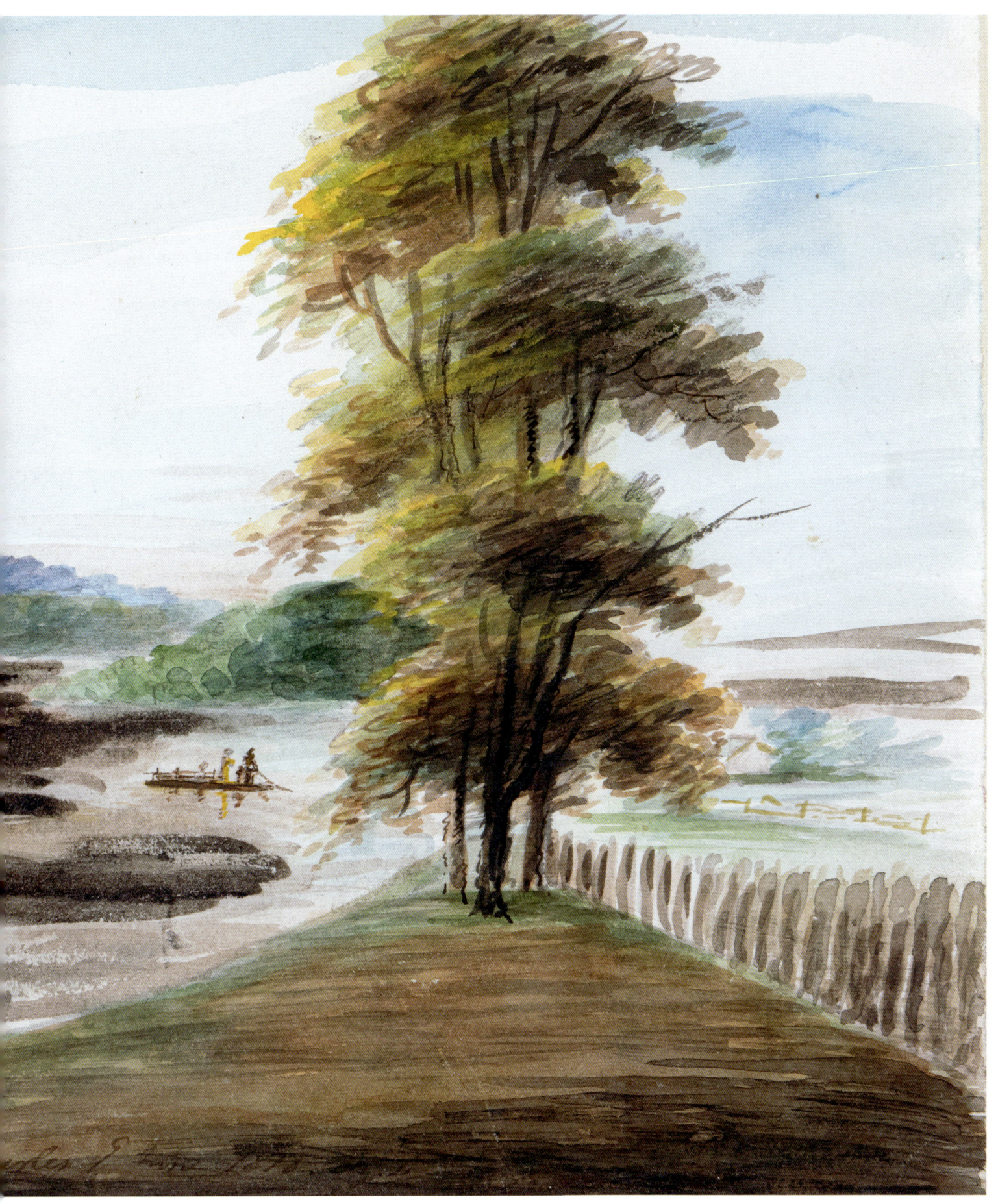

Figure 60 (Book 5)

Study of *A view from St. Charles on the Missouri*
Graphite on paper
8½" × 6¾"
1818

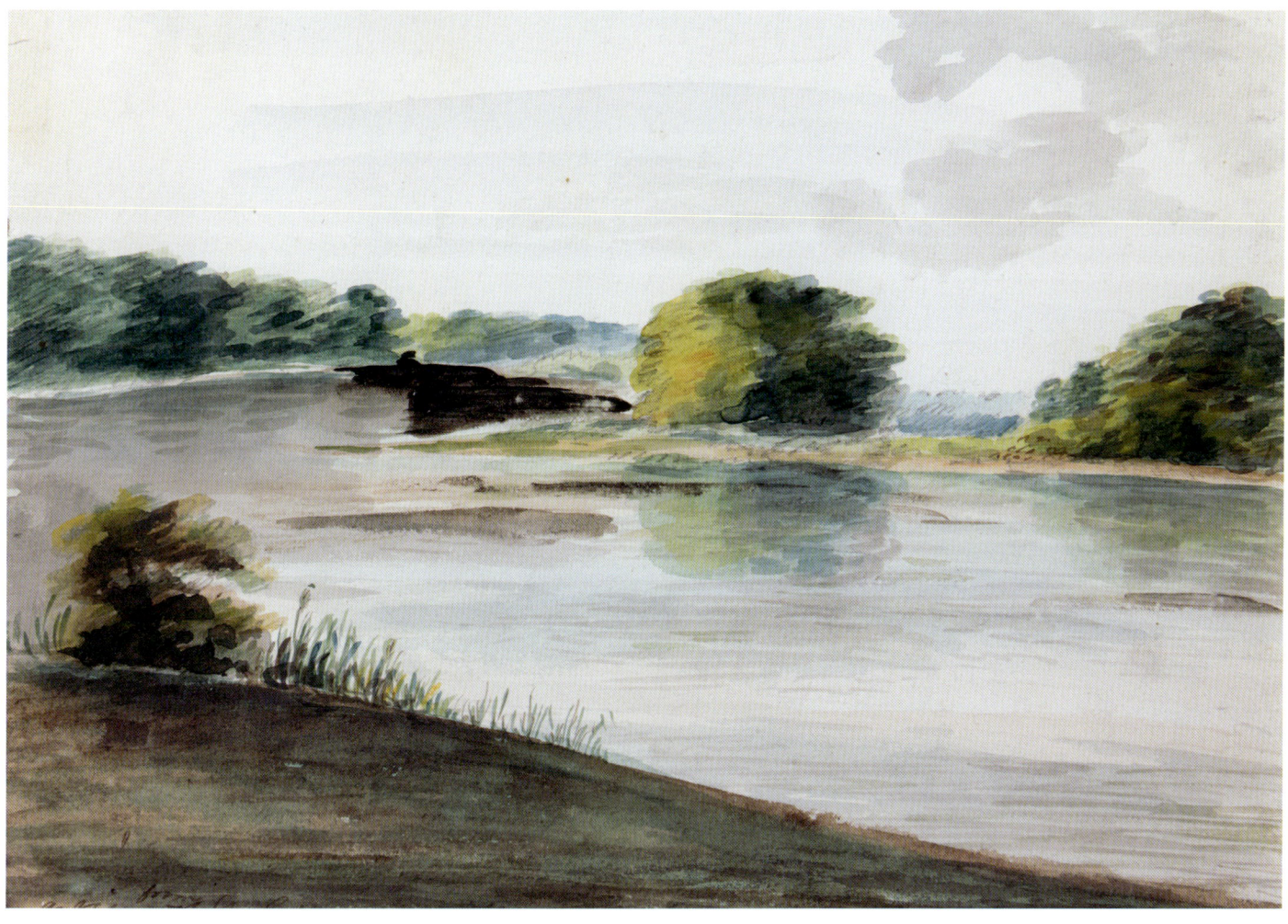

Figure 61 (Book 5)

A view from St. Charles on the Missouri
Watercolor on paper
8½" × 6¾"
1818

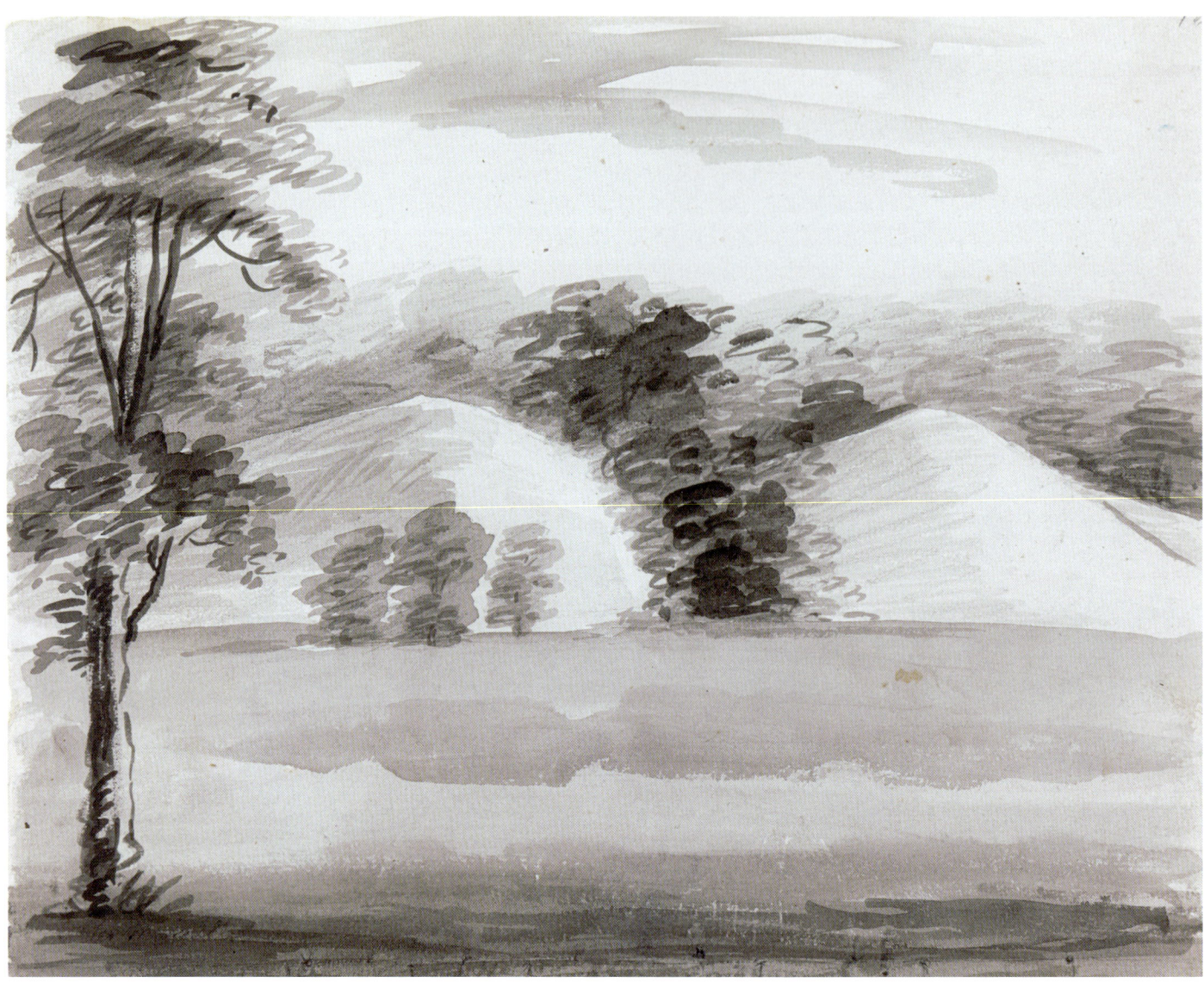

Figure 62 (Book 5)

Les Mamelles (presumed)
Ink and wash on paper
8½" × 6¾"
June 8, 1818

Located near St. Charles, Les Mamelles were two large mounds rising some 150 feet above the surrounding countryside. The view from the top made these mounds popular local landmarks for many decades.

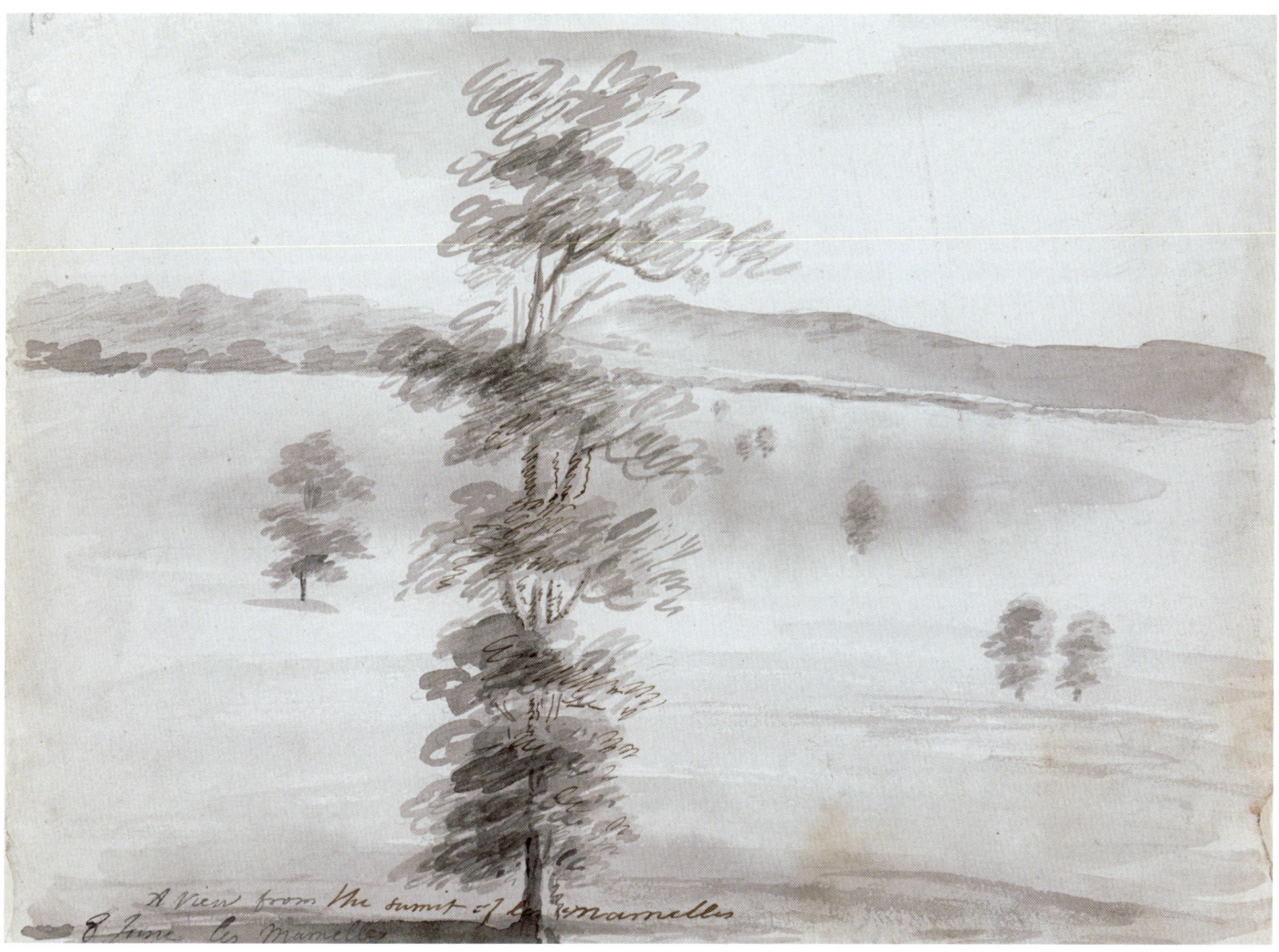

Figure 63 (Book 5)

Les Mamelles
Ink and wash on paper
8½" × 6⅝"
June 8, 1818

Inscribed "A View from the sumit of les Mamelles 8 June les Mamelles."

MORE THAN ORDINARY | 95

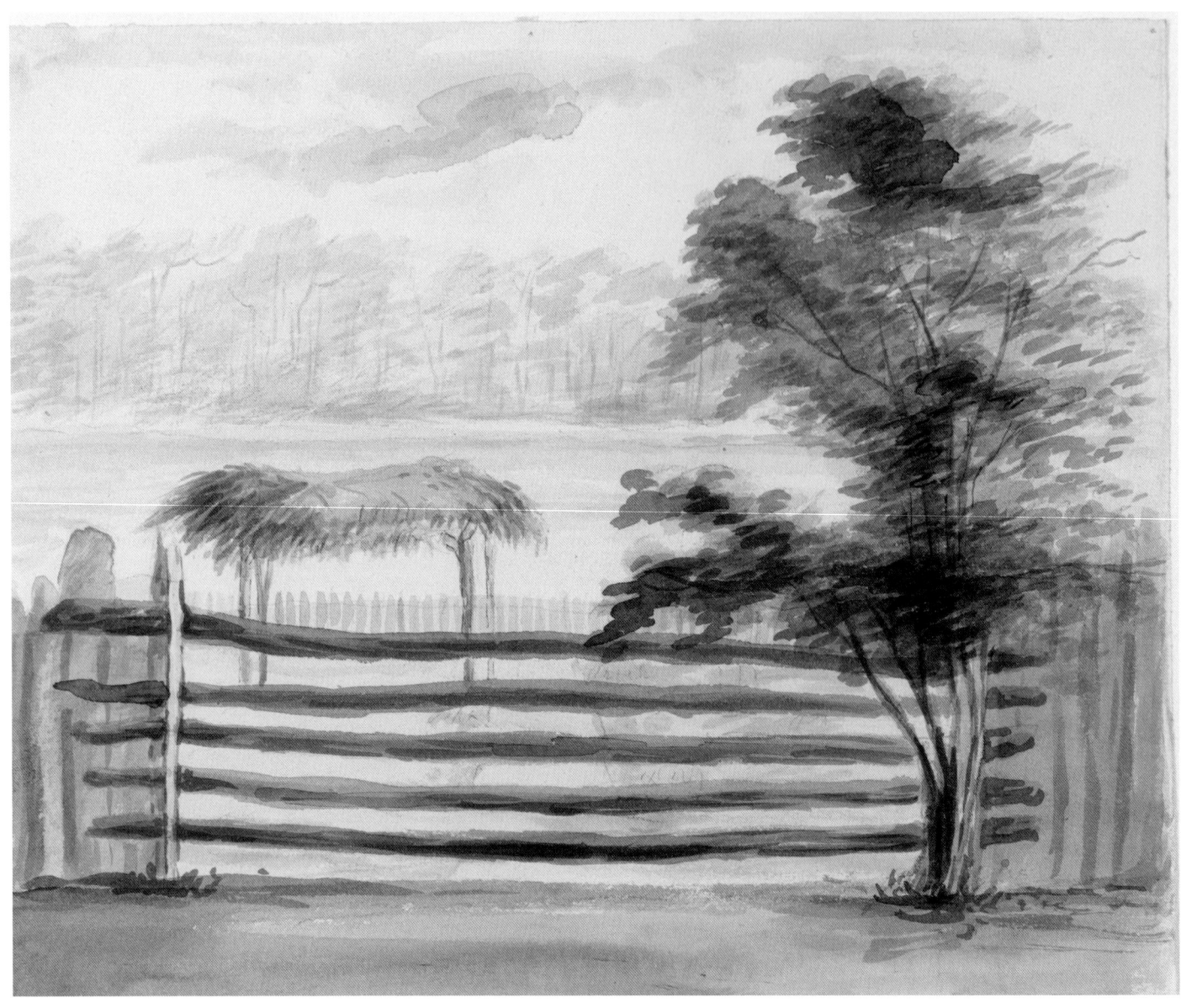

Figure 64 (Book 5)

View of the river
Ink and wash on paper
7⅞" × 7¼"
1818

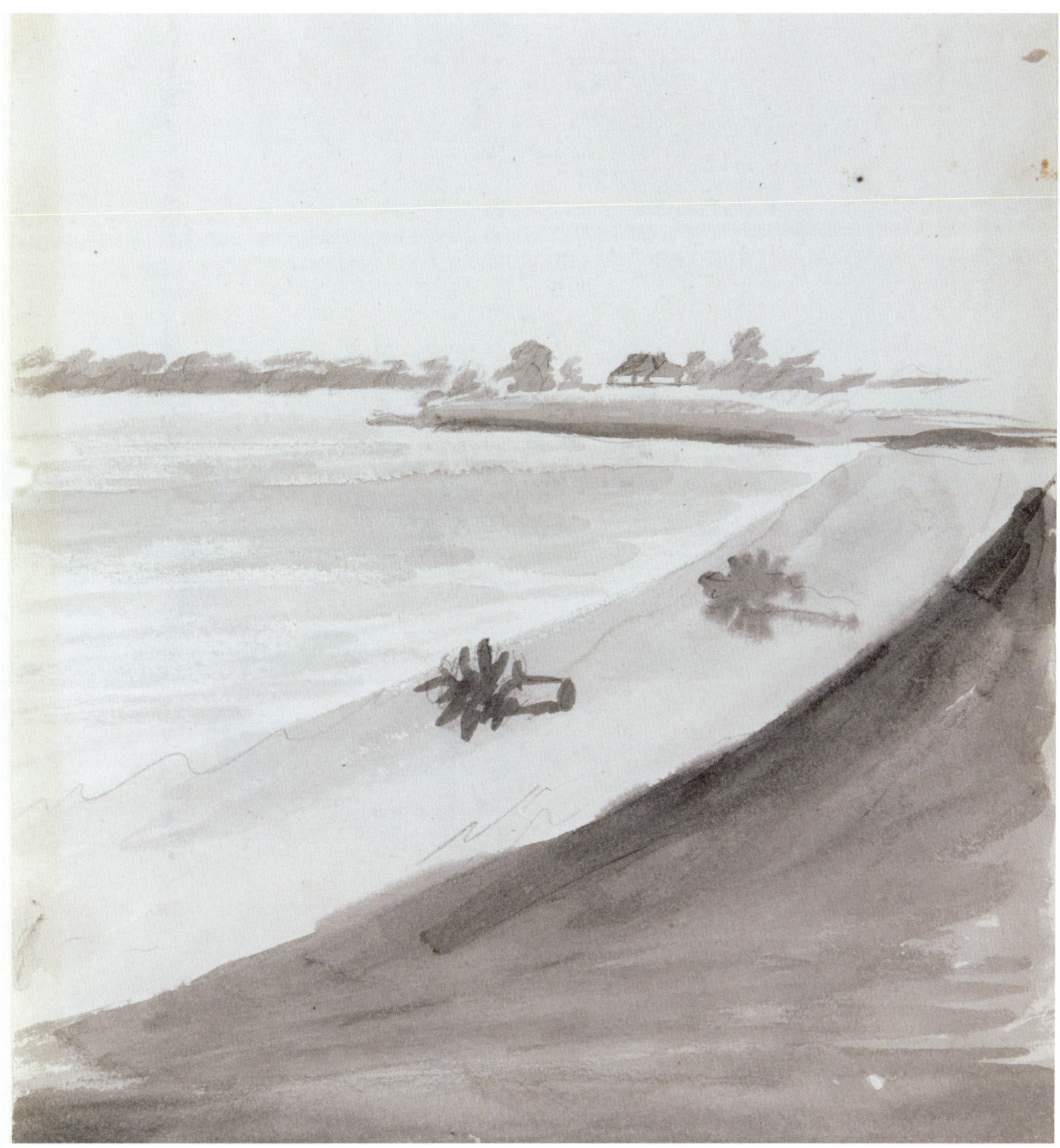

Figure 65 (Book 5)

View of the river
Wash on paper
7¾" × 9⅞"
1818

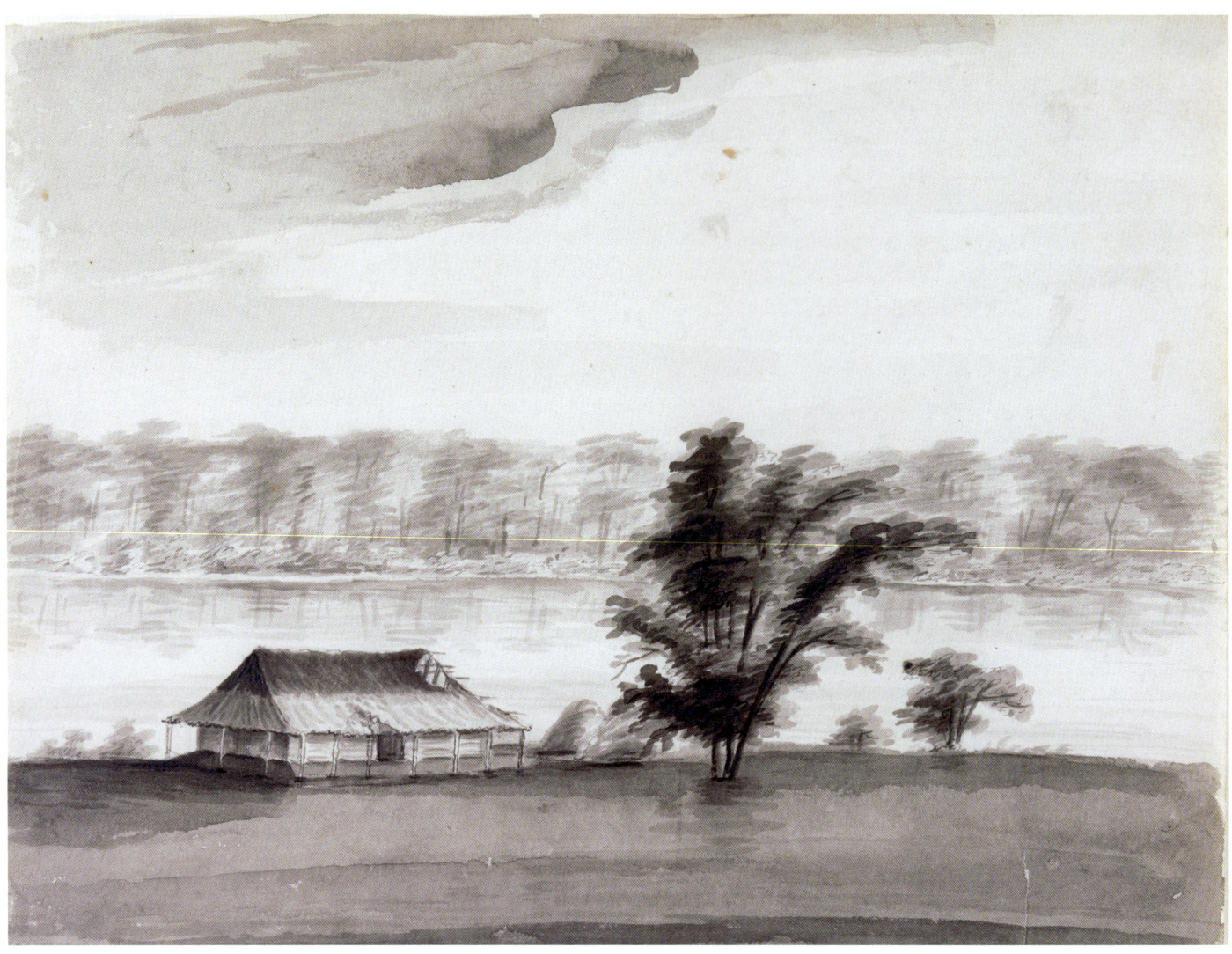

Figure 66 (Book 5)

Abandoned Creole home along the river
Ink and wash on paper
9¾" × 7¾"
1818

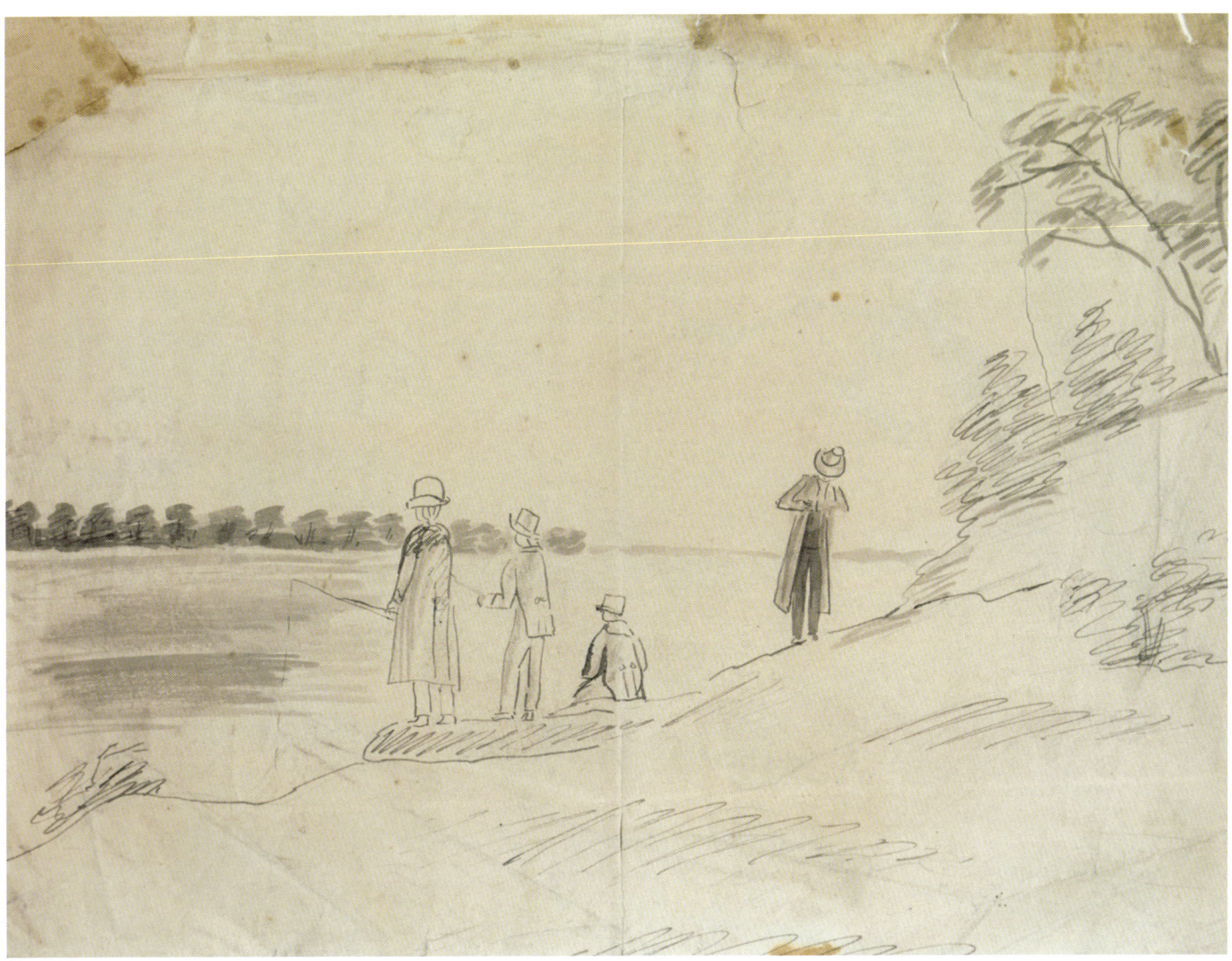

Figure 67 (Book 5)

Study of four men fishing
Graphite and wash on paper
15⅜" × 12¼"
1818

MORE THAN ORDINARY | 99

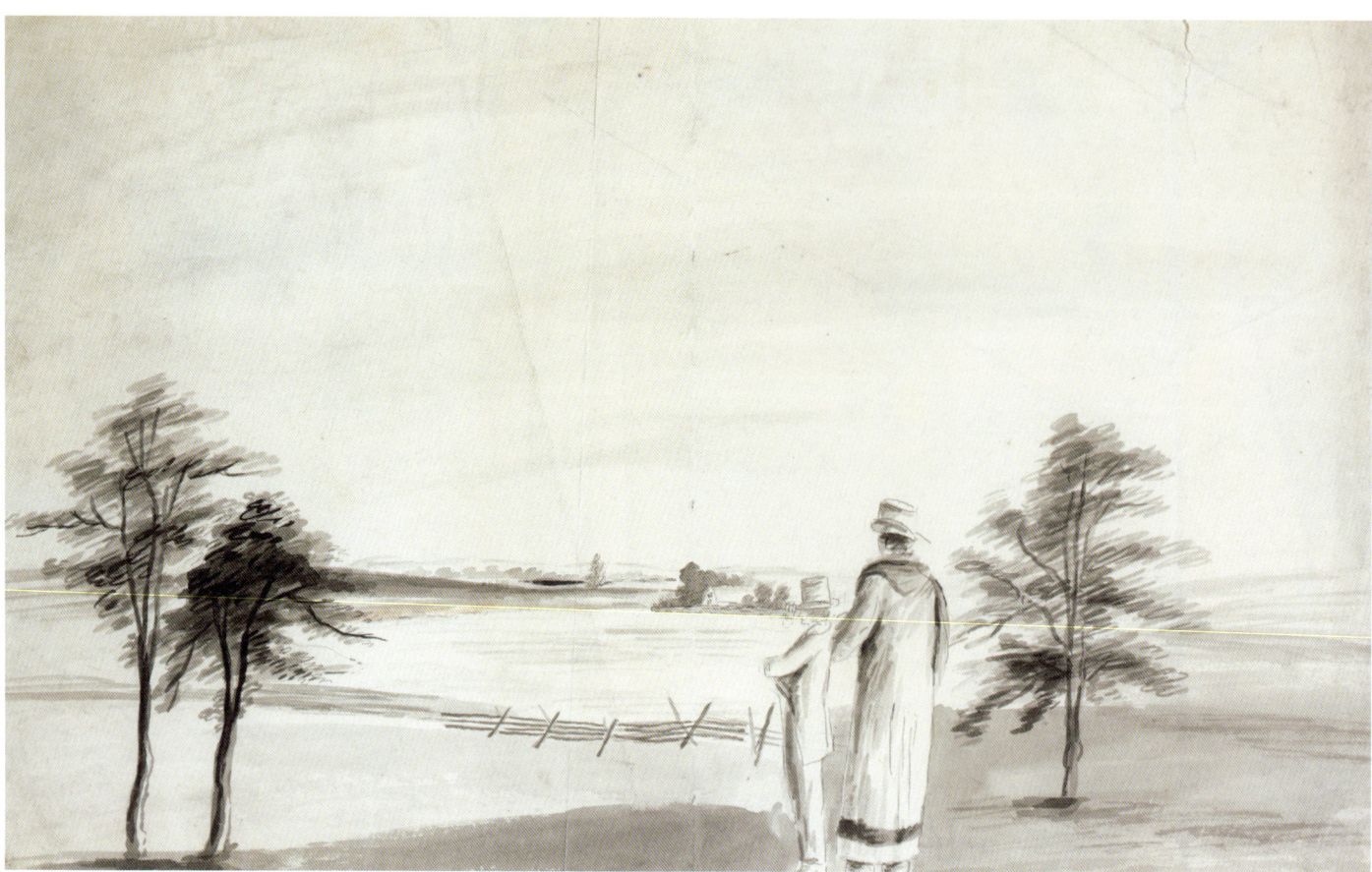

Figure 68 (Book 5)

Landscape with two men
Ink and wash on paper
15½" × 9⅞"
1818

100 | MORE THAN ORDINARY

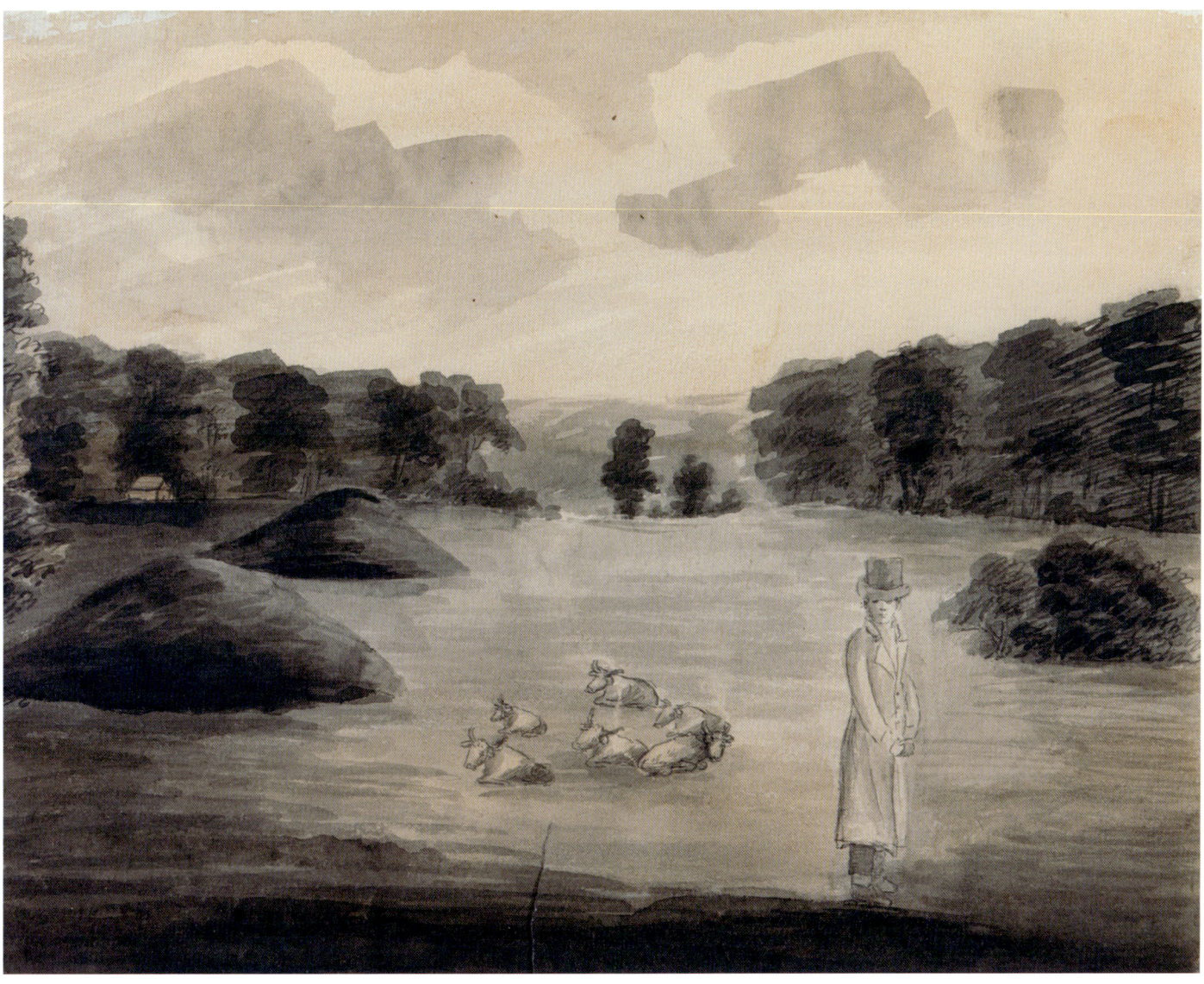

Figure 69 (Book 5)

Landscape with mounds, man, and cattle
Ink and watercolor on paper
9¾" × 7¾"
1818

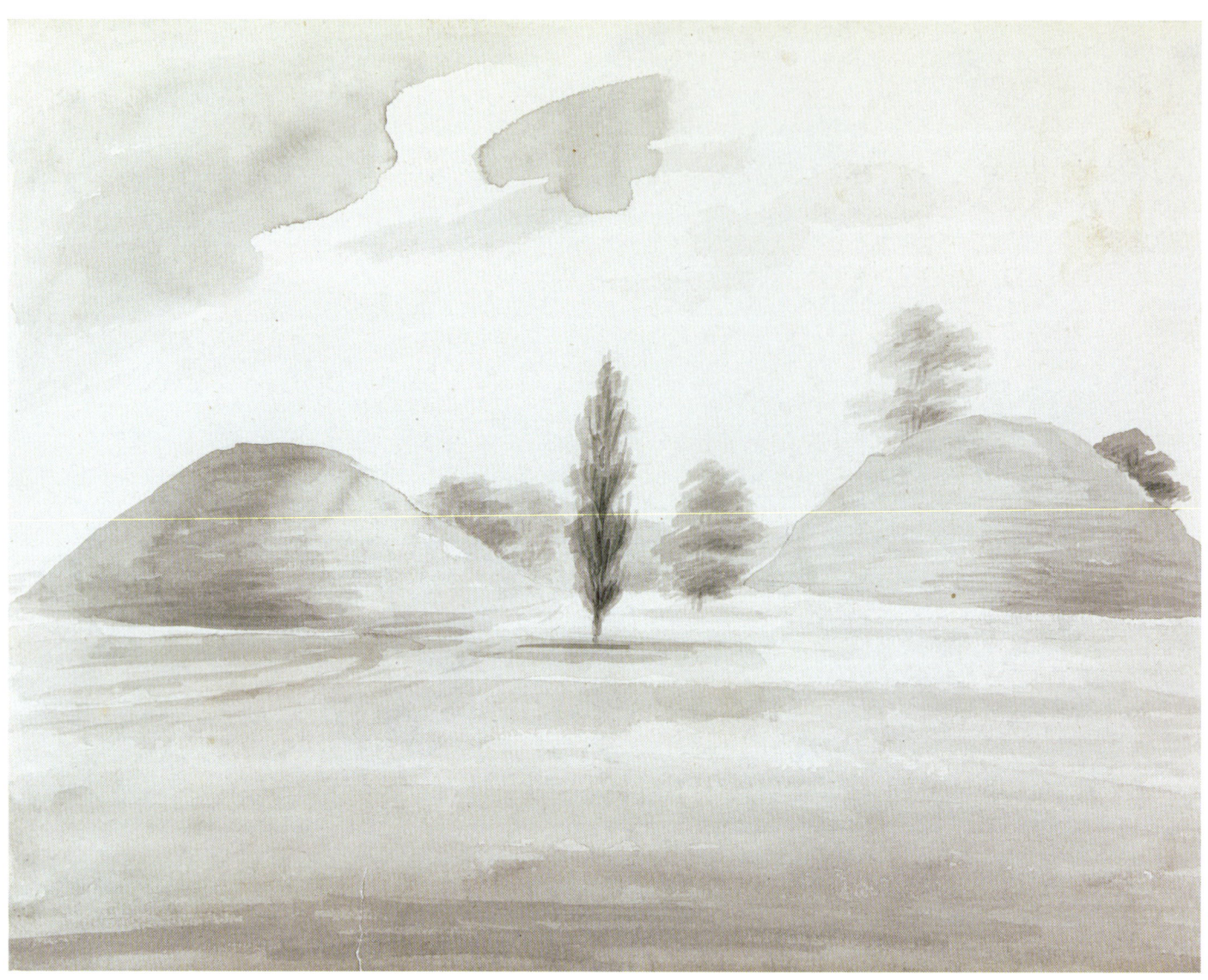

Figure 70 (Book 5)

Landscape with mounds
Wash on paper
9⅞" × 7¾"
1818

Figure 71 (Book 5)

Man and woman with cart
Graphite, ink, and wash on paper
7¾" × 9⅞"
1818

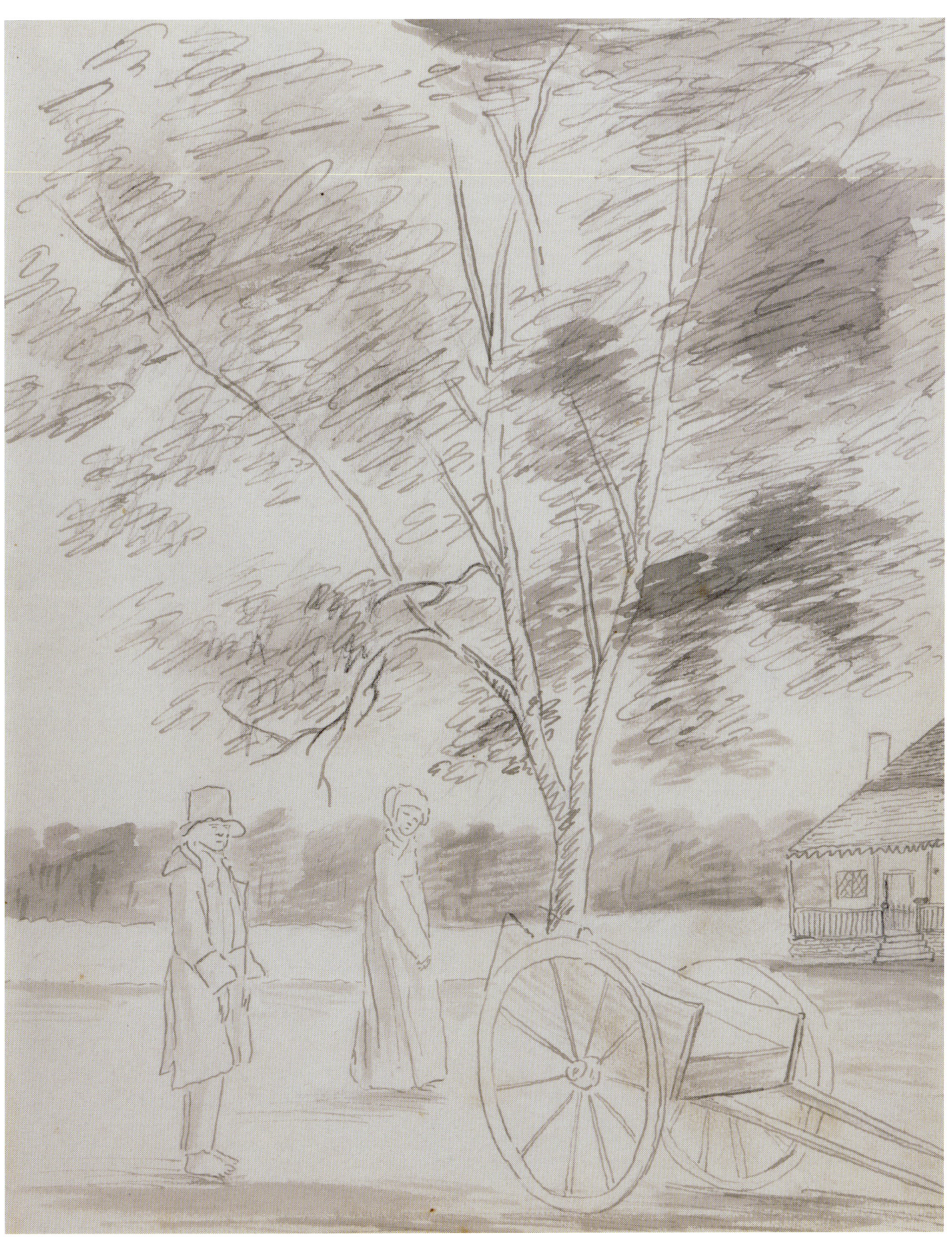

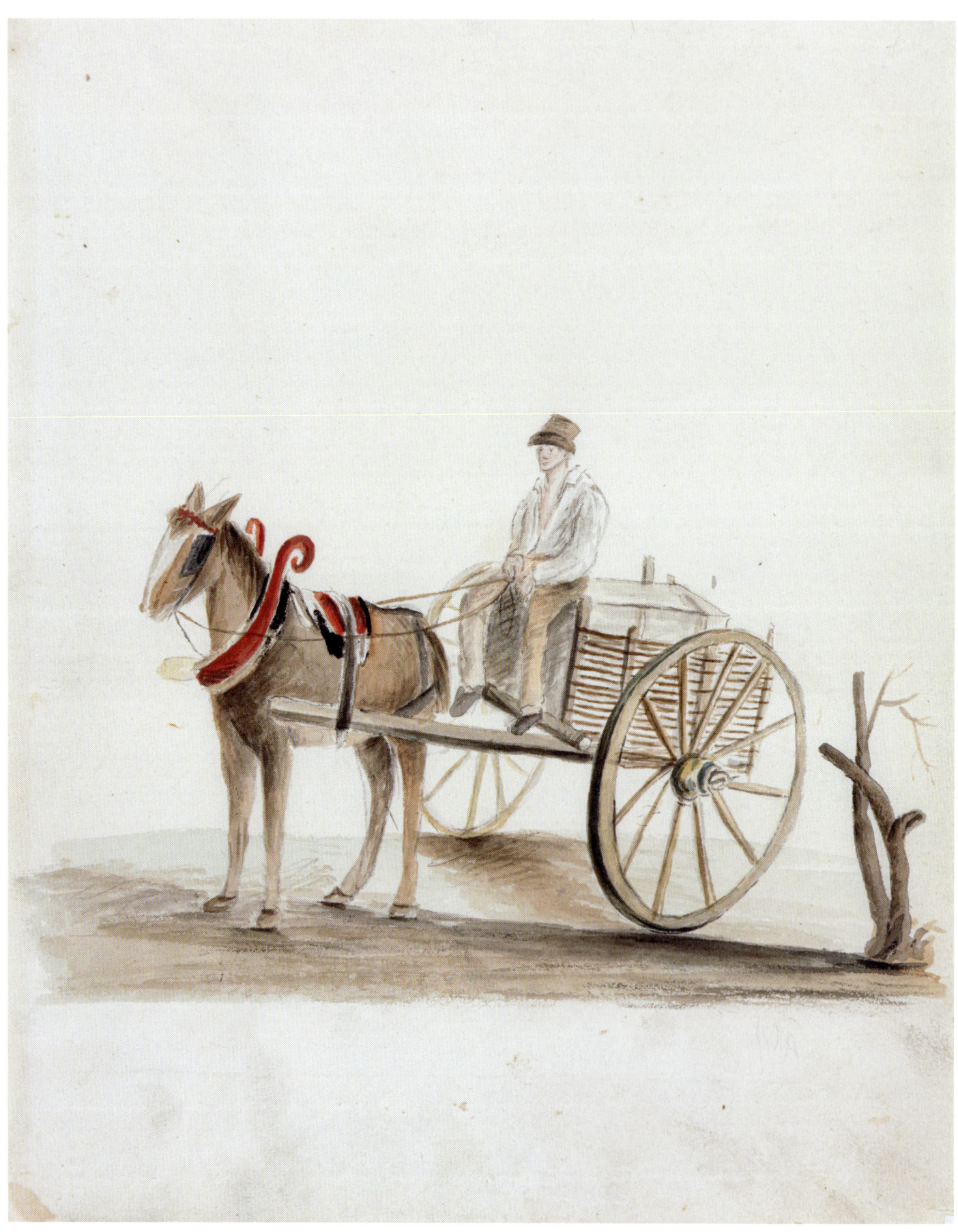

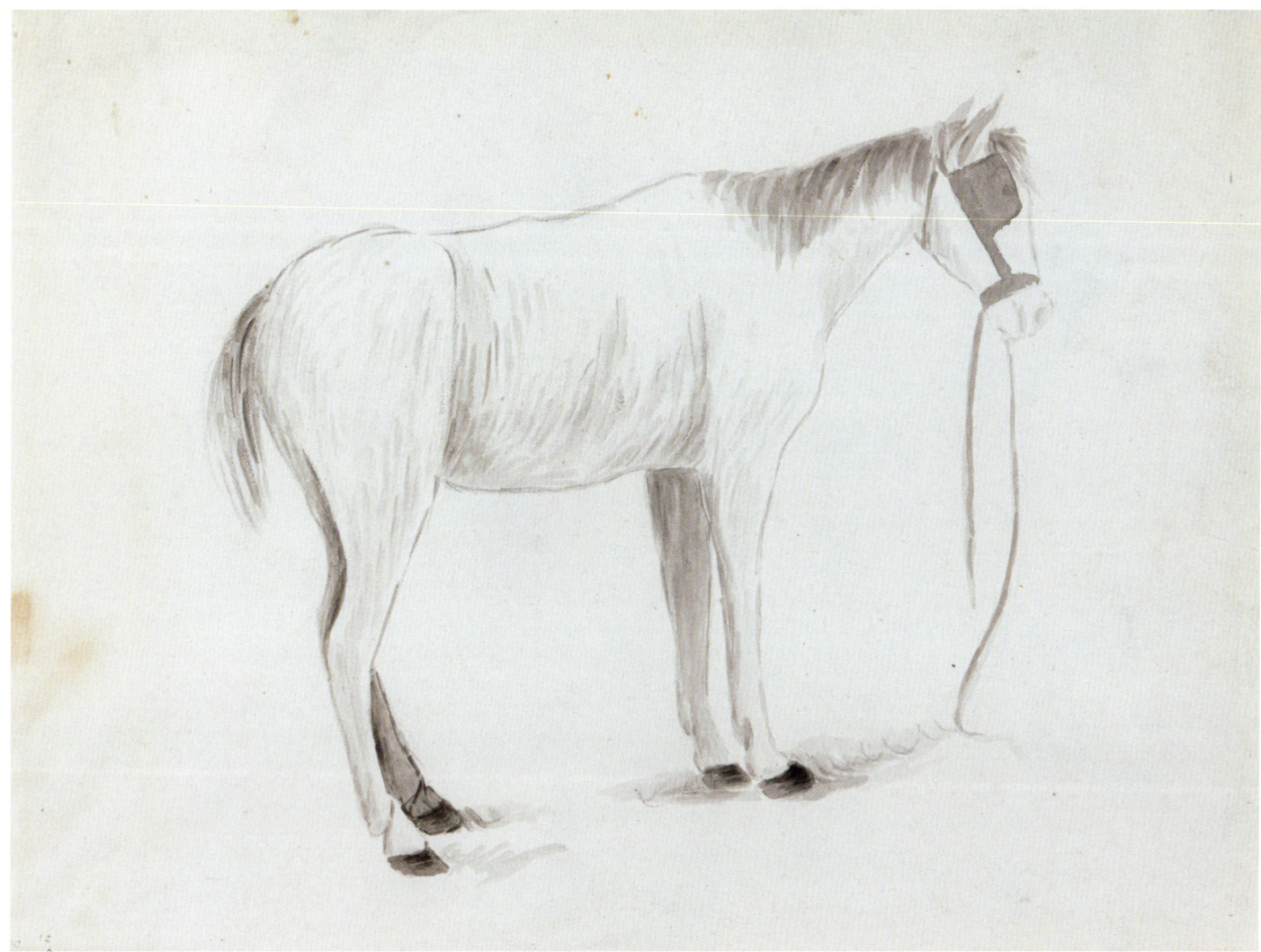

Figure 73 (Book 5)

Horse with blinders
Ink on paper
10" × 8"
1818

Figure 72 (Book 5)

Man driving a horse and cart
Graphite, ink, and watercolor on paper
7¾" × 9⅞"
1818

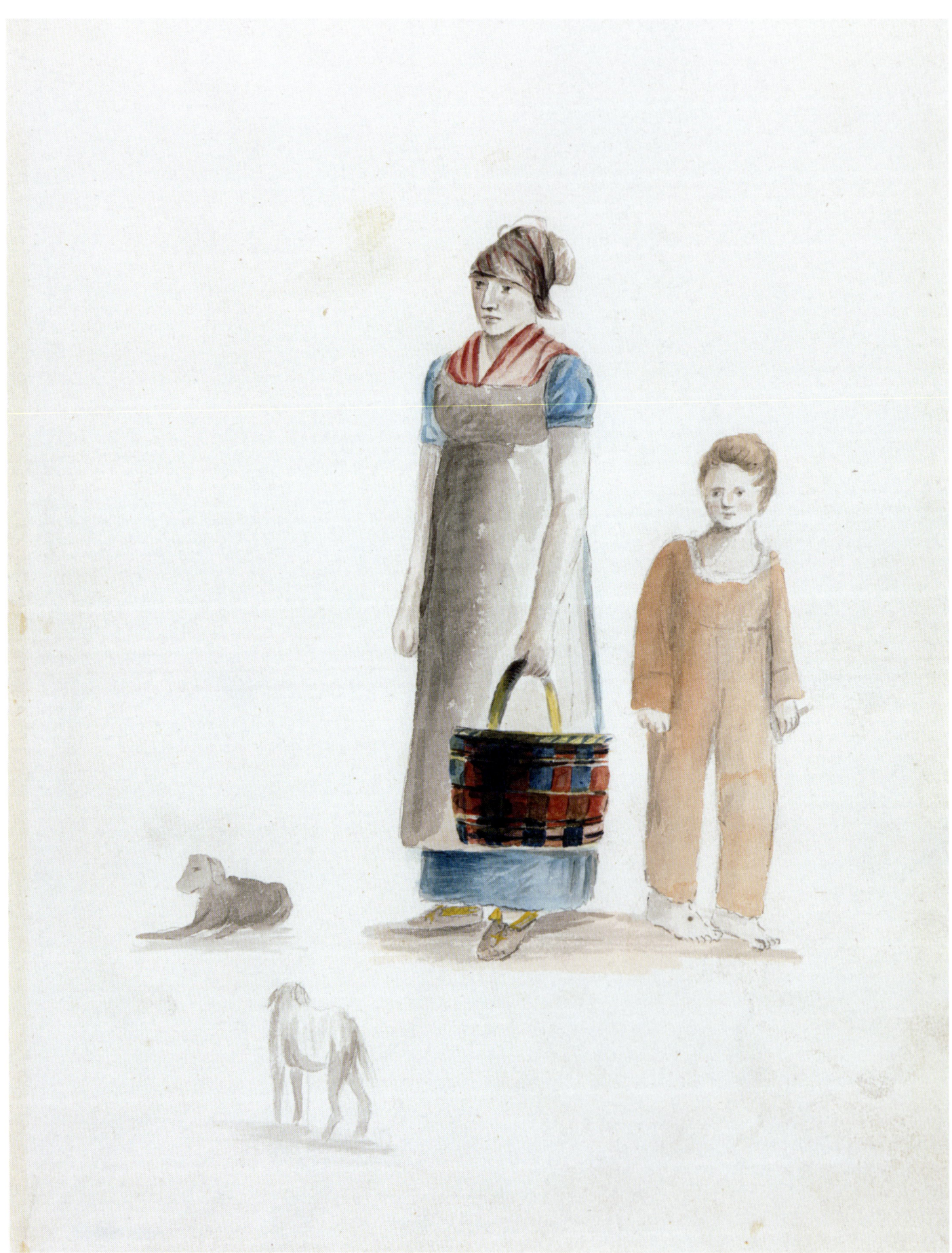

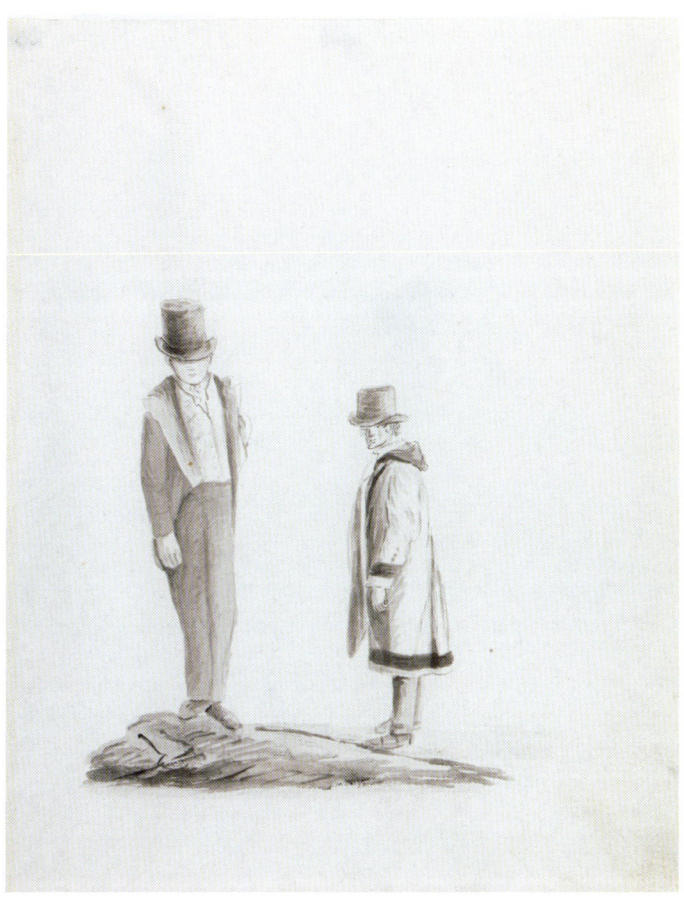

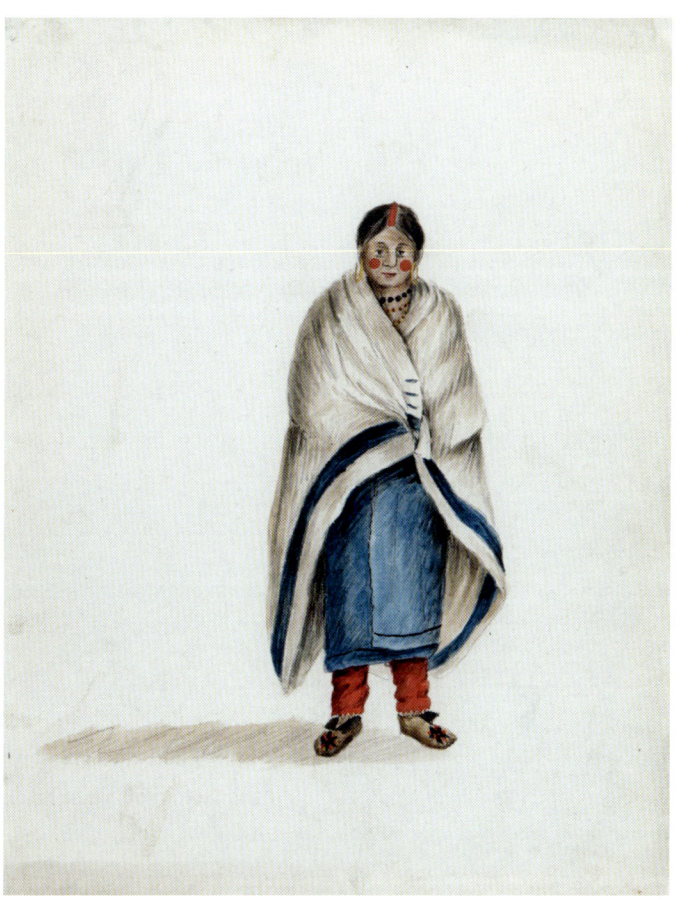

Figure 75 (Book 5)

Two men
Ink and wash on paper
7¾" × 9¾"
1818

Figure 76 (Book 5)

Native American woman wearing a point blanket
Watercolor on paper
7½" × 9⅞"
1818

The detail, color, and expressiveness of this piece make it one of the standout portraits from Anna Maria's time in St. Louis. The unidentified woman is a rare depiction of a Native American in the American West in the 1810s. Her red leggings, blue coat, blue-striped point blanket, gold hoop earrings, and three beaded necklaces are all accessories that were commonly used as trade and gift items between French and American traders and the Osage. The paint visible on her cheeks and hair part is likely vermilion, another trade item. Intensely pigmented Chinese vermilion quickly became a sought-after alternative to mineral and plant dyes that were used in symbolic Osage face-painting traditions.

Figure 74 (Book 5)

Woman with a child
Graphite, ink, and watercolor on paper
7¾" × 9⅞"
1818

Although the identities of this working woman and her child are unknown, Anna Maria chose to imbue the woman's clothing and accessories with color, pattern, and texture. Her head scarf is checked or striped in red and gray, about her neck is a crimson fichu, her day dress is a vivid blue, and on her feet are moccasins trimmed in yellow. She carries a red, blue, and yellow woven work basket. It's a delightful peek at the daily attire of a busy early 19th century woman.

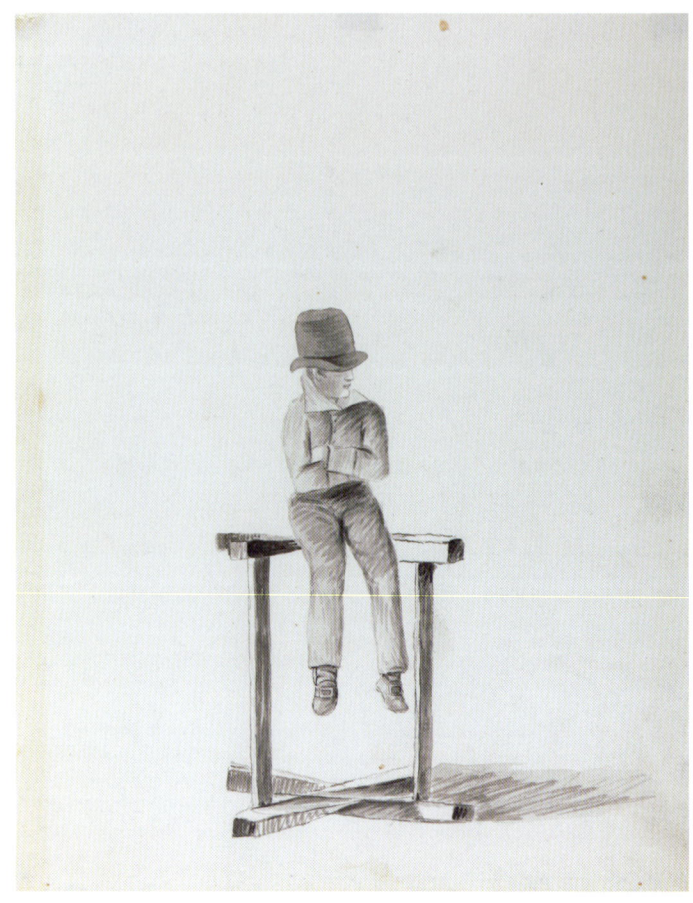

Figure 77 (Book 5)

Boy sitting on a sawbuck
Ink on paper
7¾" × 9⅞"
1818

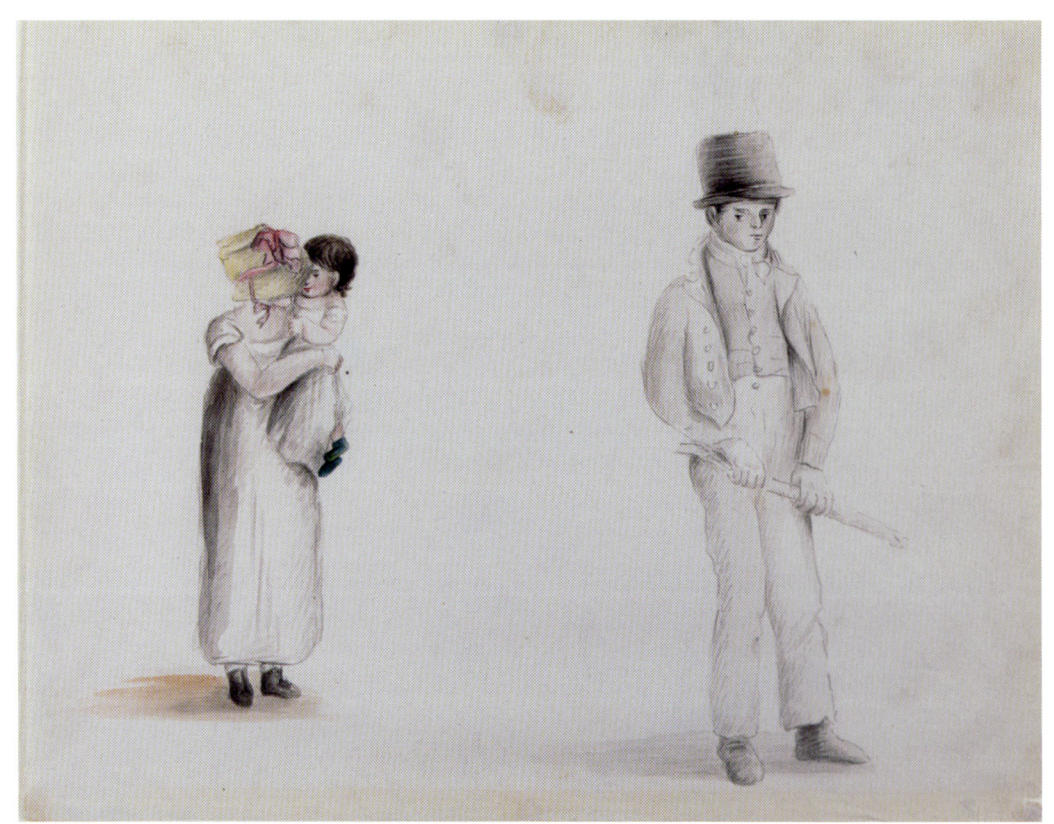

Figure 78 (Book 5)

Woman, child, and boy with a cane
Graphite and watercolor on paper
9⅞" × 7¾"
1818

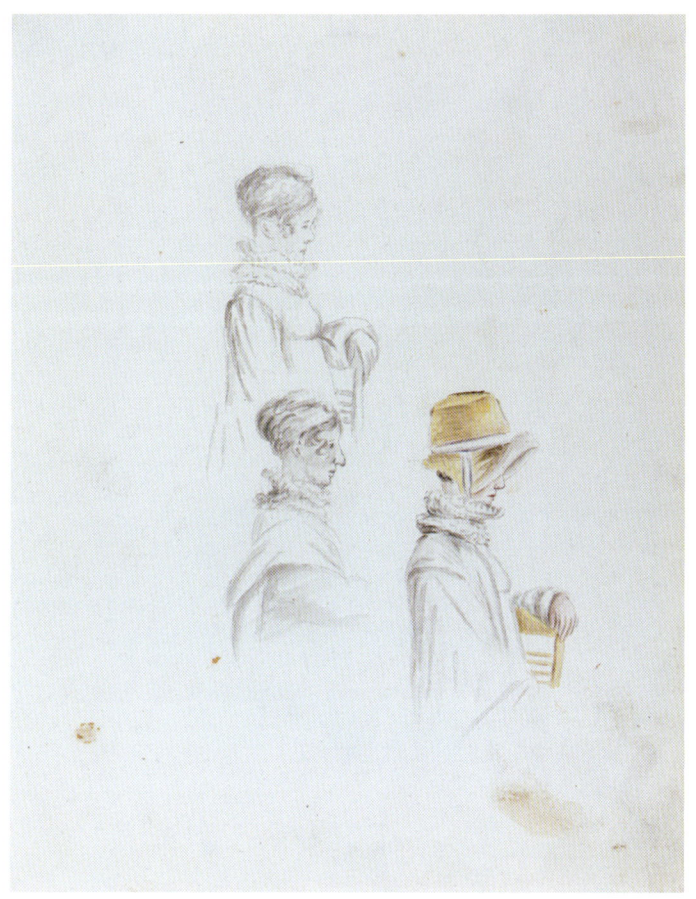

Figure 79 (Book 5)

Studies of three women in profile
Graphite, ink, and watercolor on paper
7¾" × 9⅞"
1818

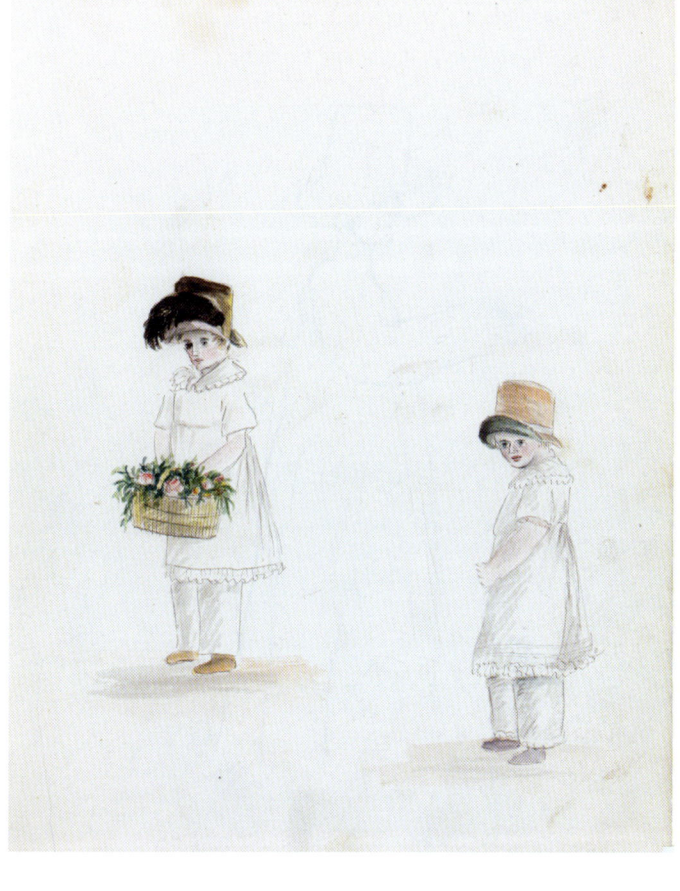

Figure 80 (Book 5)

Studies of two children in hats
Ink and watercolor on paper
7¾" × 9⅞"
1818

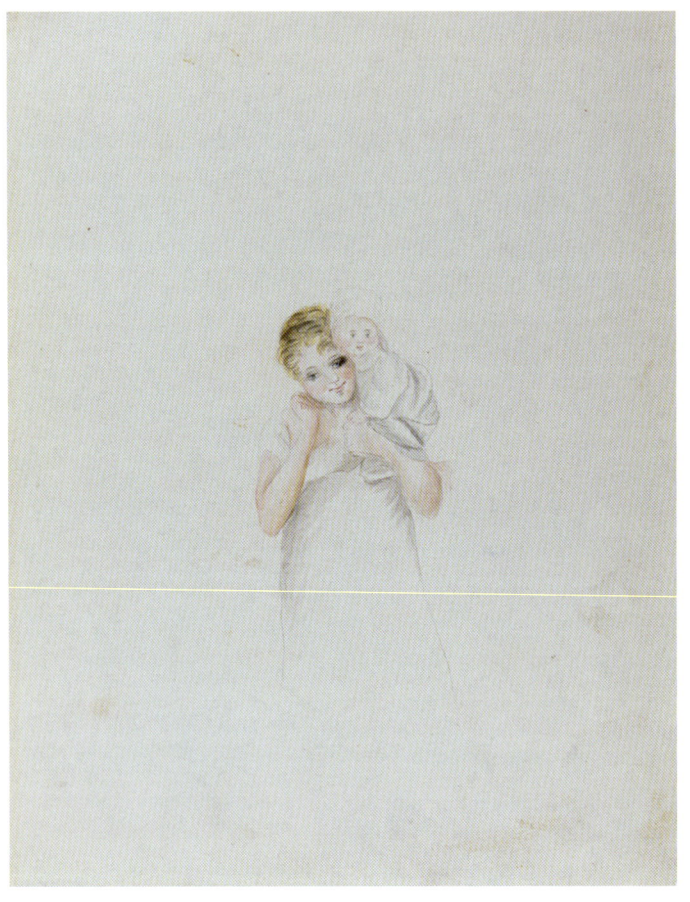

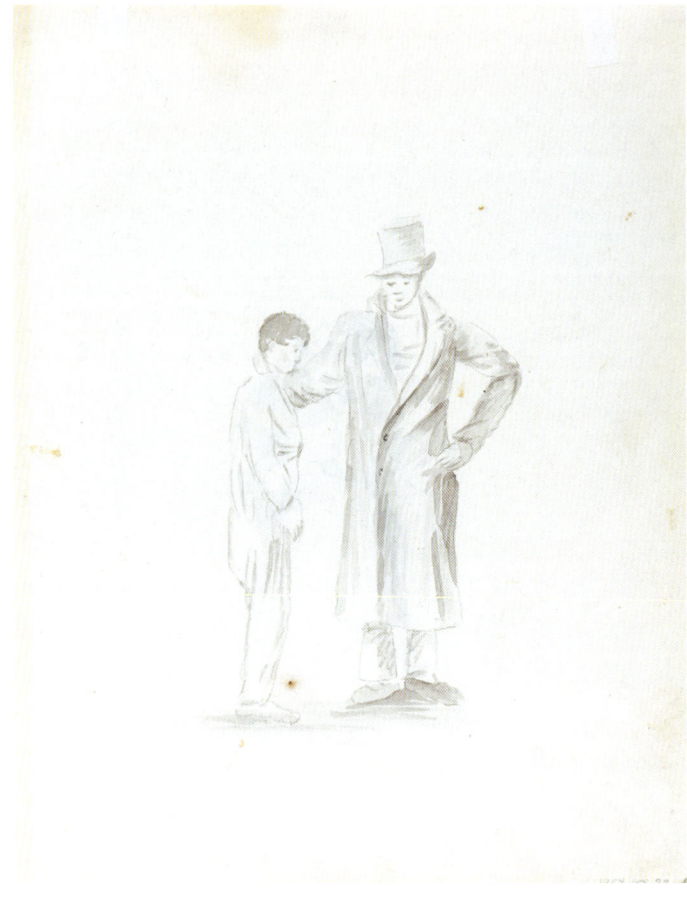

Figure 81 (Book 5)

Study of a woman holding a baby
Ink and watercolor on paper
7¾" × 9⅞"
1818

Figure 83 (Book 5)

Study of a man and boy
Graphite and ink on paper
7¾" × 9¾"
1818

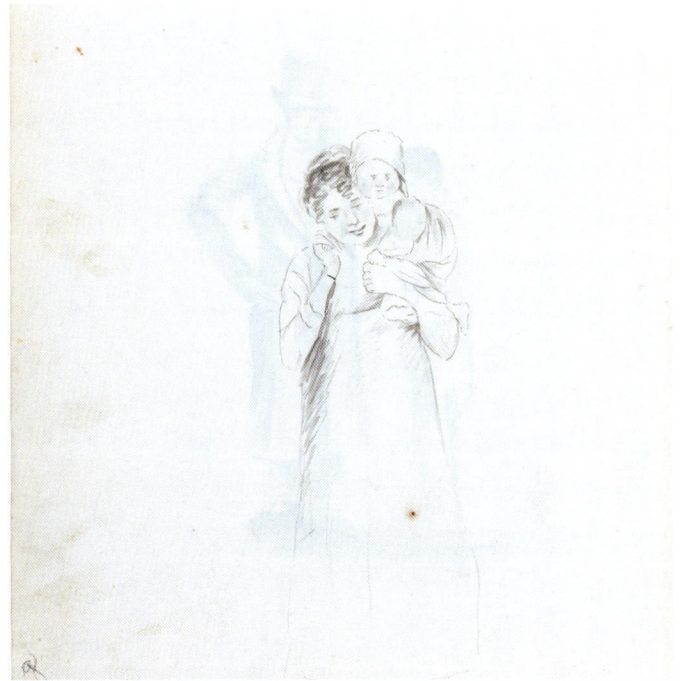

Figure 82 (Book 5)

Study of a woman holding a baby
Ink on paper
7¾" × 9¾"
1818

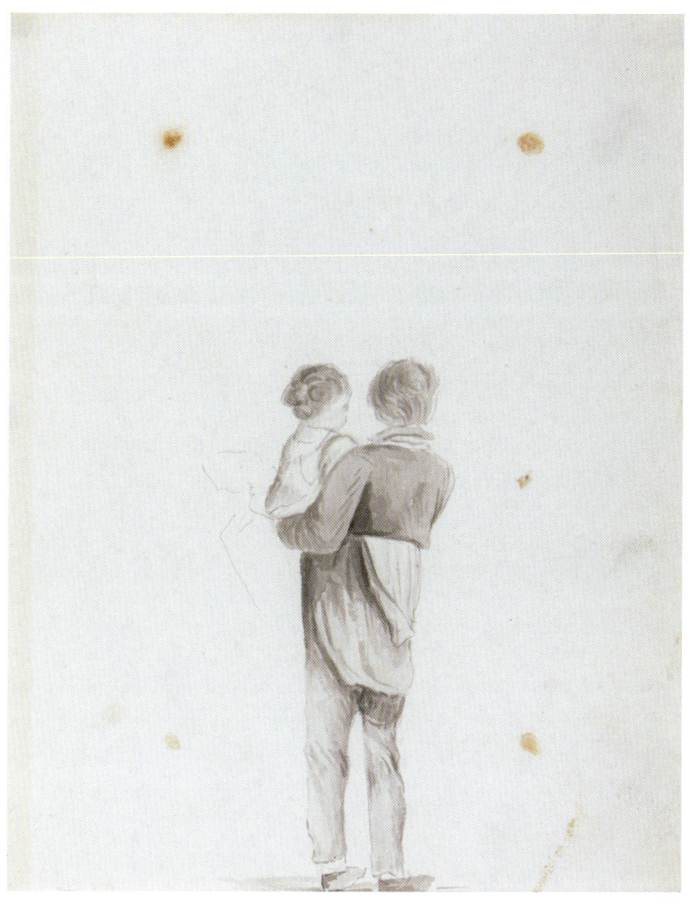

Figure 84 (Book 5)

Study of a boy holding a baby
Graphite and ink on paper
7⅞" × 9⅞"
1818

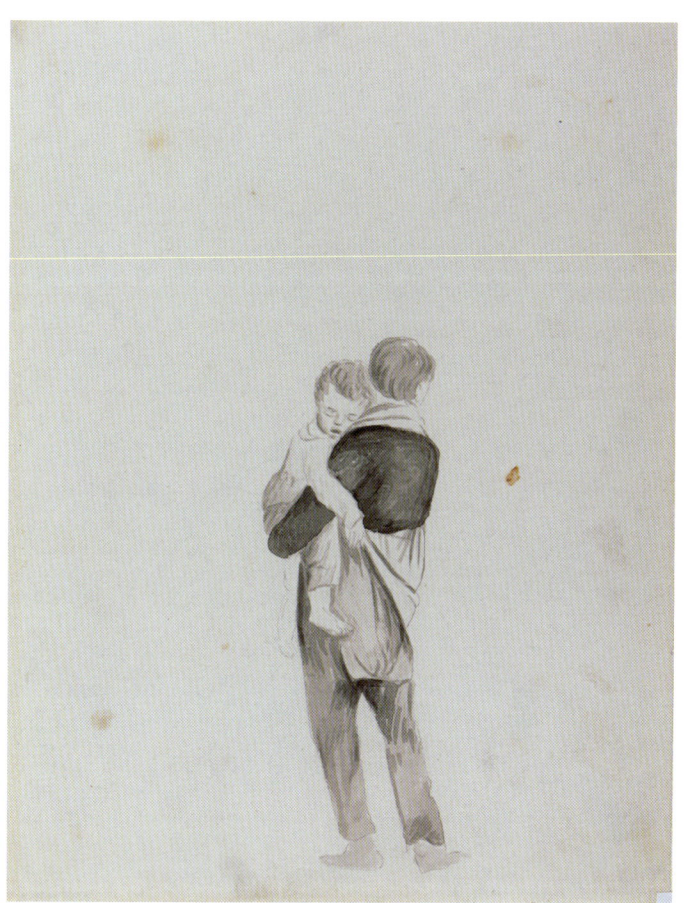

Figure 85 (Book 5)

Study of a boy holding a baby
Graphite and ink on paper
7¾" × 9¾"
1818

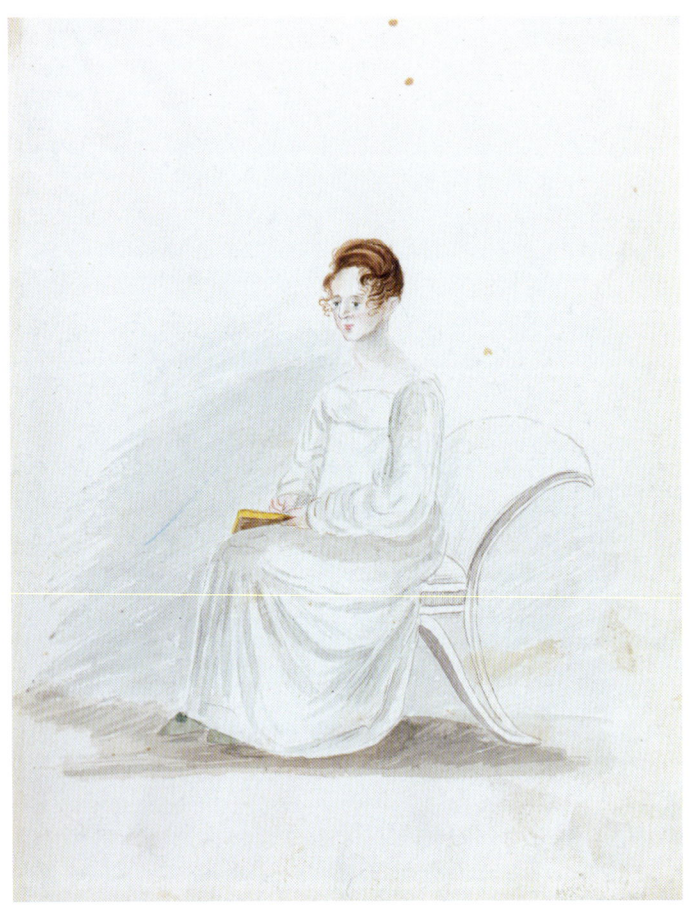

Figure 86 (Book 5)

Woman sitting with a book
Ink, watercolor, and wash on paper
7¾" × 9¾"
1818

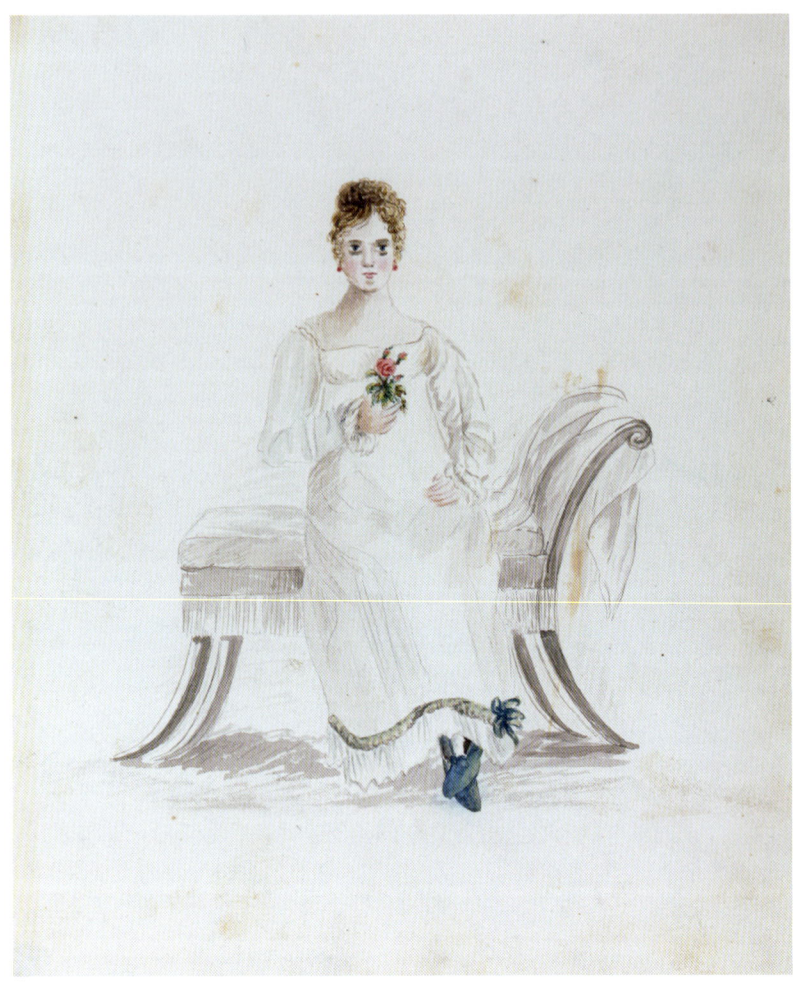

Figure 87 (Book 5)

Woman holding a rose
Ink and watercolor on paper
7¾" × 10"
1818

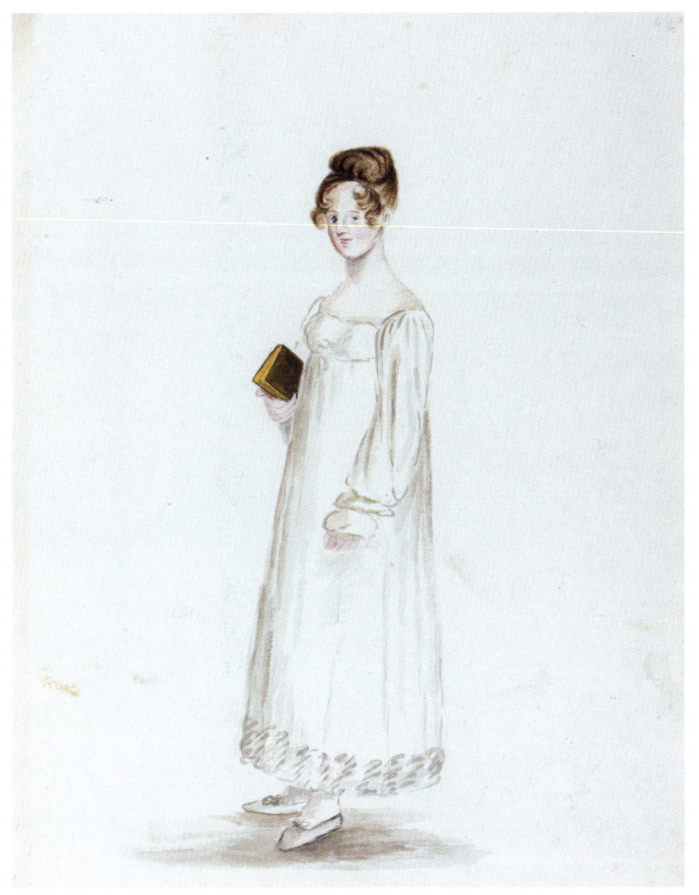

Figure 88 (Book 5)

Woman holding a book
Ink and watercolor on paper
7¾" × 9⅞"
1818

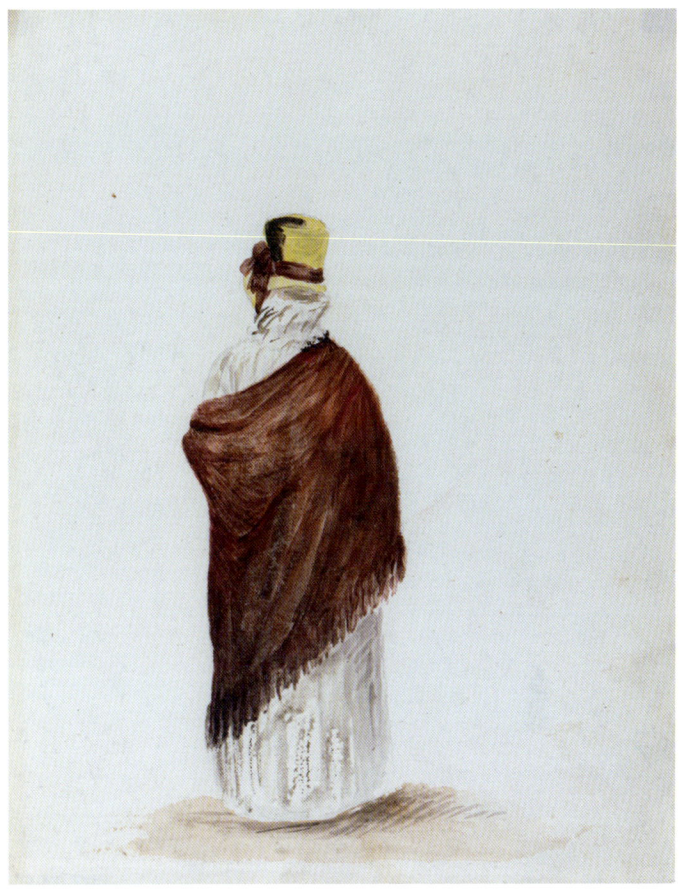

Figure 90 (Book 5)

Woman wearing a shawl
Watercolor on paper
7¾" × 9⅞"
1818

MORE THAN ORDINARY | 113

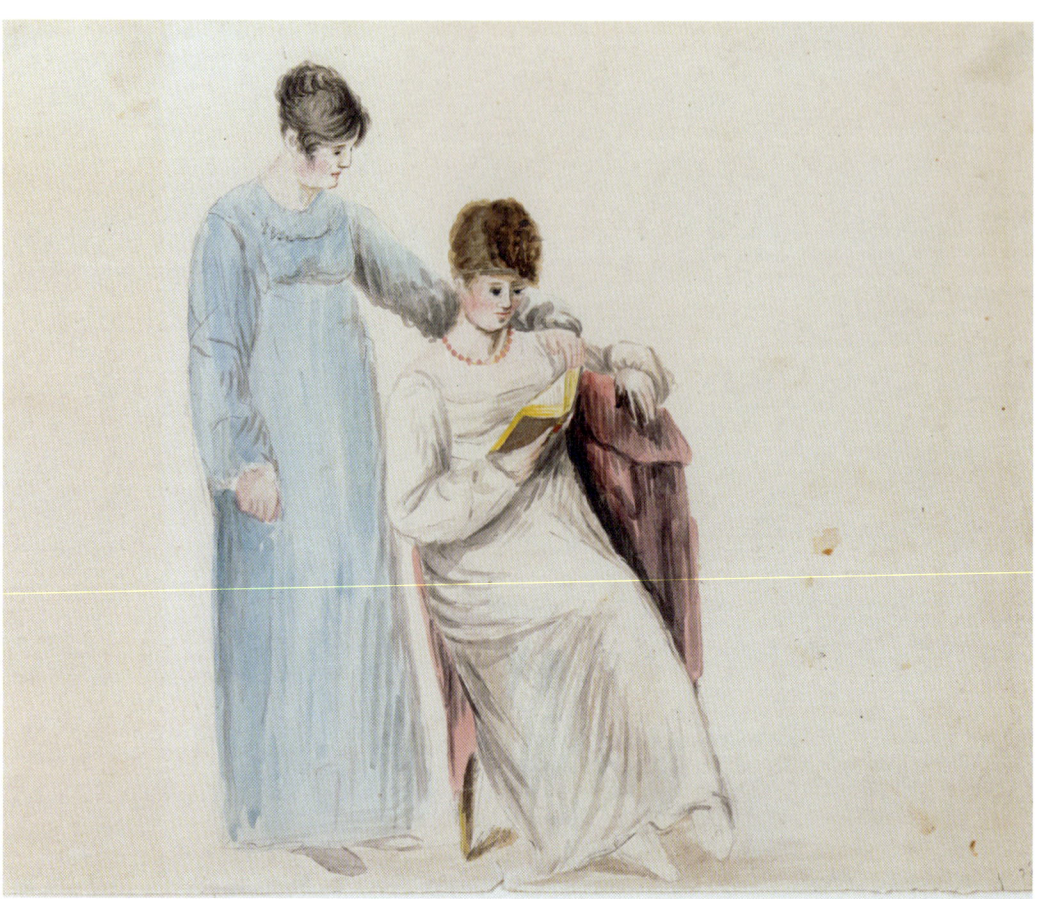

Figure 89 (Book 5)

Two women reading
Ink and watercolor on paper
8¾" × 7⅛"
1818

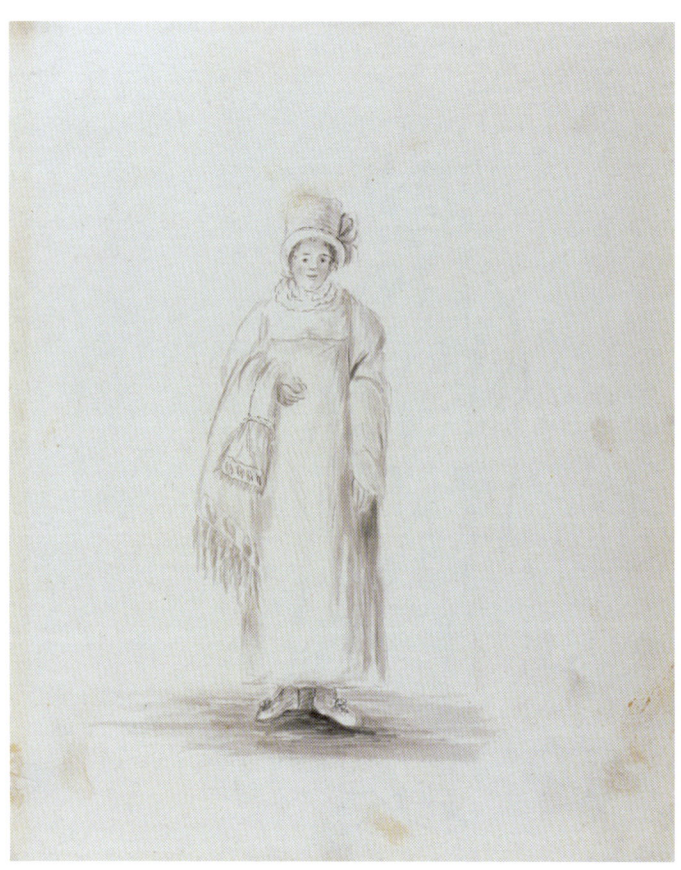

Figure 91 (Book 5)

Study of a woman holding a purse and wearing a shawl
Ink on paper
7¾" × 9⅞"
1818

Figure 92 (Book 5)

Woman wearing a red fichu
Watercolor on paper
7¾" × 9⅞"
1818

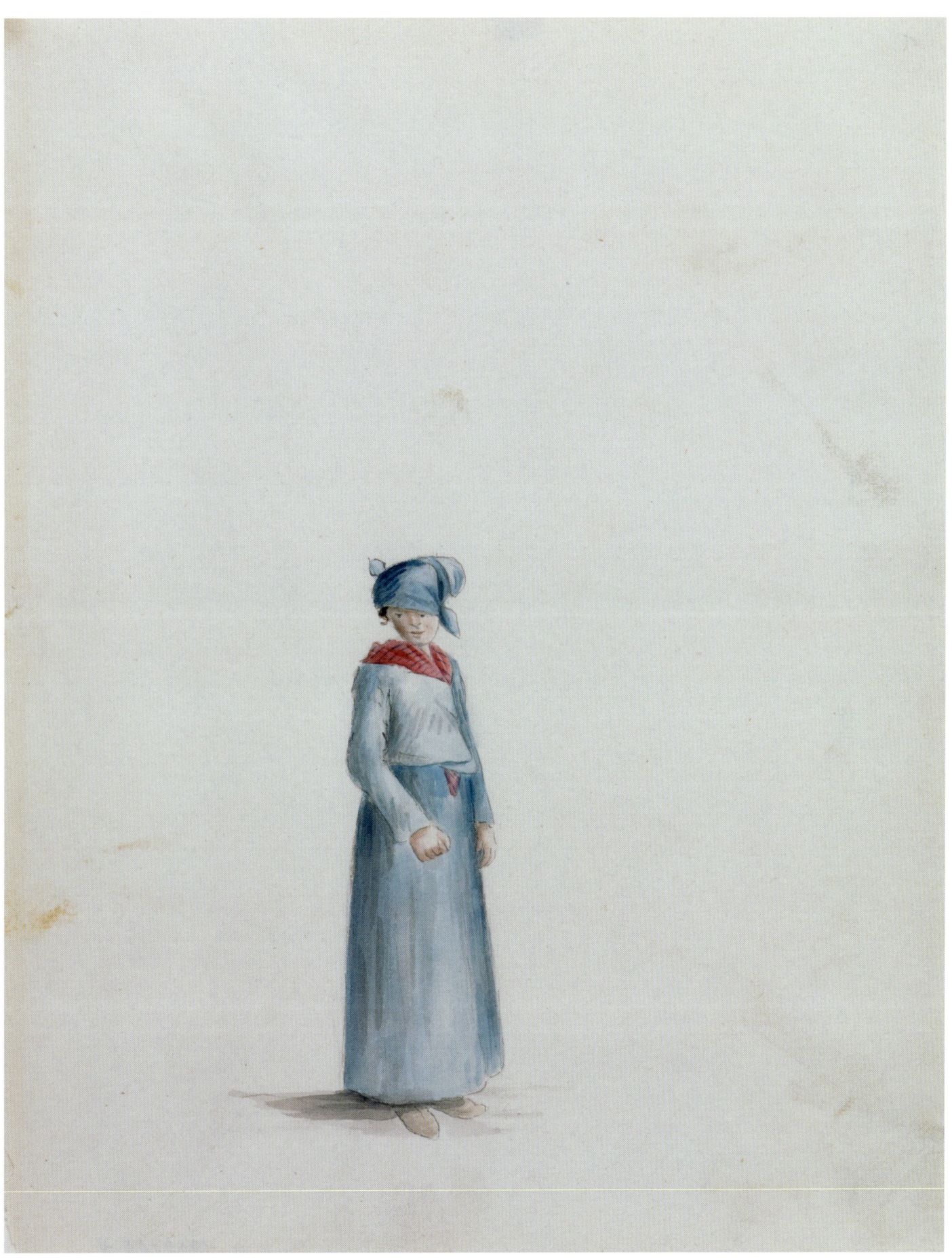

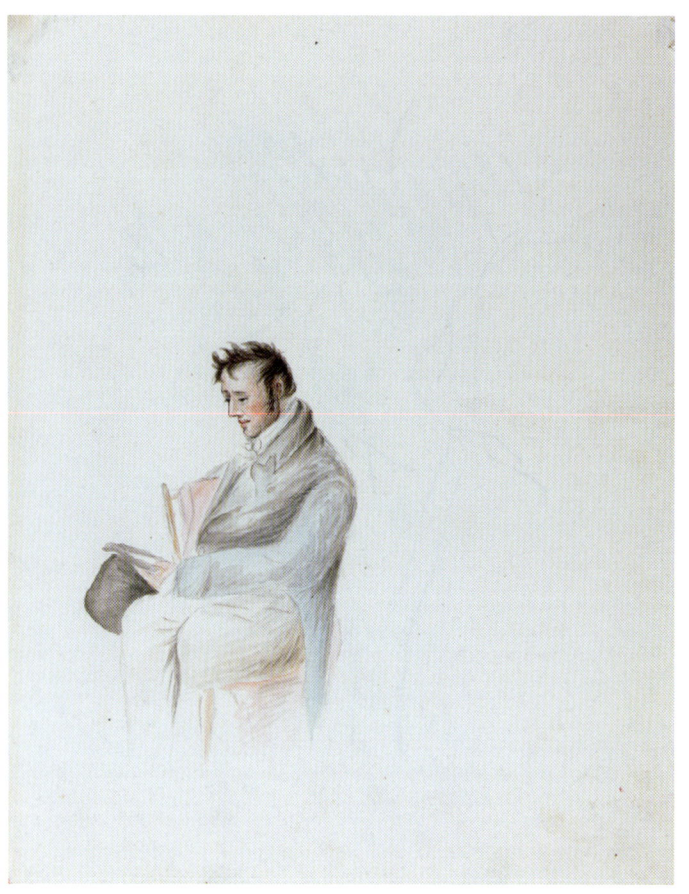

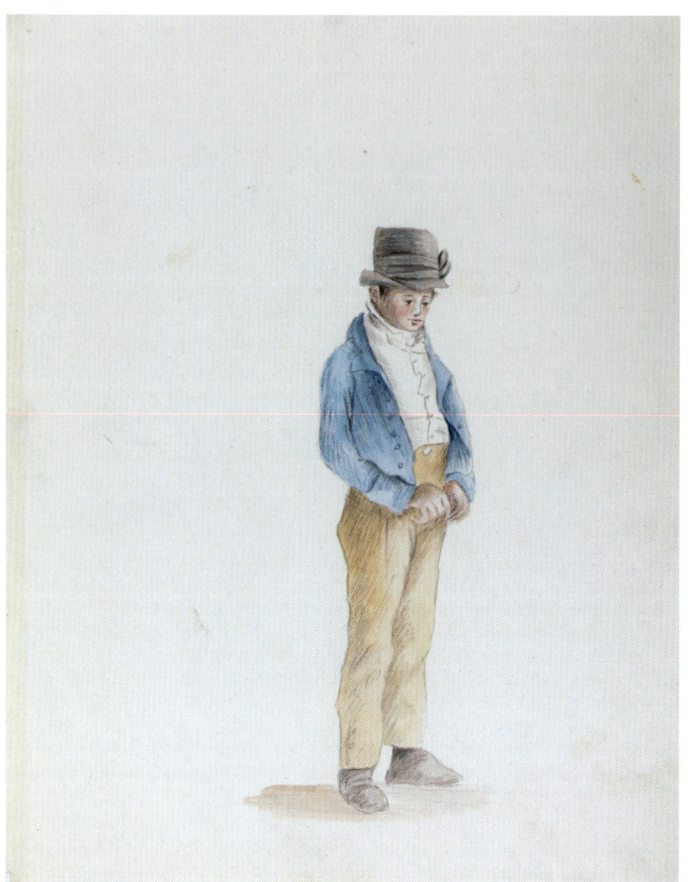

Figure 93 (Book 5)

Study of a man sitting
Graphite and watercolor on paper
7⅝" × 9⅞"
1818

Figure 94 (Book 5)

Boy wearing a beaver hat
Watercolor on paper
7¾" × 9⅞"
1818

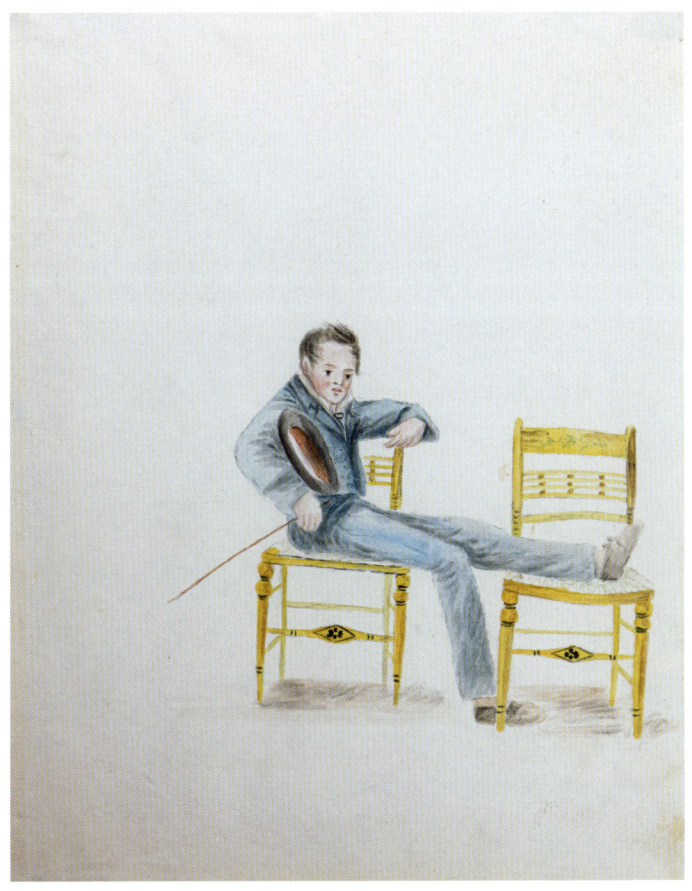

Figure 95 (Book 5)

Boy reclining on two fancy chairs
Watercolor on paper
7¾" × 9⅞"
1818

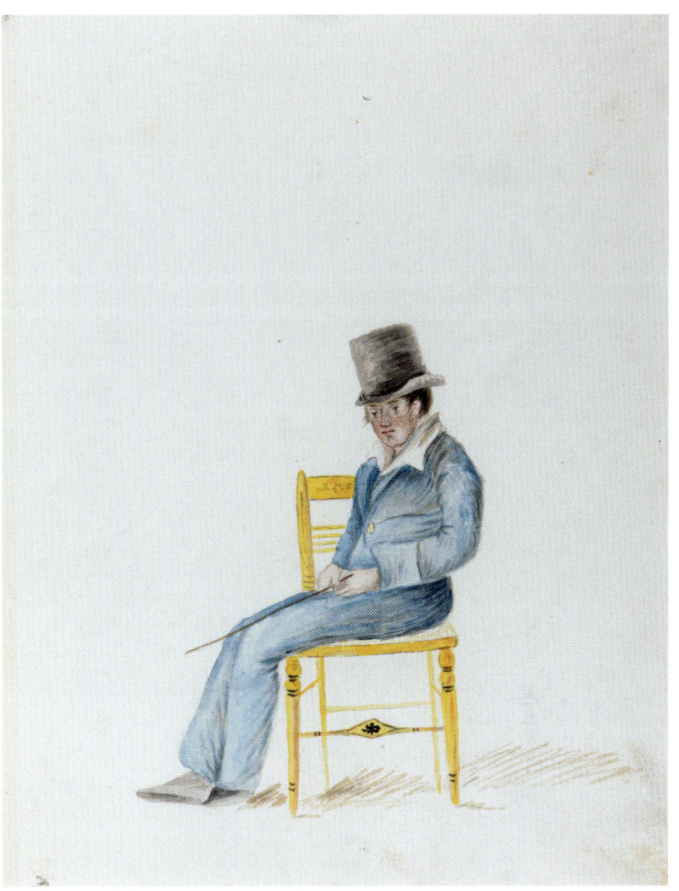

Figure 96 (Book 5)

Boy sitting in a fancy chair
Watercolor on paper
7¾" × 9⅞"
1818

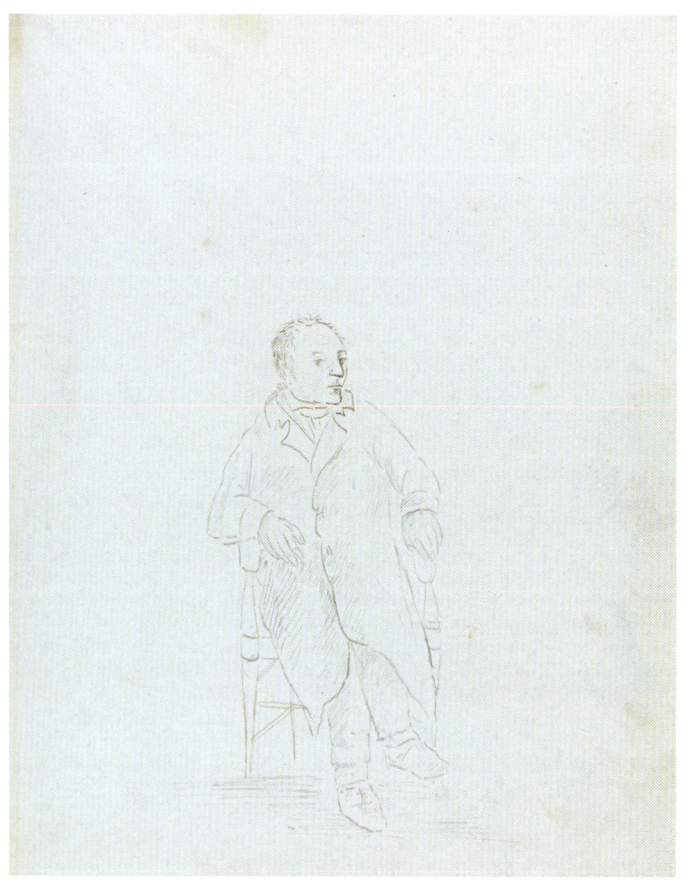

Figure 97 (Book 5)

Study of a seated man
Graphite on paper
7¾" × 9⅞"
1818

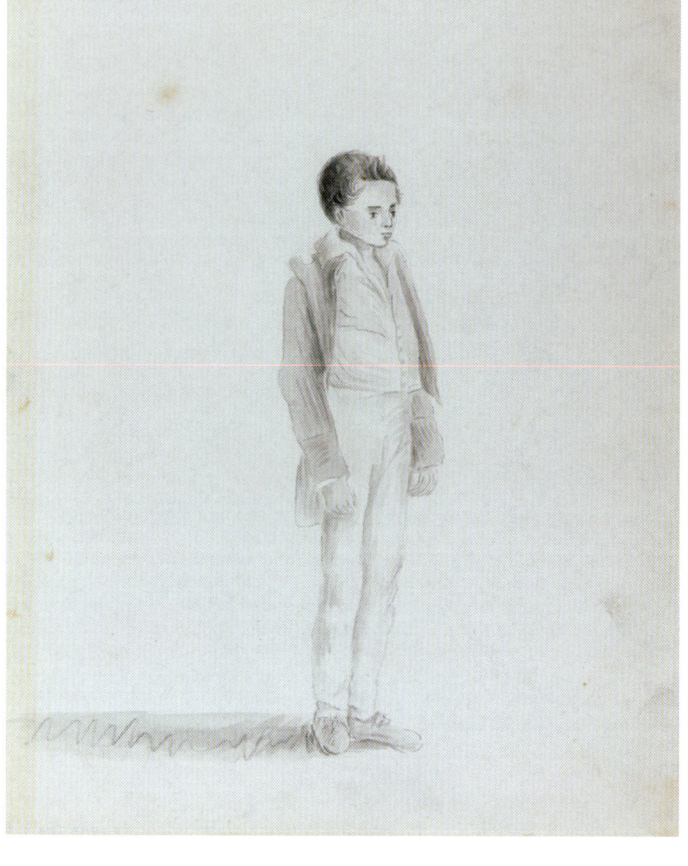

Figure 98 (Book 5)

Boy
Graphite and ink on paper
7¾" × 9⅞"
1818

Figure 99 (Book 5)

Boy reading
Graphite and ink on paper
7¾" × 9⅞"
1818

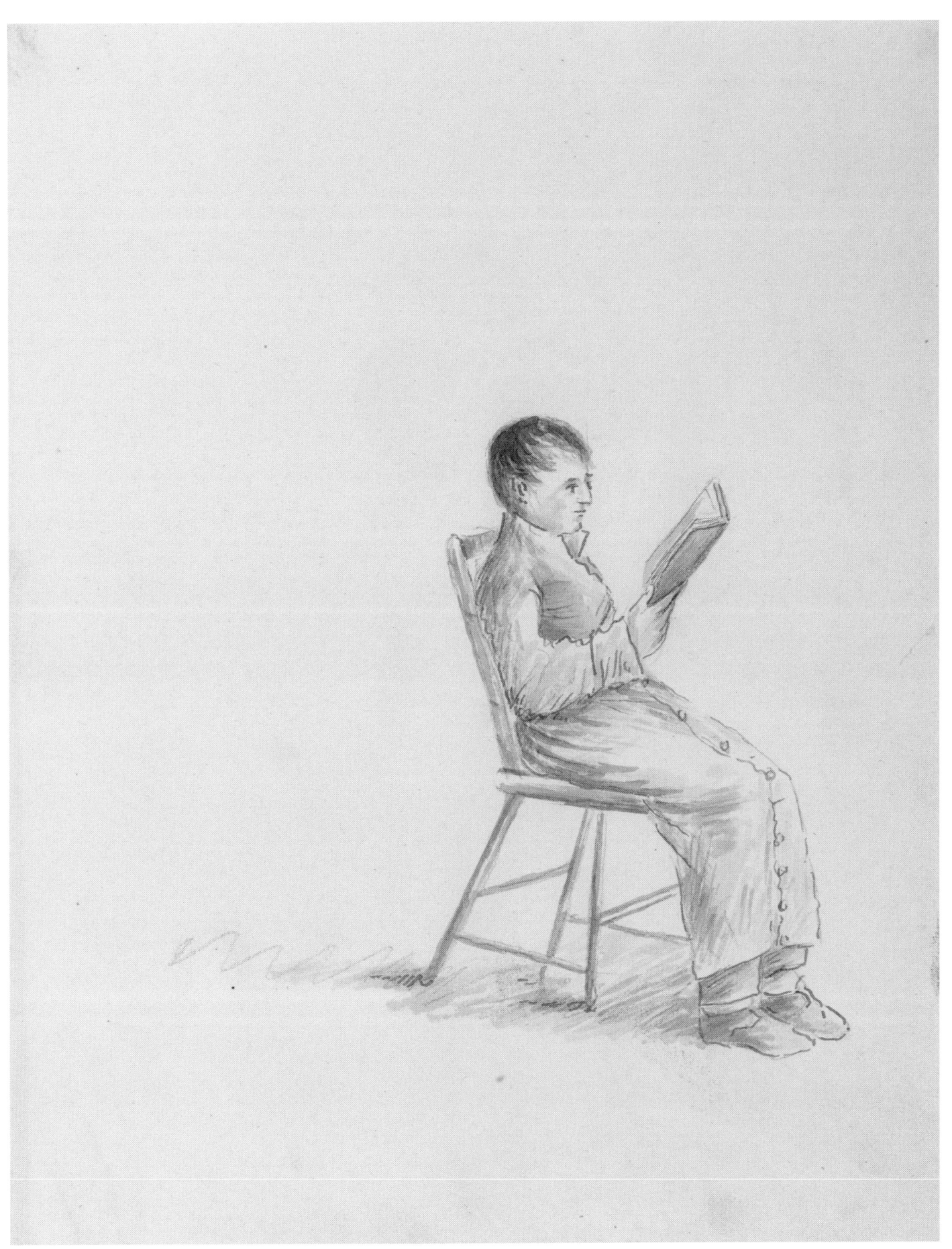

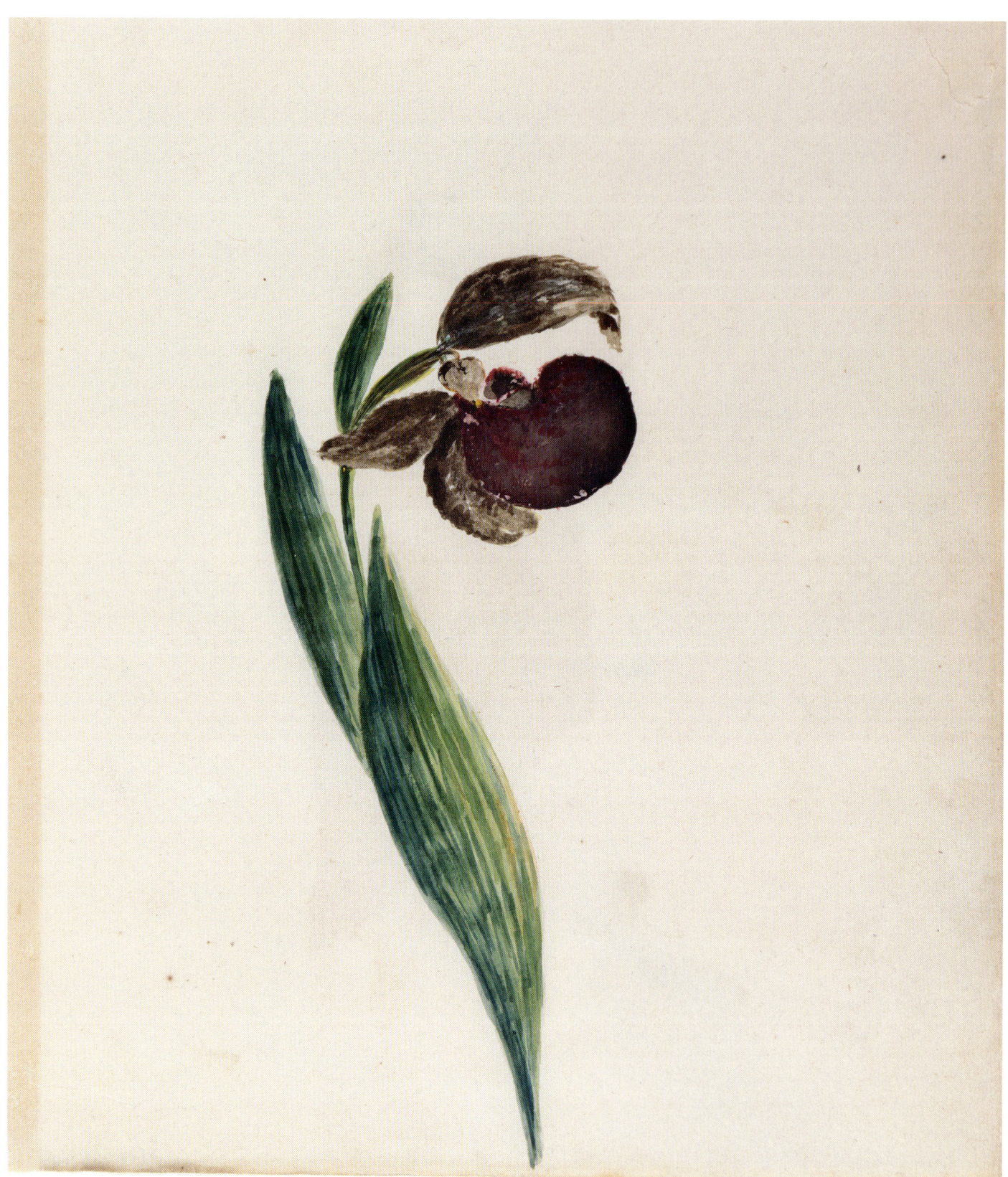

Figure 100 (Book 5)

Purple flower
Watercolor on paper
8" × 10"
1818

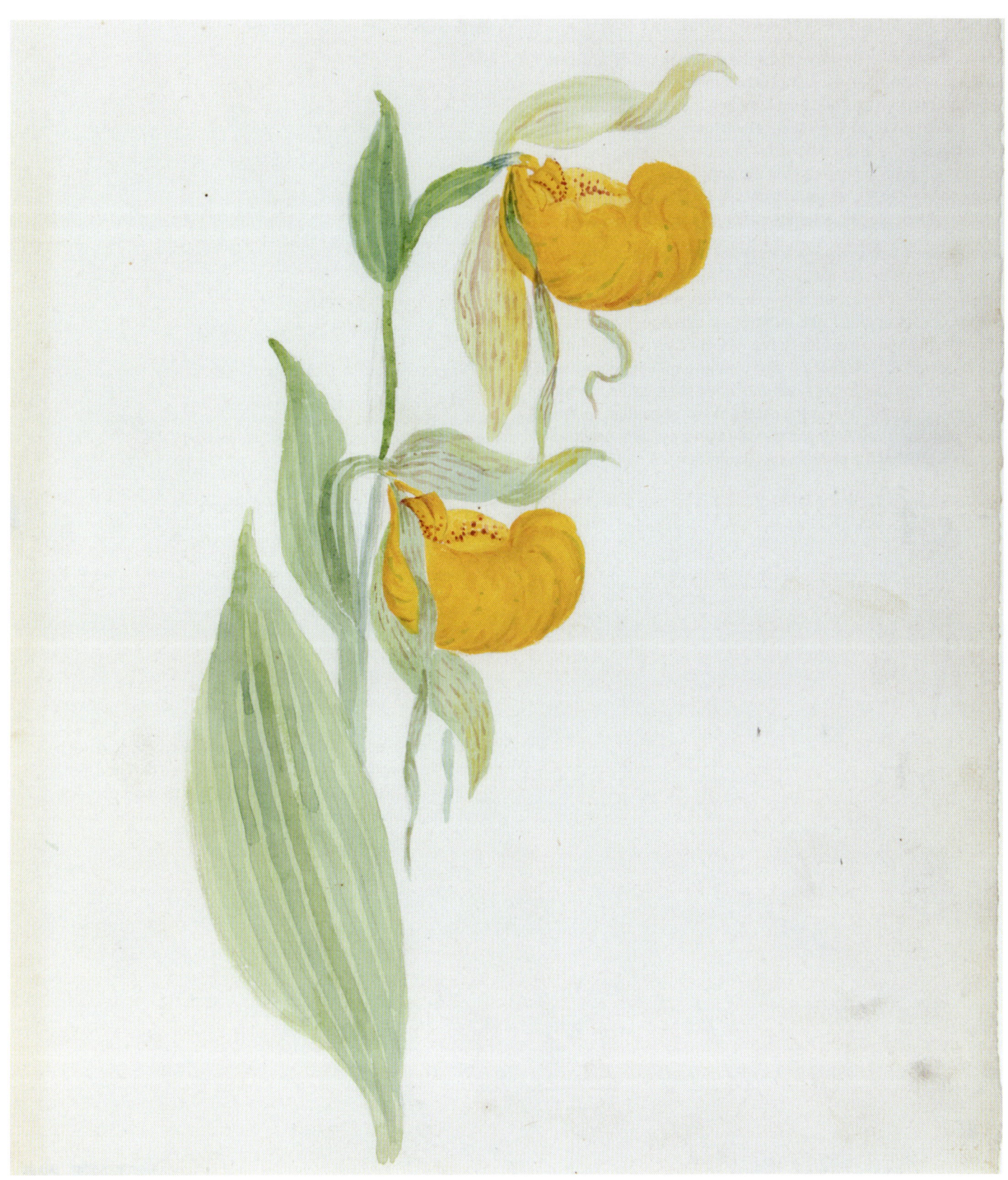

Figure 101 (Book 5)

Yellow lady's slipper flowers
Watercolor on paper
7¾" × 9⅞"
1818

SECTION 3: SILHOUETTES AND LOOSE ART

Silhouettes were at their most popular during the early 19th century, just as Anna Maria von Phul was coming into her own as an aspiring young artist. The 19 cutwork and drawn profiles included here are attributed to Anna Maria's own hand, though not all can be verified. Some of the silhouettes may have originally been pasted alongside her paintings in the sketchbooks her descendants donated to the Missouri Historical Society in 1953, but their location within specific volumes went unrecorded.

Several letters between Anna Maria von Phul and Ann Gist in the early 1800s mention terms like "profile" and "miniature portrait," which may refer to silhouettes—a word not used until decades later. In one letter dated 1806, Anna Maria tells Ann, "I enclose you a profile which I must confess is not thought a verry correct resemblance of my face." Anna Maria also created a miniature portrait of Ann, which she sent to her along with a few short verses. The poem hints that the portrait lacks the details of Ann's beautiful smile and face—perhaps it was Anna Maria's way of expressing modesty, or it may indicate that the portrait is a silhouette.

Written under a miniature portrait,

of

Miss A. E. G_'s

To do thee justice, I did not pretend,

I only sketch'd the features of my friend;

Had I a Titian's pencil, warm,

Or soft Corregio's magic charm;

O! with what rapture would I trace,

The mind illumin'd, in thy speaking face;

Thy sweetest smile should there be seen,

Thy waving tresses and thy graceful mien;

No lovelier subject could the canvass warm,

And it should breath the every charm.

To future ages would thy beauty bloom,

A deathley laurel then would clasp my tomb

Yet would I all their praises resign,

For one approving smile of thine.

Lexington April 1808(?) A. M. v.P.

The other 16 pieces of art included in this section could not be reassociated with their original volumes, were donated loose, or—in the case of Figures 135 and 136—exist as part of the von Phul archival collection.

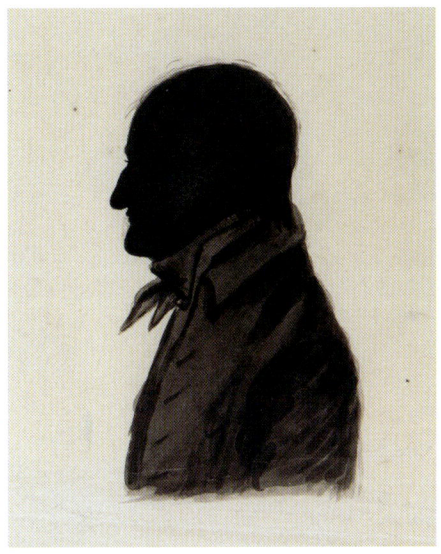

Figure 102

Silhouette
Ink on paper
3⅝" × 7⅛"
Unknown date

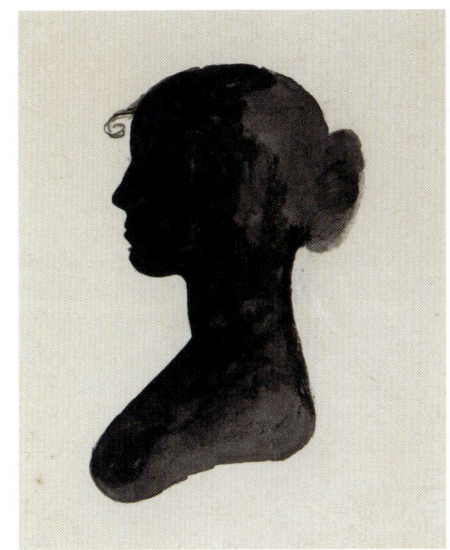

Figure 103

Silhouette
Ink on paper
3⅝" × 5⅛"
Unknown date

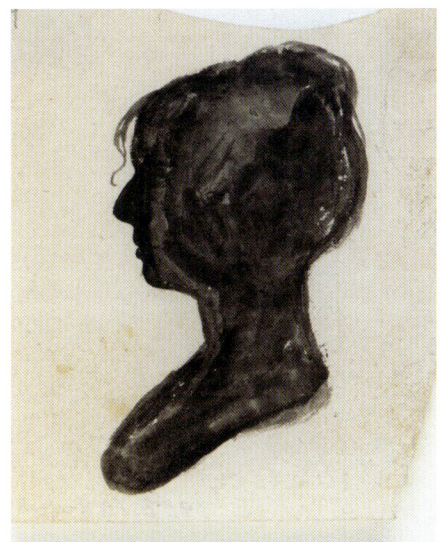

Figure 104

Silhouette
Ink on paper
2⅛" × 2⅝"
Unknown date

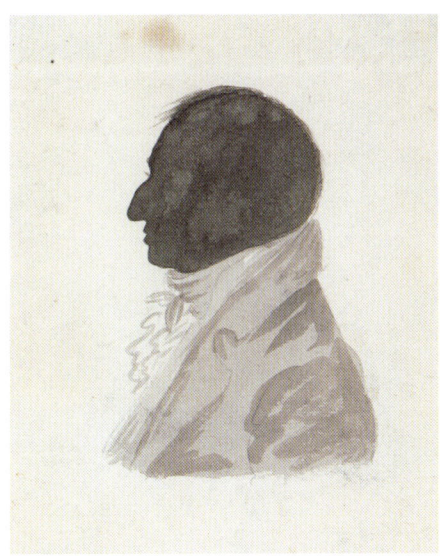

Figure 105

Silhouette
Ink on paper
6" × 5⅝"
Unknown date

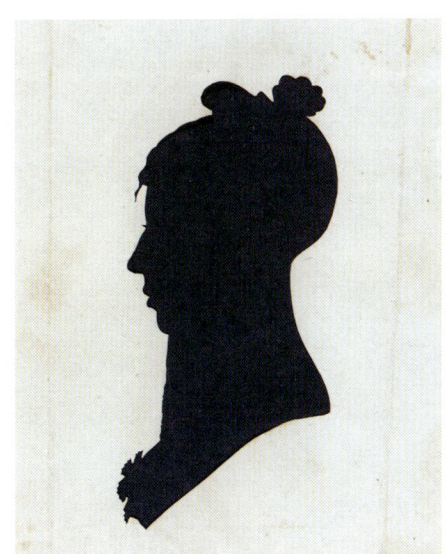

Figure 106

Silhouette
Hollow cut on white paper
4" × 5¼"
Unknown date

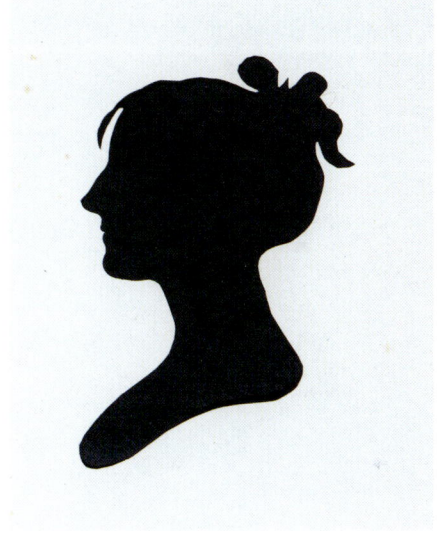

Figure 107

Silhouette
Hollow cut on white paper
4⅜" × 5"
Unknown date

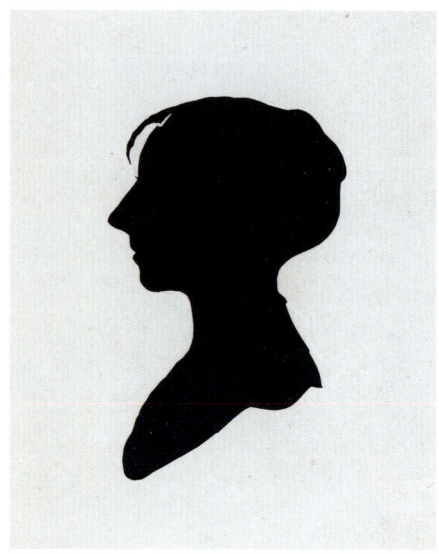

Figure 108

Silhouette
Hollow cut on white paper
4½" × 5¼"
Unknown date

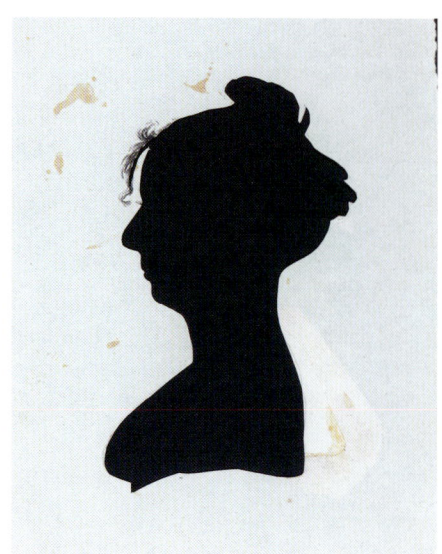

Figure 109

Silhouette
Hollow cut on white paper with ink details
3⅞" × 5⅛"
Unknown date

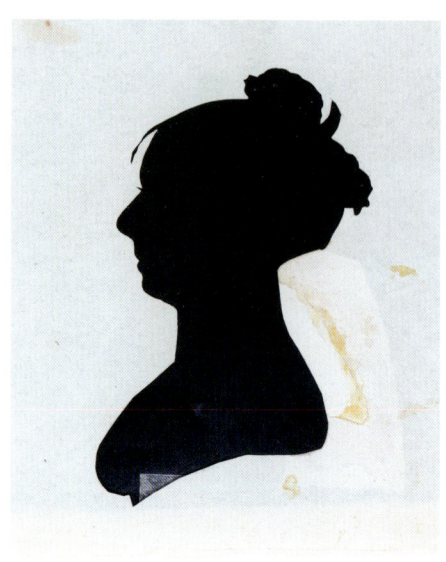

Figure 110

Silhouette
Hollow cut on white paper
4⅜" × 4¾"
Unknown date

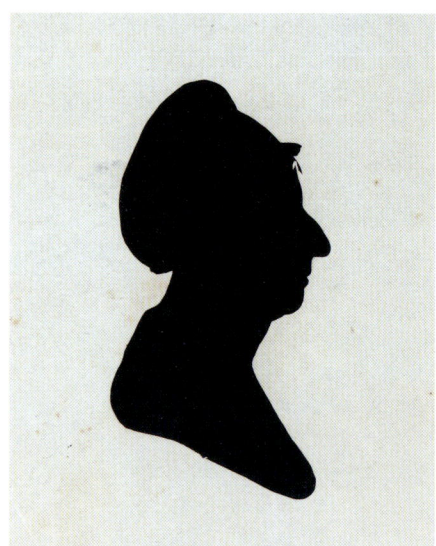

Figure 111

Mrs. Von Phul silhouette
Hollow cut on white paper
3⅞" × 4⅞"
Unknown date

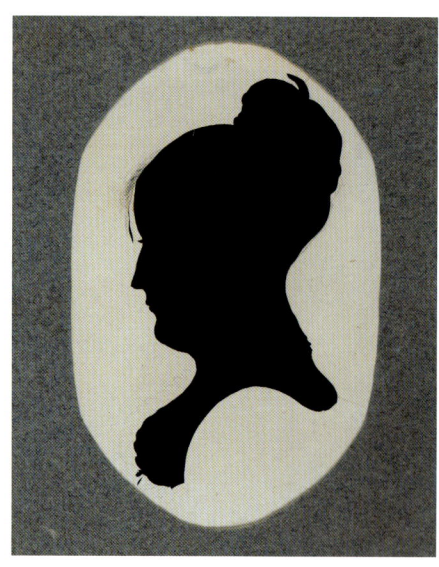

Figure 112

Silhouette
Hollow cut on white paper with graphite details and tracing lines
4¾" × 6⅛"
Unknown date

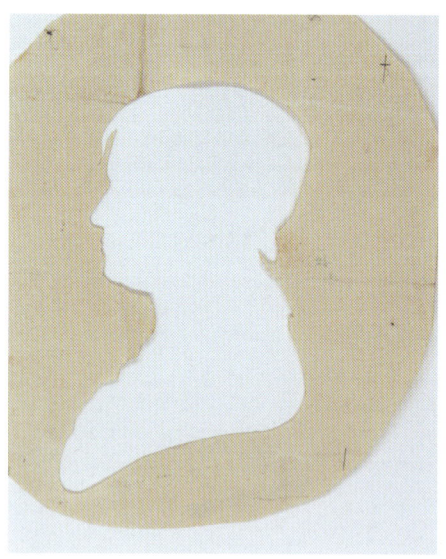

Figure 113

Silhouette
Hollow cut on white paper
4⅜" × 5⅝"
Unknown date

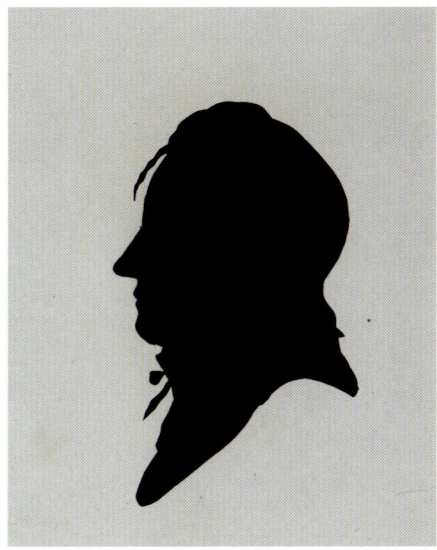

Figure 114

Silhouette
Hollow cut on white paper
3⅞" × 4½"
Unknown date

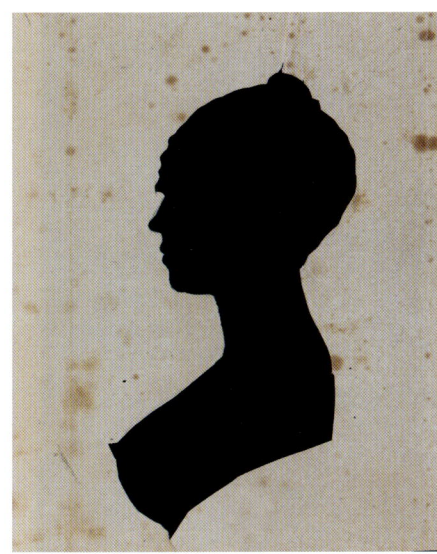

Figure 115

Silhouette
Hollow cut on white paper
4⅛" × 4⅞"
Unknown date

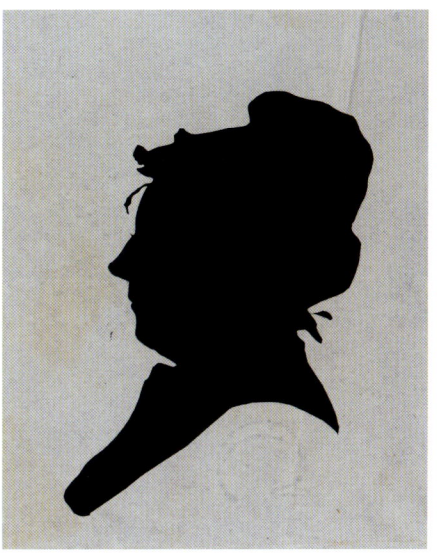

Figure 116

Silhouette
Hollow cut on white paper
5⅝" × 5⅛"
Unknown date

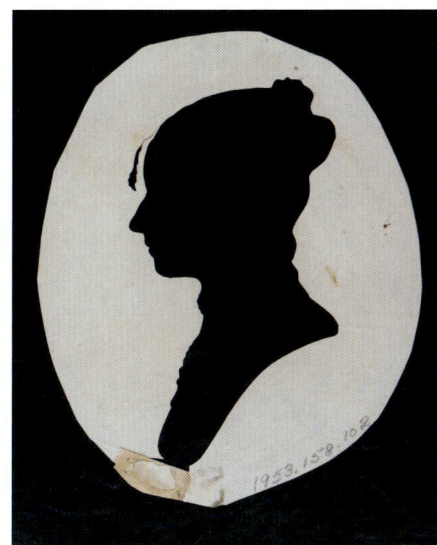

Figure 117

Silhouette
Hollow cut on white paper
3⅛" × 3¾"
Unknown date

MORE THAN ORDINARY | 125

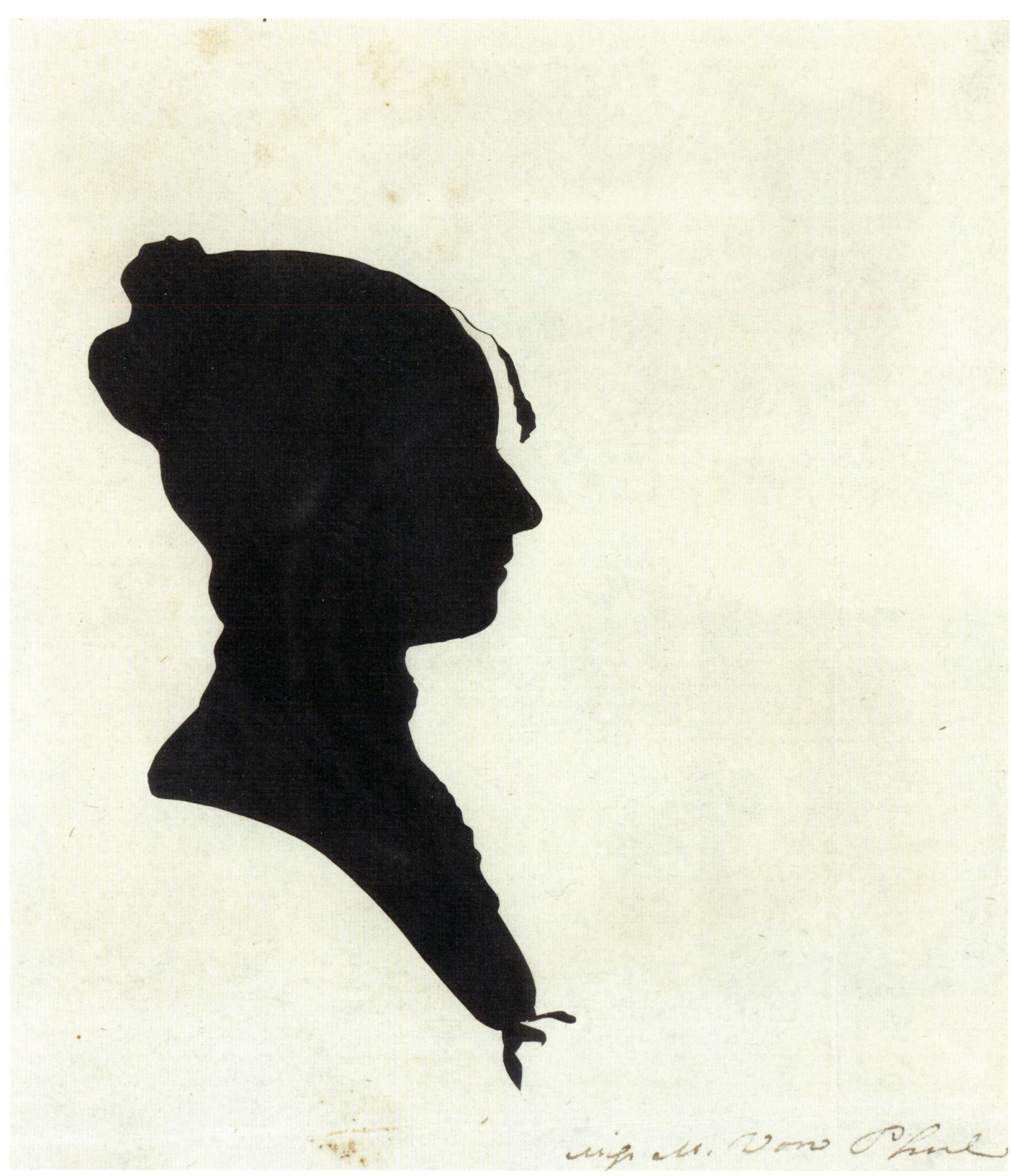

Figure 118

Miss M. Von Phul silhouette (possible self-portrait)
Hollow cut on white paper
4" × 4⅝"
Unknown date

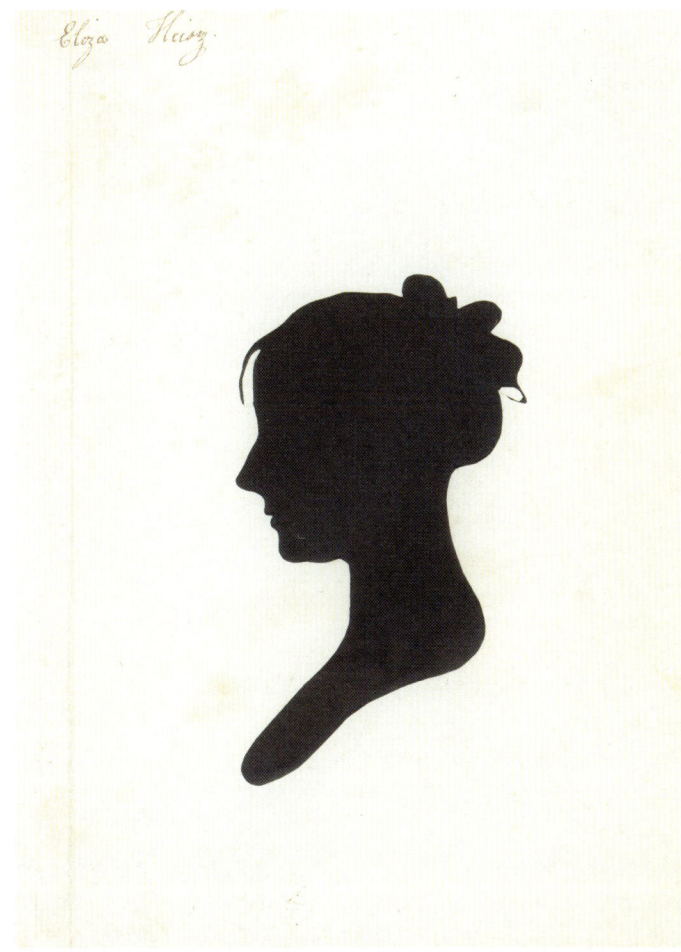

Figure 119

Eliza Heisz silhouette
Hollow cut on white paper
3⅝" × 5"
Unknown date

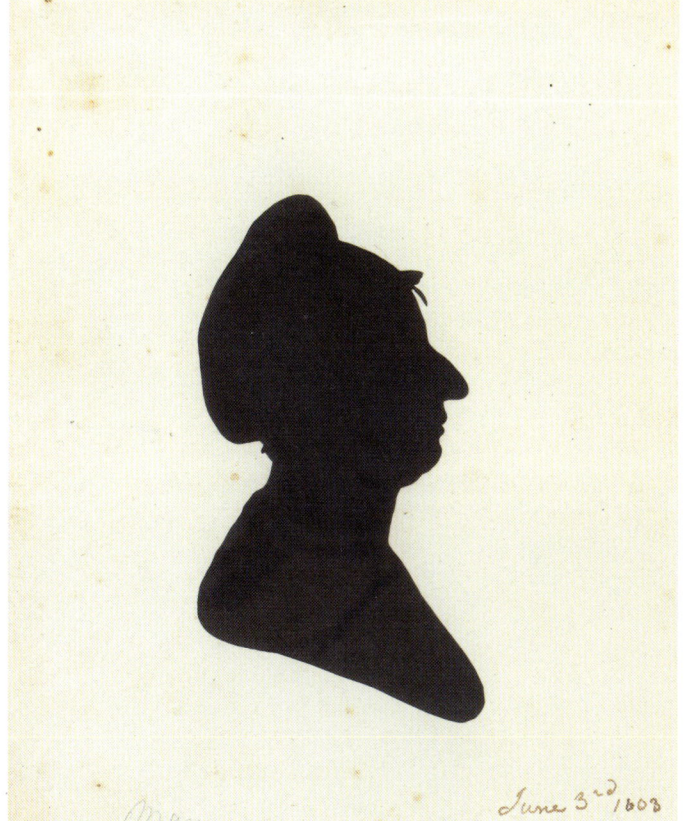

Figure 120

Mama (Catharine von Phul) silhouette
Hollow cut on white paper
3⅝" × 4¾"
June 3, 1803

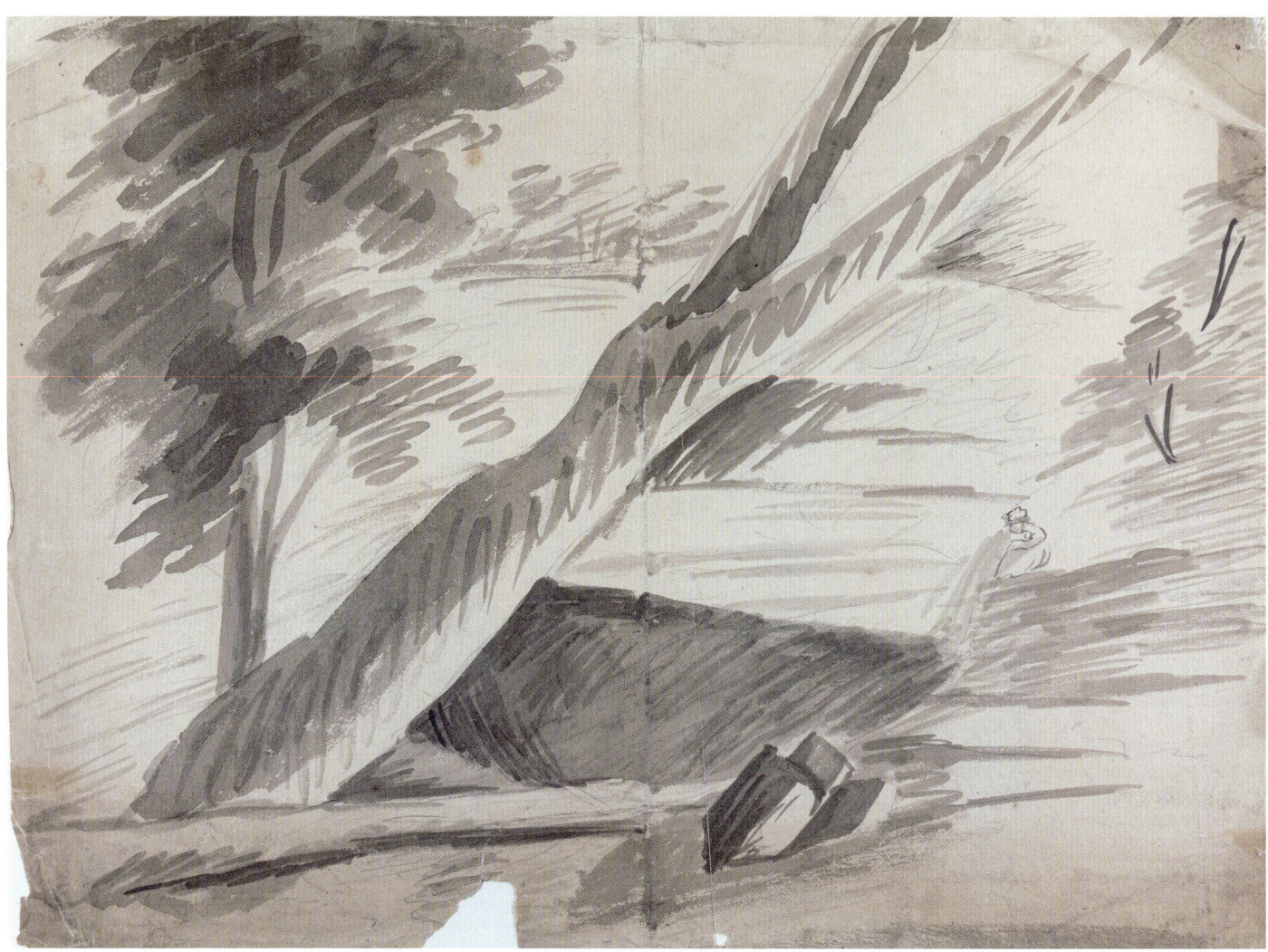

Figure 121

Landscape study
Graphite, ink, and wash on paper
15¼" × 11¾"
Unknown date

This oversize study of a landscape includes a small figure wearing a bonnet and crouching near the right side of the frame. Figure 122 is on the reverse and includes the same woman, this time depicted with a companion.

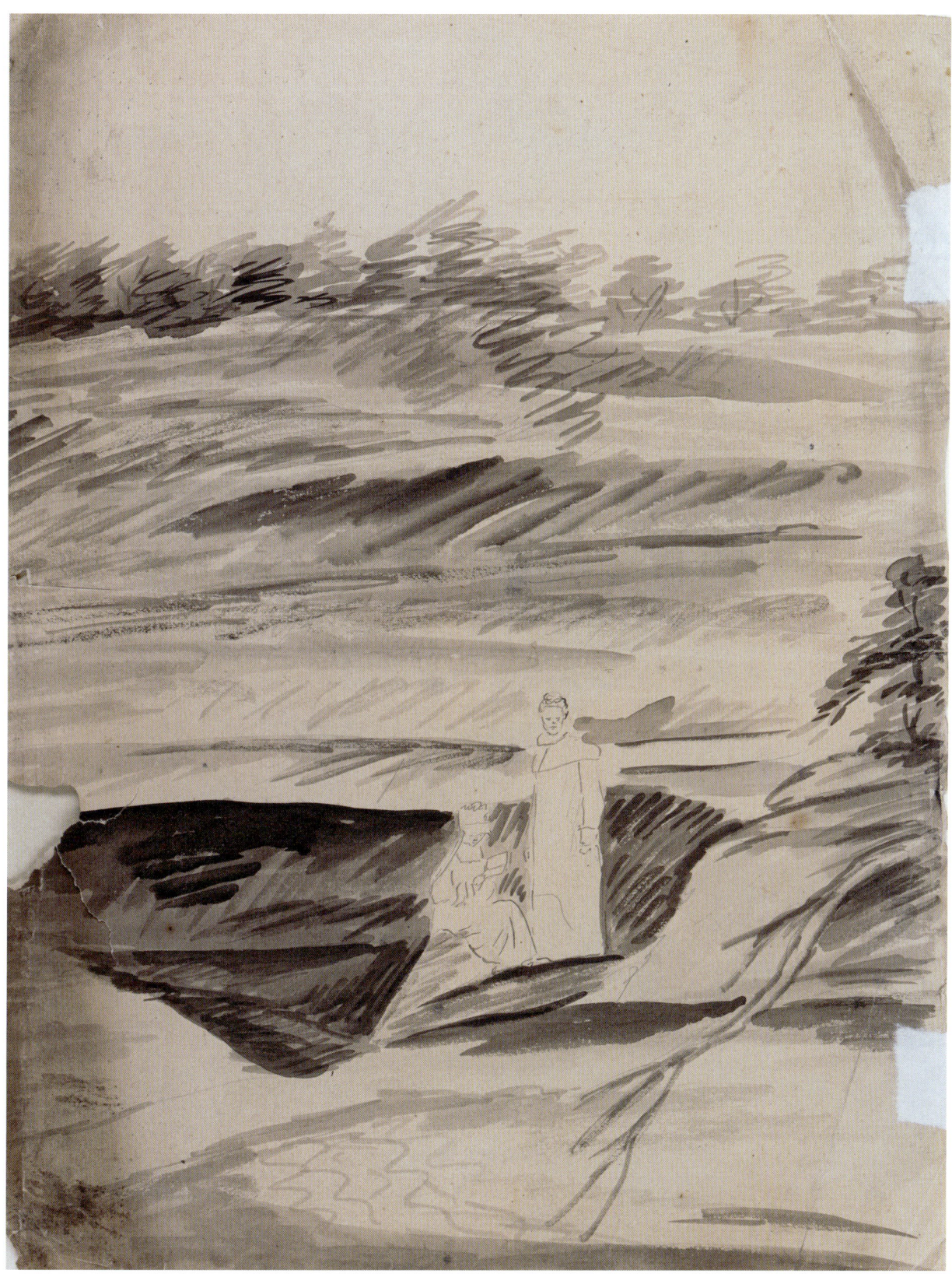

Figure 122

Landscape study with two women
Graphite, ink, and wash on paper
11¾" × 15¼"
Unknown date

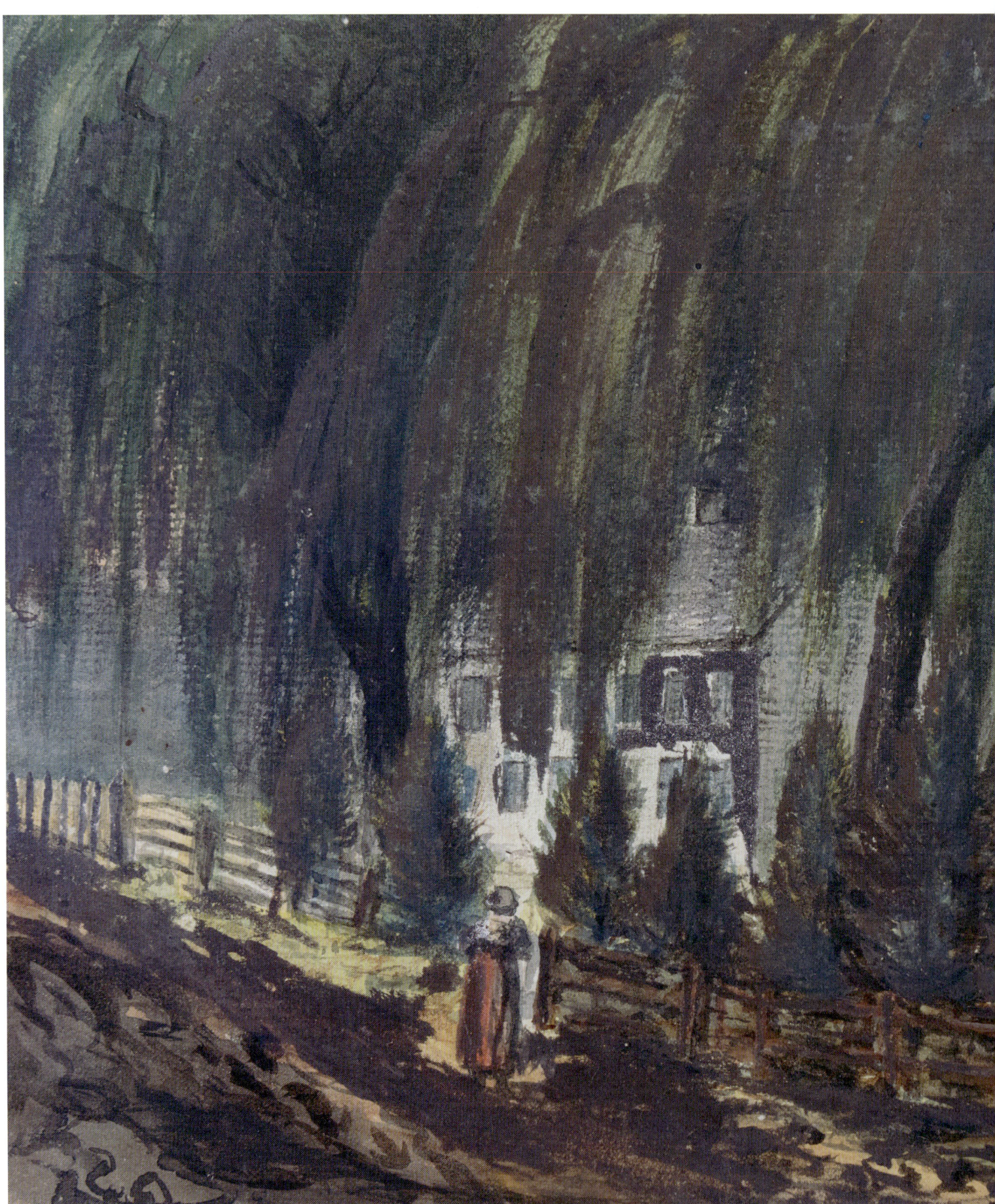

Figure 123

Chaumiere du Prairie
Watercolor, ink,
and gouache on paper
8½" × 6⅝"
Unknown date

The large, rambling house featured in this landscape painting is thought to be Chaumiere du Prairie, David Meade's estate in Jessamine County, Kentucky, constructed after the original home had been expanded and improved.

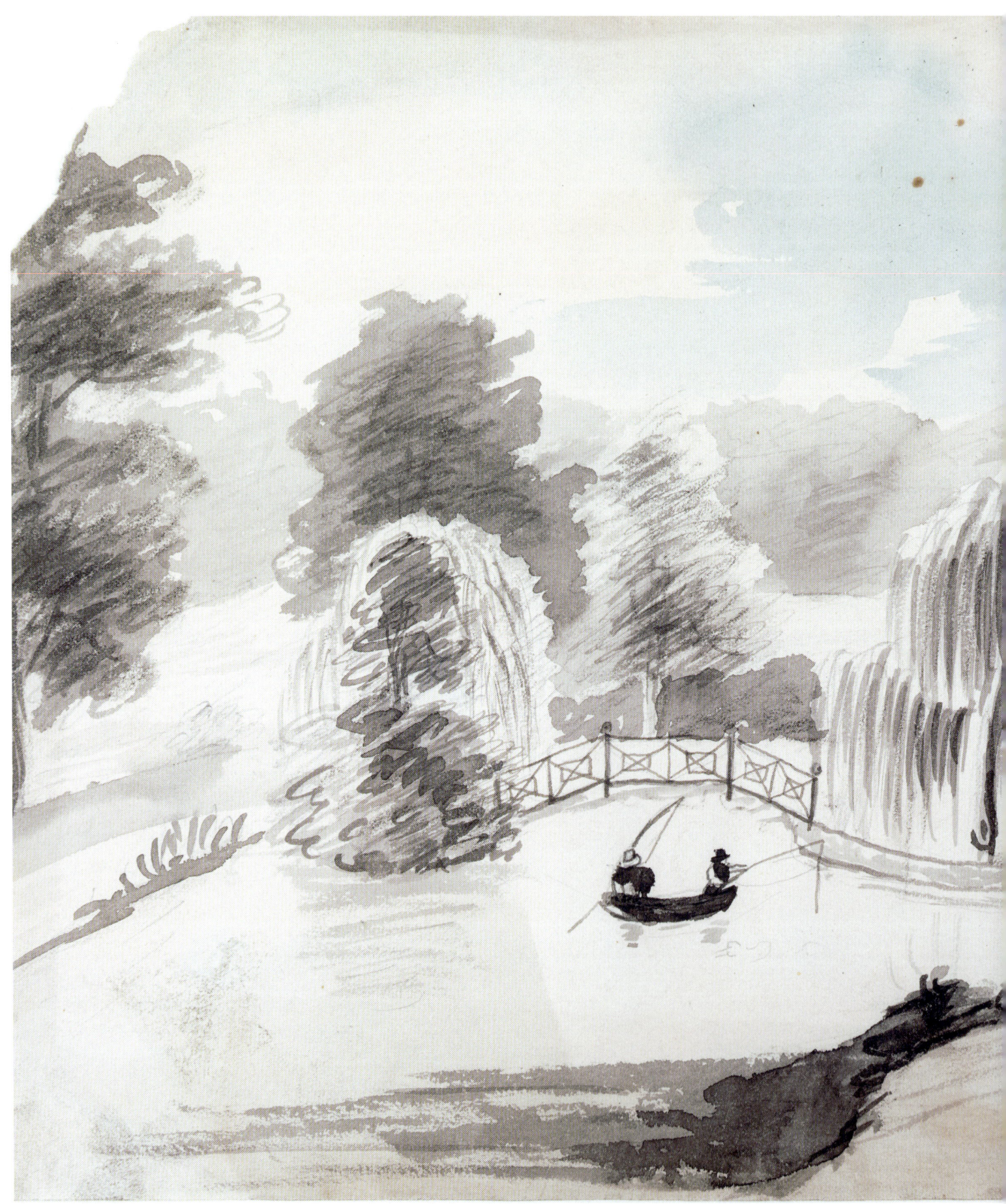

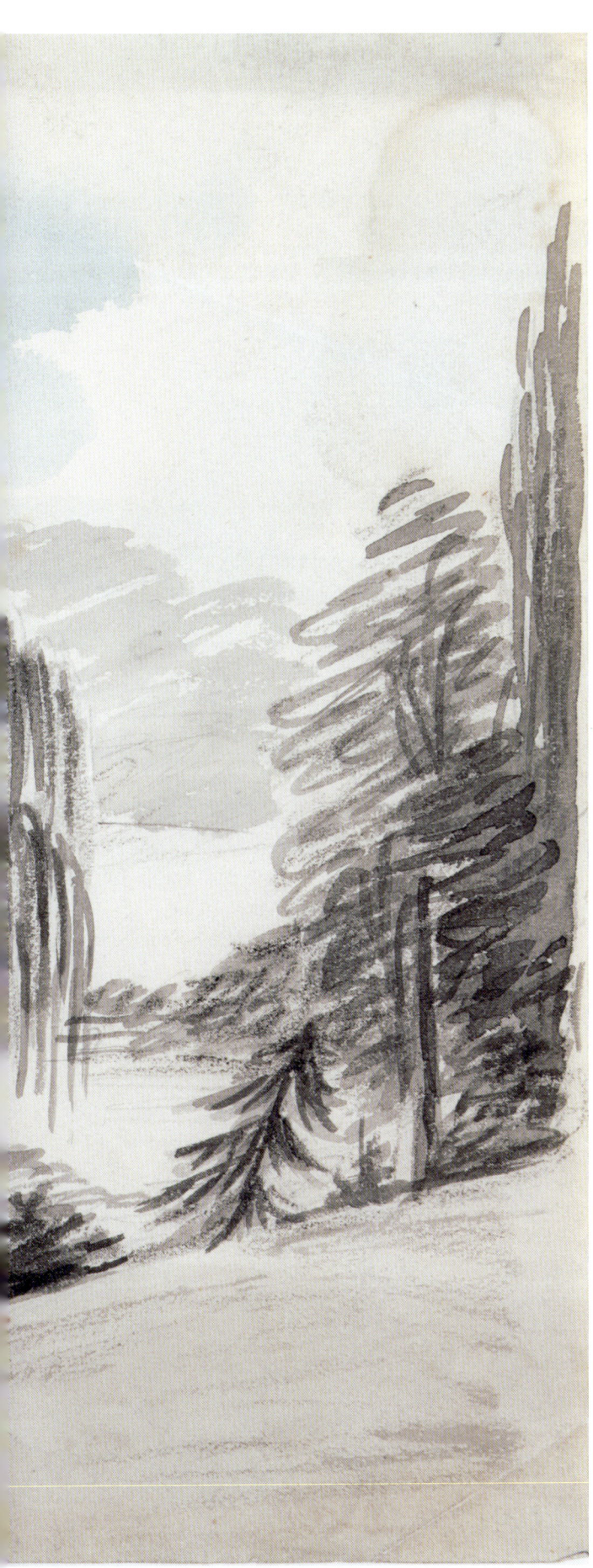

Figure 124

Lake at Chaumiere du Prairie
Graphite, ink, and wash on paper
10" × 7⅞"
Unknown date

Visitors to Chaumiere often wrote about the estate in a rush of compliments and wonder. The lake and its small bridge were frequently mentioned, as in this 1823 account, published in William and Ophia Smith's 1953 book *A Buckeye Titan*, written for the Historical and Philosophical Society of Ohio:

> Ornamental walks led off to the most beautiful parts of the grounds. There was a small islet at the head of the lake, with a picturesque Chinese bridge leading to it. At the foot of the lake, in a deep dell, was a fine spring that disappeared into the ground a few feet away. In another part of the dell, the waters of the lake cascaded over a natural wall, at the same time passing through a rude arch which was a fine imitation of Gothic ruins. On the bank of the lake was a white Doric portico at the end of a walk arched over by the boughs of cherry and plum trees.

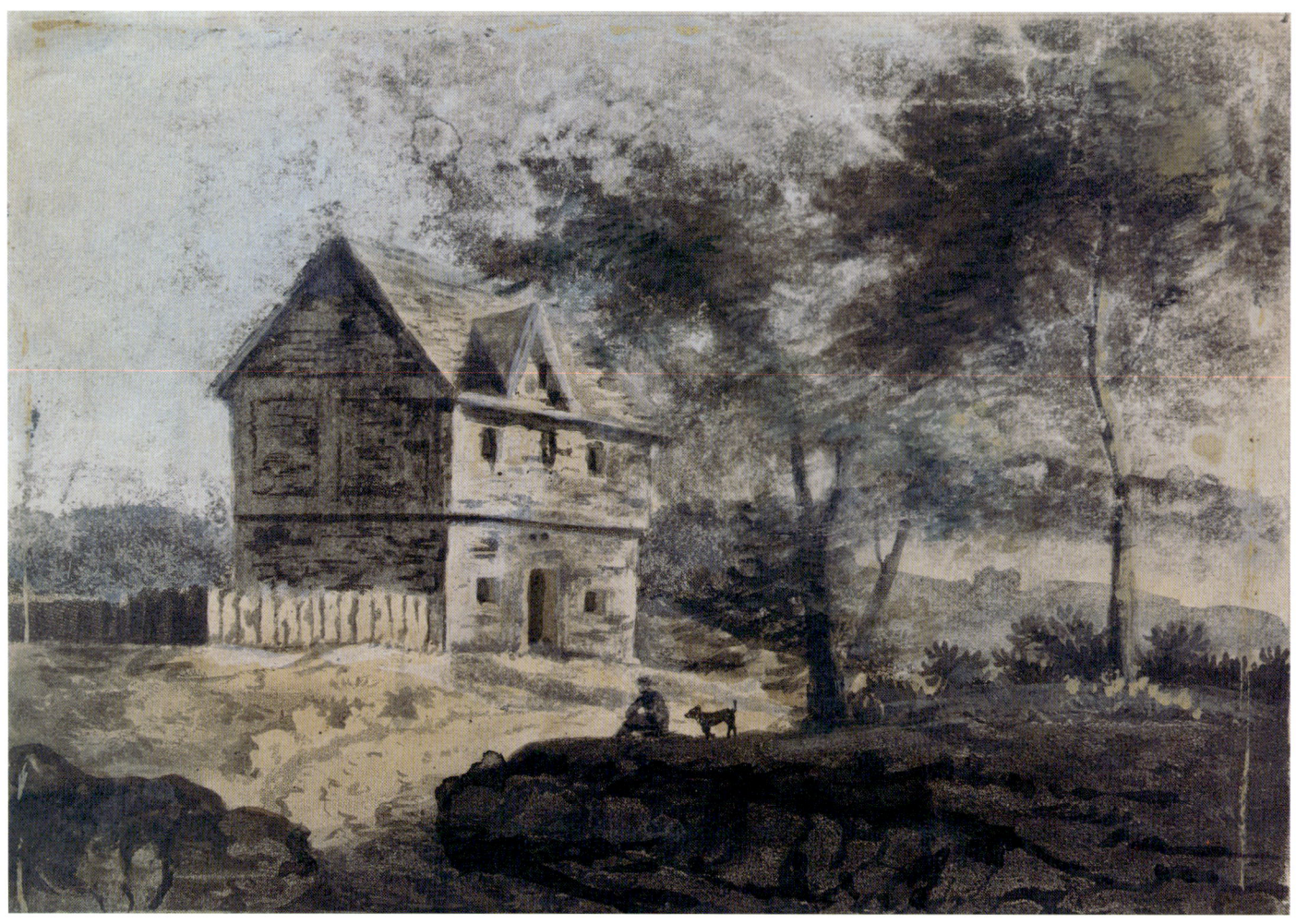

Figure 125

Untitled
Watercolor over a print
8⅜" × 6⅜"
Unknown date

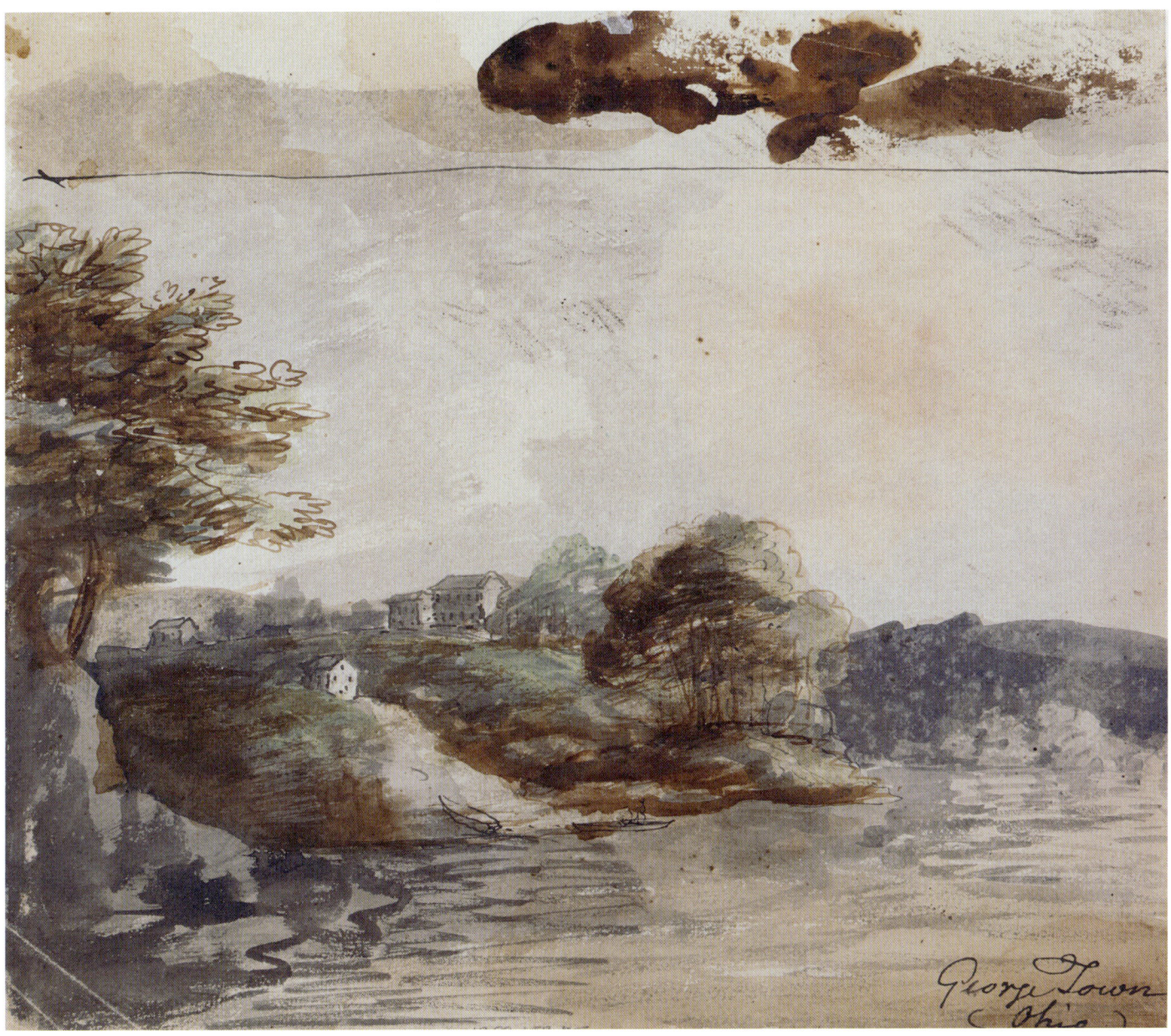

Figure 126

George Town (Ohio)
Ink and watercolor on paper
8¾" × 7⅞"
Unknown date

Inscribed "George Town (Ohio)." The exact location of the "George Town" Anna Maria painted in this piece is unknown, although it likely refers to Georgetown, Pennsylvania, a small town adjacent to the Ohio River, not far from that state's border with West Virginia. She may have created this piece and the riverscape on the reverse (Figure 127) during a return trip to Philadelphia.

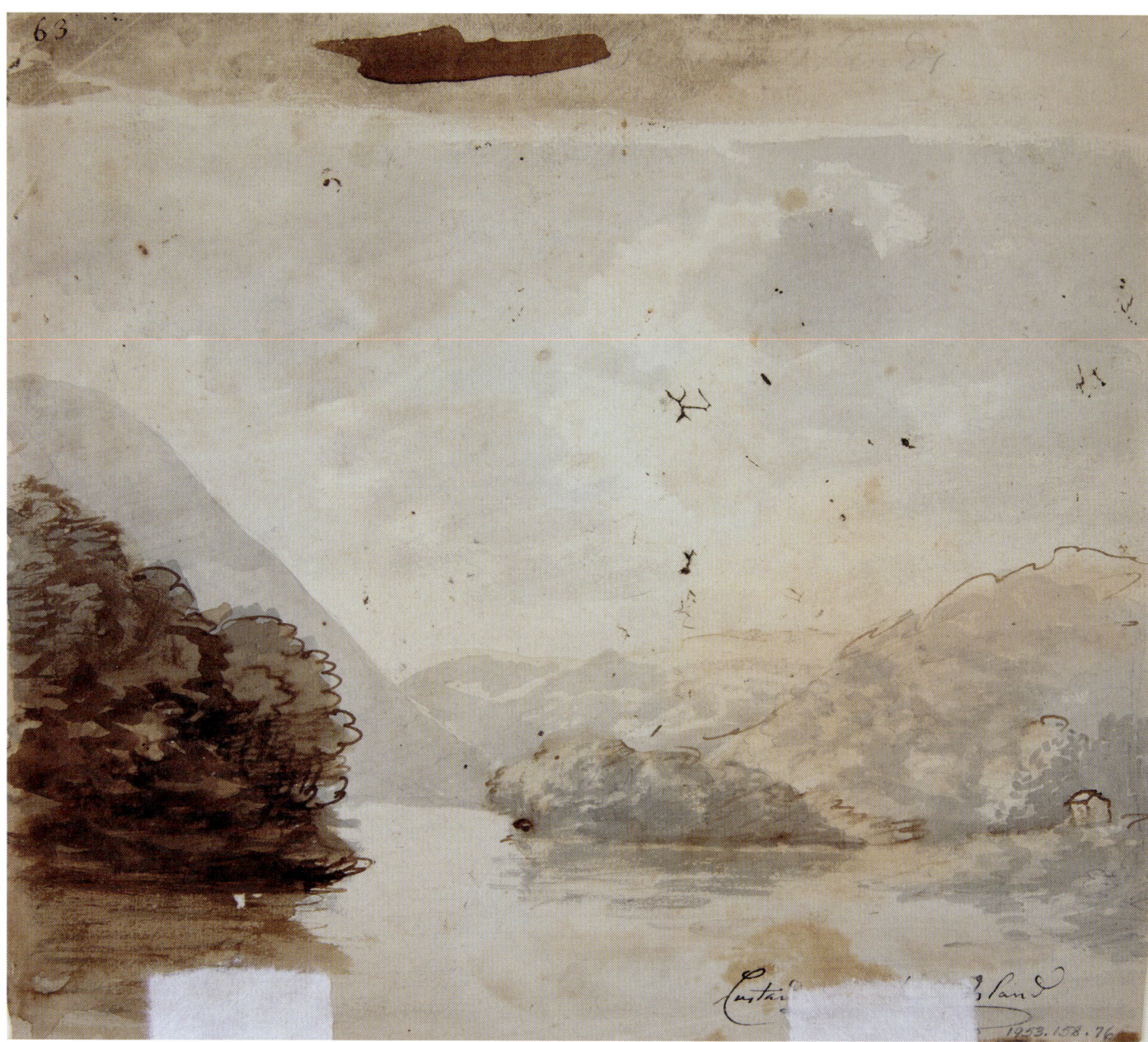

Figure 127

Custard & Baker's Island
Ink, wash, and watercolor on paper
8¾" × 7⅞"
Unknown date

Inscribed "Custard & Baker's Island." Baker's Island, demolished during the 20th century, was a small island in the Ohio River in eastern West Virginia.

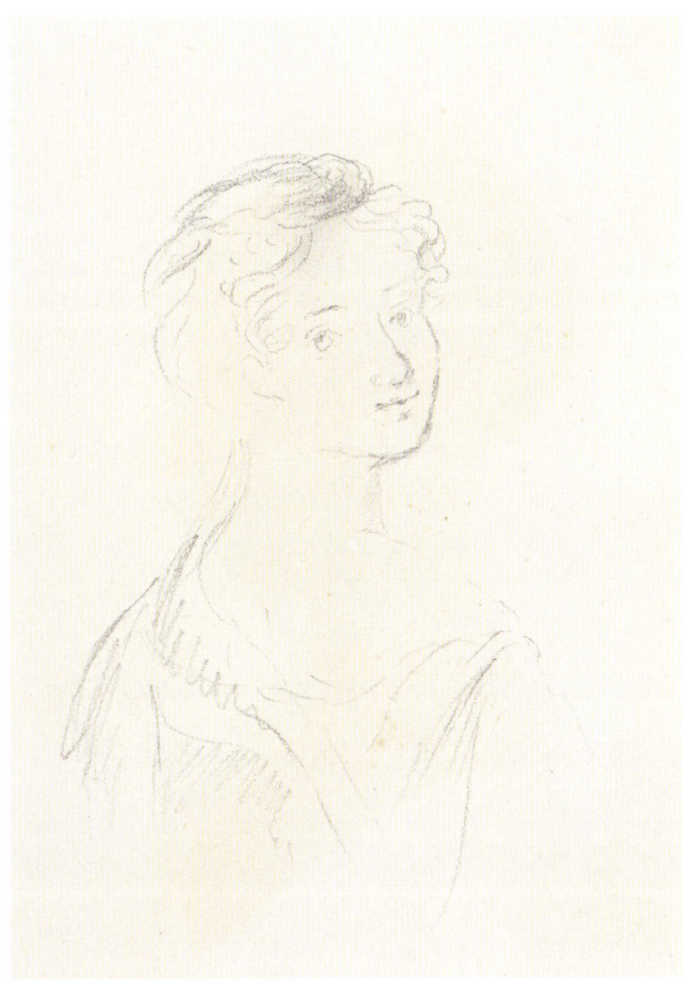

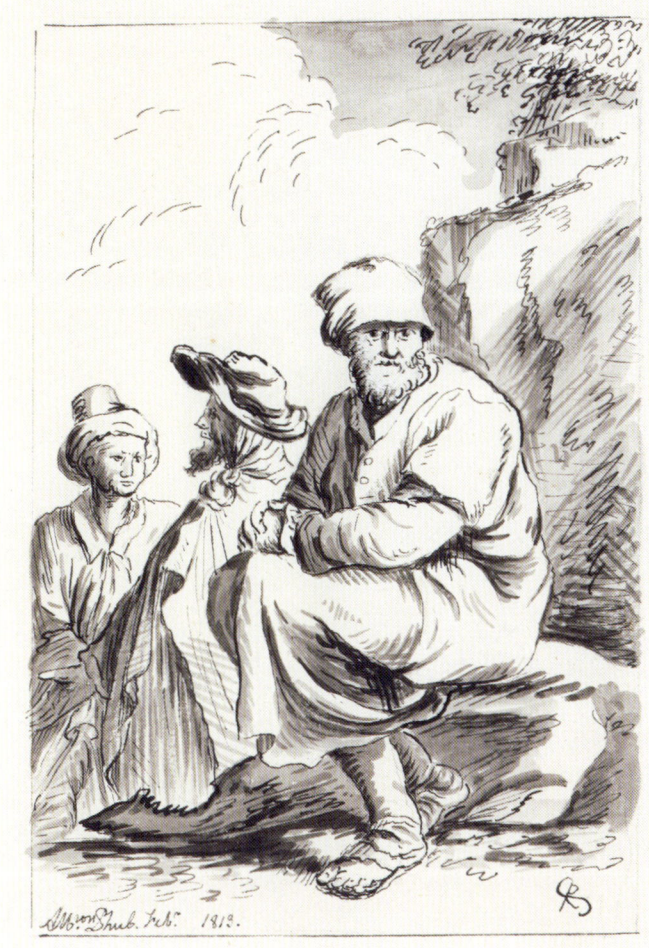

Figure 128

Study of a woman
Graphite on paper
2 ⅝" × 4½"
Unknown date

Figure 129

Copy of an unidentified print
Ink on paper
6½" × 8"
February 1813

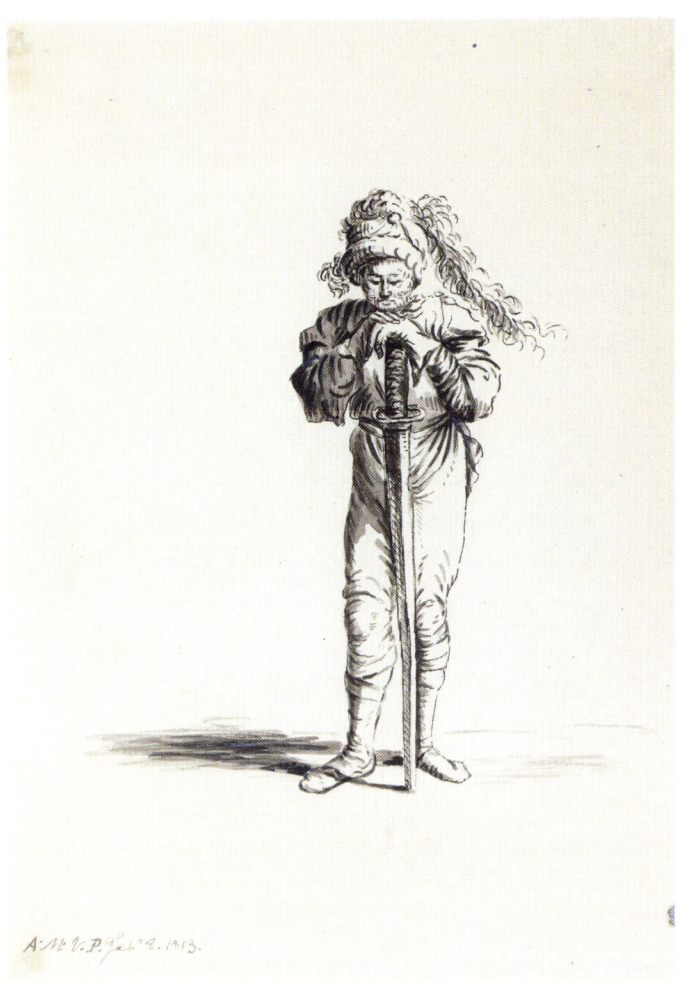

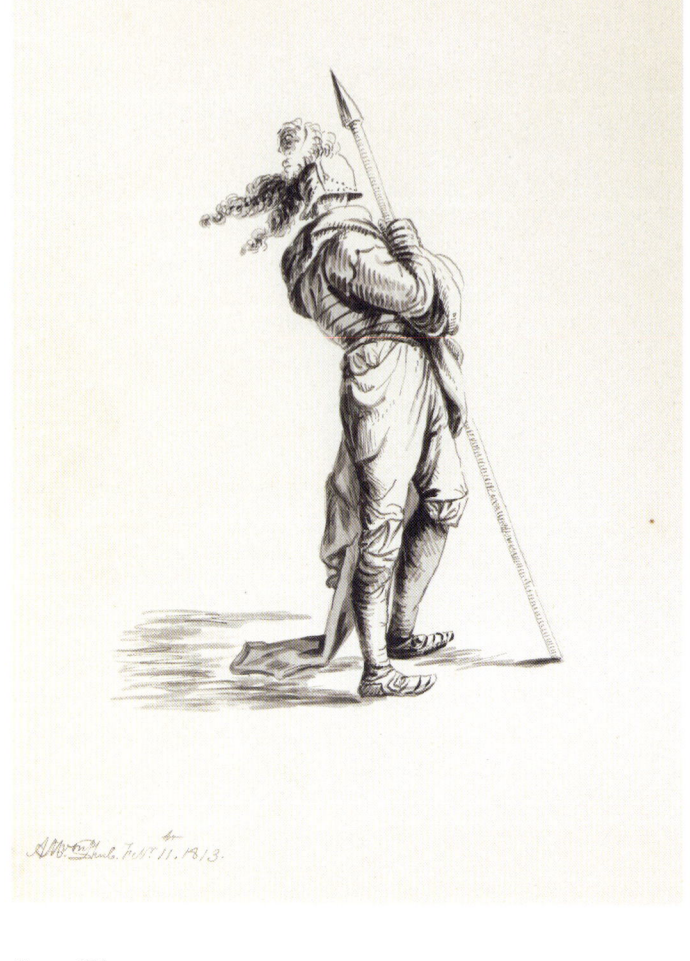

Figure 130

Copy of an unidentified print
Ink on paper
6½" × 8"
February 8, 1813

Figure 131

Copy of an unidentified print
Ink on paper
6½" × 8"
February 11, 1813

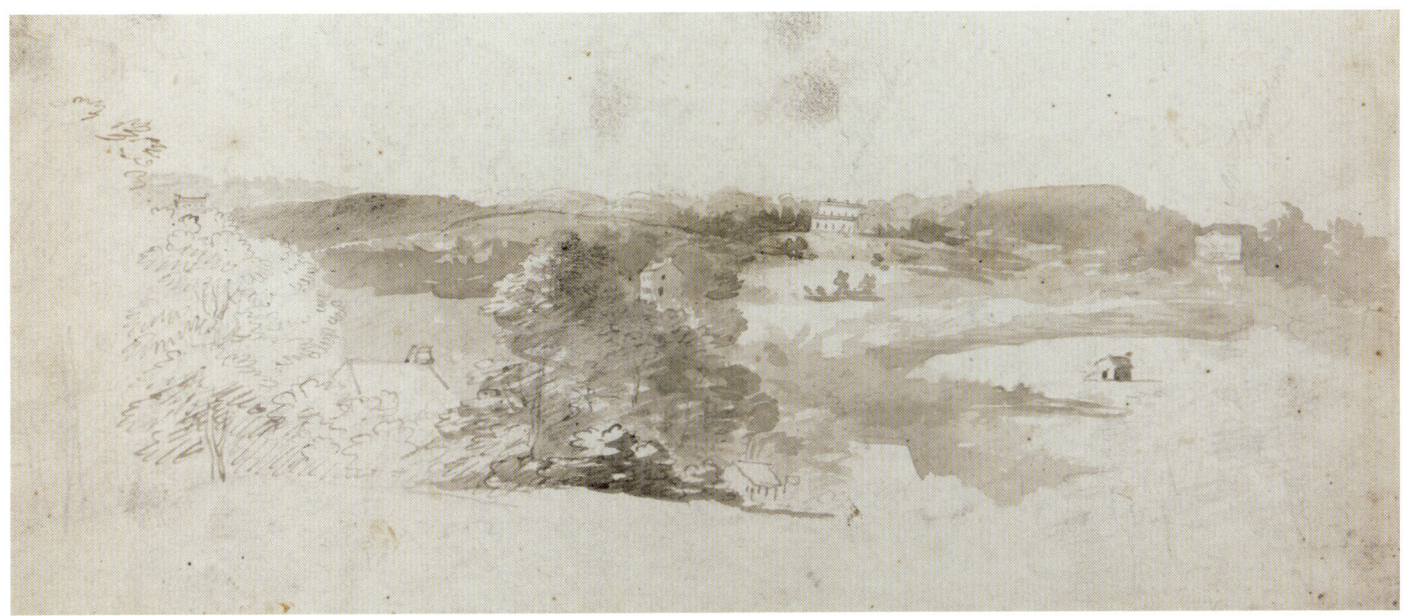

Figure 132

Landscape with houses
Graphite, ink, and wash on paper
13¼" × 8⅜"
Unknown date

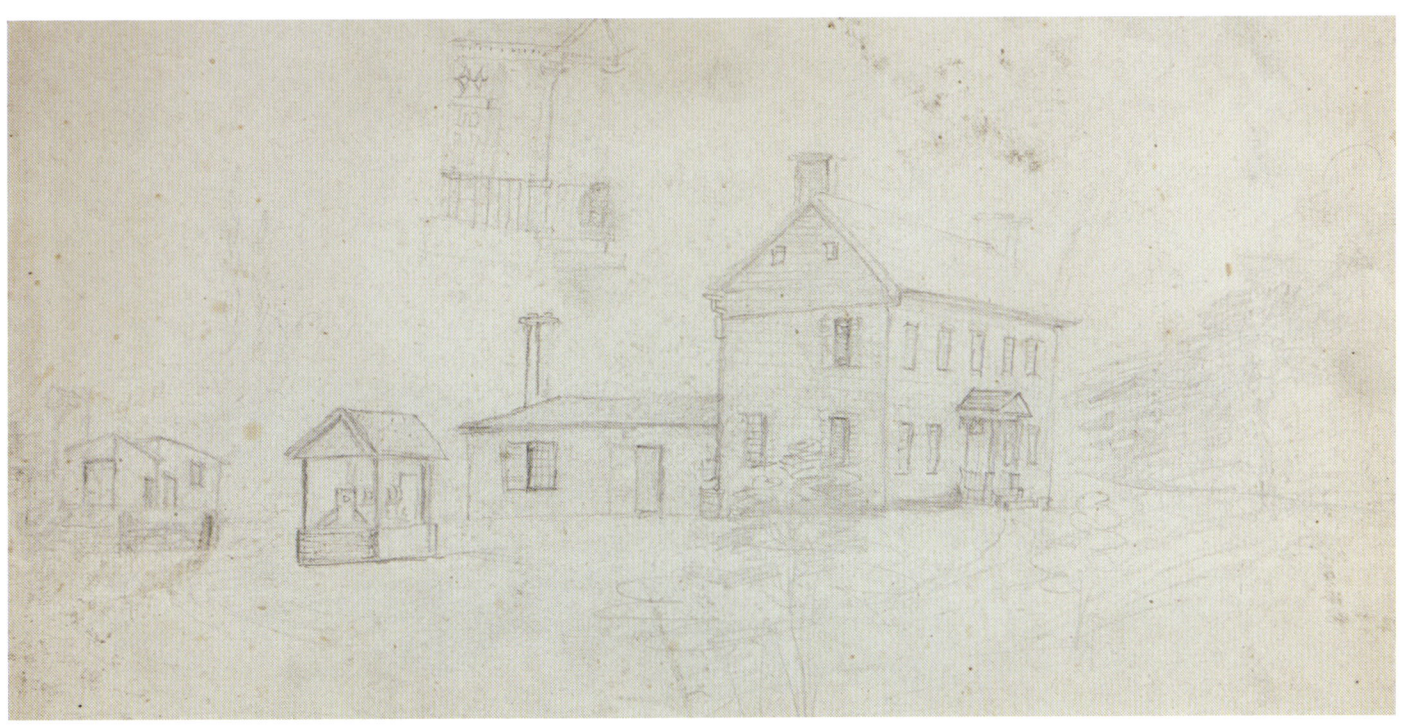

Figure 133

Study of a house and outbuildings
Graphite on paper
13¼" × 8⅜"
Unknown date

MORE THAN ORDINARY | 139

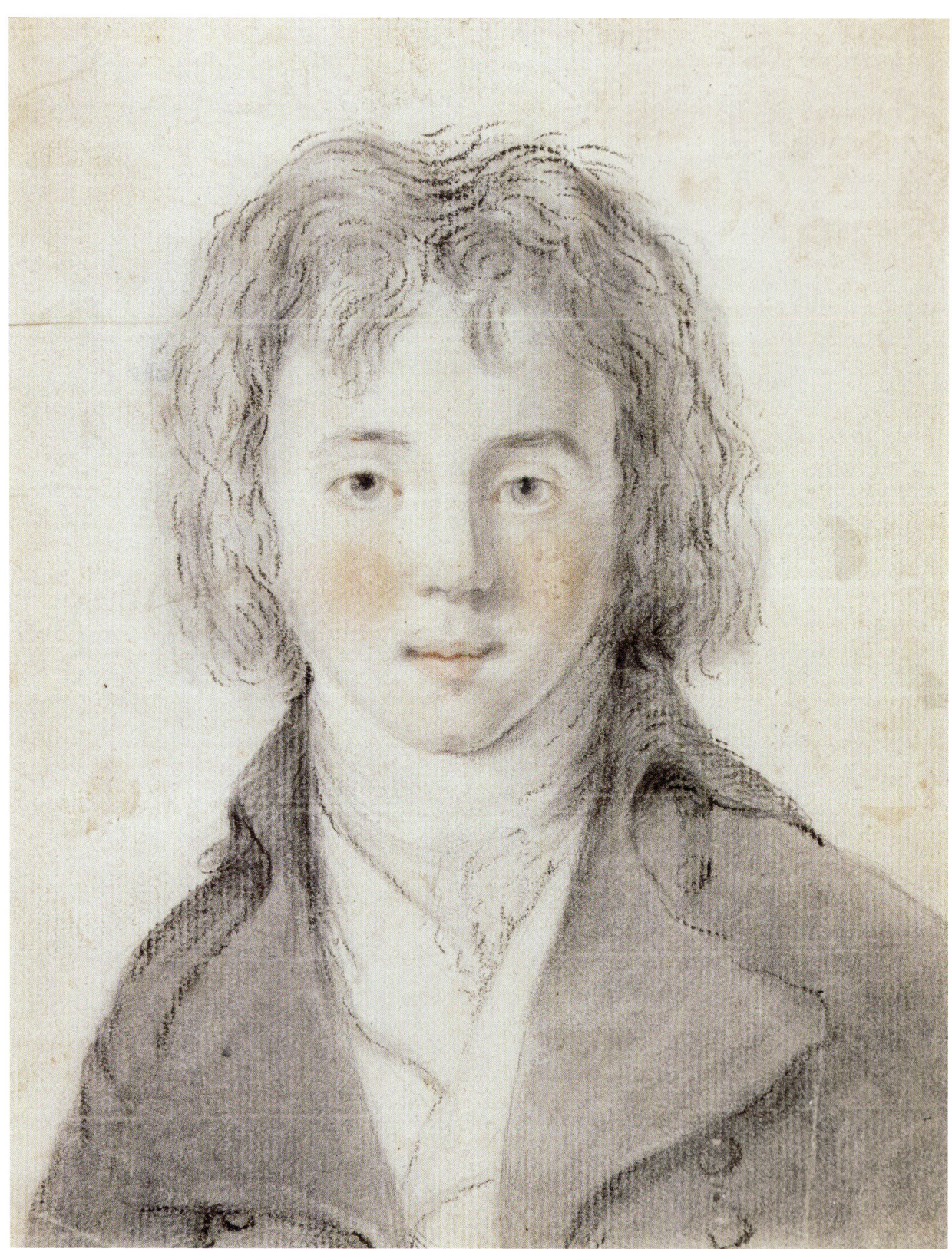

Figure 134

Portrait of a boy
Unknown medium on paper
6¼" × 8⅛"
Unknown date

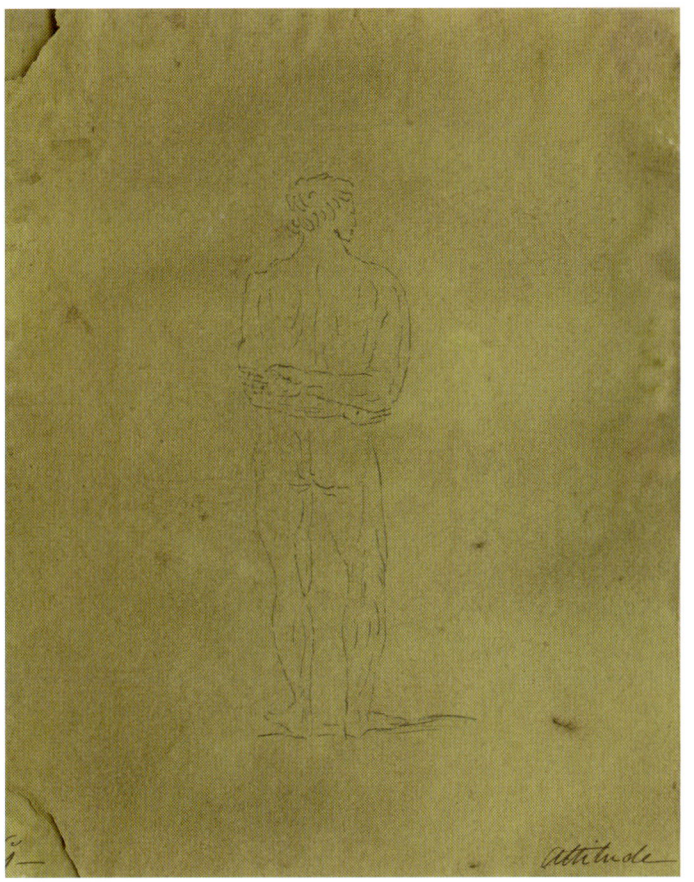

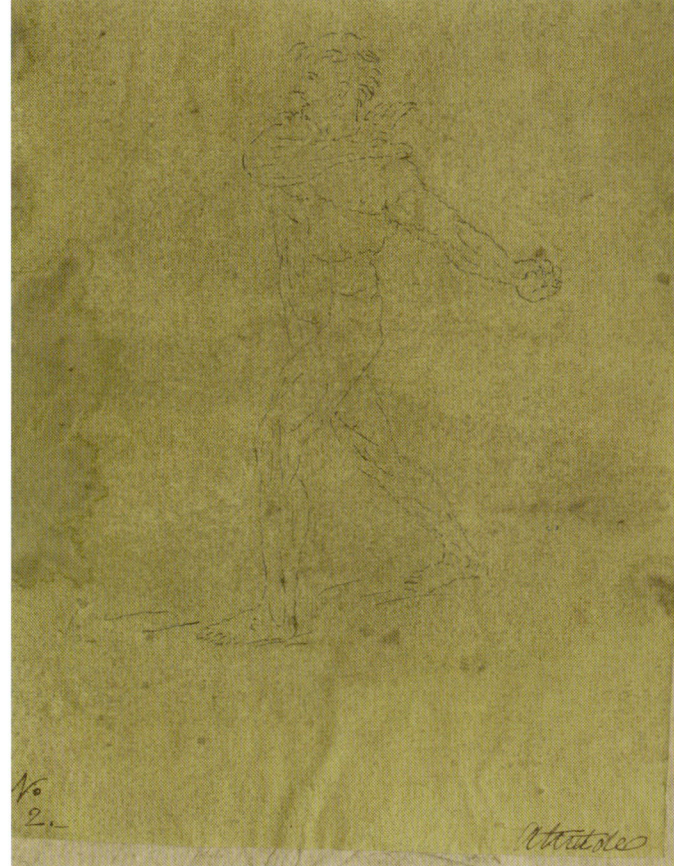

Figure 135

Attitude No. 1 (academy figure study)
Ink on paper
Unknown date

While access to live models and anatomy classes were generally unavailable to women artists, Anna Maria nevertheless practiced depicting the nuances of the human form and movement through her copywork. These two diminutive figure studies were pasted onto a page in one of her receipt books.

Figure 136

Attitude No. 2 (academy figure study)
Ink on paper
Unknown date

MORE THAN ORDINARY | 141

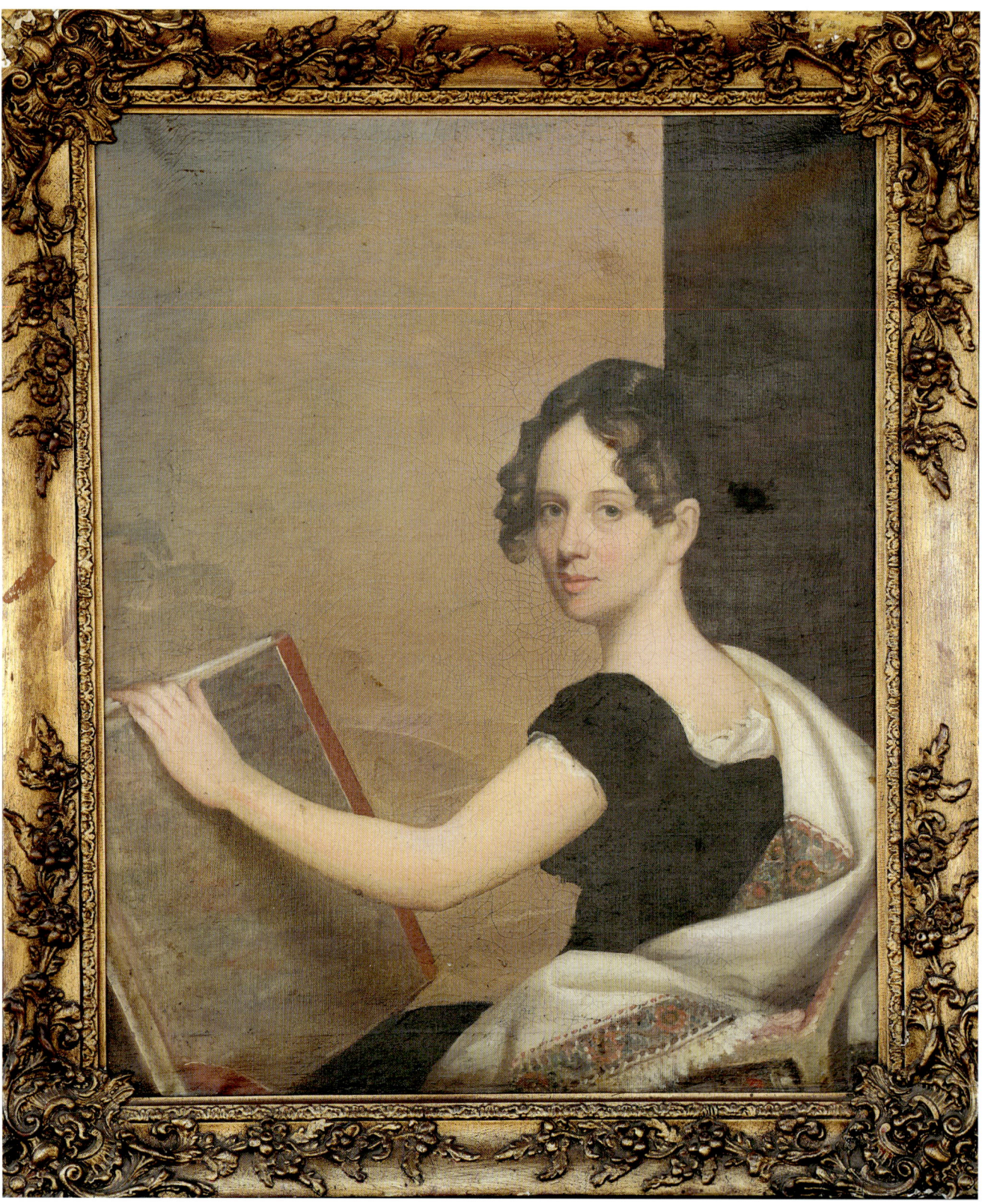

ABOUT THE AUTHOR

Hattie Felton is the senior curator for the Missouri Historical Society and holds a master's degree in public history from the University of Arkansas at Little Rock. She stewards the institution's fine- and decorative-arts collections. Her research explores the material culture of the domestic sphere as well as the lives and work of 19th- and 20th-century St. Louis artists and artisans. As part of her curatorial practice, Felton finds creative ways to collaborate with colleagues and community members to foster engagement in every part of museum work. Her previous publications include contributions to *Arkansas Made*, volumes 1 and 2. On the weekends she can be found curating the garden and bookshelves at the University City home she shares with her husband and their cat and dog.

With gratitude to
Ed & H. Pillsbury Foundation
for sponsoring this publication

With additional support from
Les Amis St. Louis